THEODORE ROOSEVELT
AND THE ART OF CONTROVERSY

WILLARD B. GATEWOOD, JR.

THEODORE ROOSEVELT AND THE ART OF CONTROVERSY

Episodes of the
White House Years

LOUISIANA STATE UNIVERSITY PRESS / Baton Rouge

For my friend: Joseph H. Parks

Copyright © 1970 by
Louisiana State University Press

Library of Congress Catalog Card Number 74–122354
ISBN 0–8071–0430–2

Chapter 3 is reprinted, with changes, from the *Journal of
Negro History*, January, 1968, by permission. Chapter 7
is reprinted, with changes, from the *American Quarterly*,
XVIII (1966), 35–51, by permission (Copyright © 1966,
Trustees of the University of Pennsylvania).

Manufactured in the United States of America by
The TJM Corporation

Designed by A. R. Crochet

Preface

During the era of Theodore Roosevelt, Winthrop Chanler and his wife belonged to a group that Owen Wister called the "Roosevelt familiars." Quite naturally when Margaret Terry Chanler published her recollections in 1934, Roosevelt received considerable attention. But unlike certain other friends and admirers of Roosevelt, she did not presume to comment on his place in history. Instead she observed, "Clio is biting her pencil while she looks for the final word." Clio may not have yet found that final word, if indeed she ever will, but the quantity and quality of Roosevelt studies in the thirty-five years since the publication of Mrs. Chanler's memoirs suggest that his place in history is at least secure. Certainly the works of George E. Mowry, John M. Blum, William H. Harbaugh, and Howard K. Beale, among others, should be sufficient to put Clio at ease.

The essays in this volume do not presume to offer a new interpretation of Theodore Roosevelt or of his presidency. They do, it is hoped, reveal something of significance about Roosevelt as a man and political leader by focusing upon his responses to diverse issues which attracted attention in the Progressive Era. Among such issues treated in this volume are the status of Negroes, the uses of patronage, the rights of organized labor, the separation of church and state, federal patronage of the arts, and the investigatory activities of the national government. As an introduction, the first essay attempts to summarize the conclusions reached by contemporary observers and historians regarding the personality and political techniques of Roosevelt which made him a persistent storm center of controversy. The other essays deal with specific incidents during his term as President. Each of these incidents provides a commentary on what has been termed the Rooseveltian affinity for combat. While these episodes in themselves may well have been minor, they involved sensitive areas of American life and had implications of major significance, especially in regard to the plausibility of the Square Deal slogan. Three of the essays deal with Roosevelt's encounters with the so-called Negro problem: his dinner with the Negro leader Booker T. Washington; his closing of the Indianola, Mississippi, post office because of the intimidation of the Negro postmaster; and his appointment of Dr. William D. Crum, a Negro, as customs collector at Charleston, South Carolina. The fifth essay explores the various ramifications of the controversy triggered in 1903 by the dismissal of William A. Miller from his position in the Government Printing Office on the grounds that he had been expelled from a labor union. The treatment of the Miller affair is followed by two essays about controversies which involved church-state relations. One of these concerns Roosevelt's troubles with Maria Longworth Storer, the rather hysterical wife of an American ambassador, whose machinations in pursuit of the cardinal's hat for Archbishop John Ireland appear in retrospect more comic than serious; the other deals with Roosevelt's efforts to provide the nation with an artistic coinage and with the agitation which greeted the absence of "In God We Trust" from the new coins. The final essay, on the controversy over the Secret Service in 1908–1909, describes the origins and progress of the dispute and analyzes the role played by Roosevelt, especially in forming the agency that became the Federal Bureau of Investigation.

Many individuals and institutions provided assistance in the preparation of this volume. Mrs. Alice Roosevelt Longworth was kind enough to share with me some of her recollections of the episodes treated here. I am also grateful for the assistance rendered by various persons in the United States Department of Justice and in the Secret Service Division of the Treasury Department and by librarians and archivists at the Library of Congress, National Archives, University of Georgia, University of North Carolina at Chapel Hill, Duke University, Atlanta University, Emory University, Mississippi State Department of Archives and History, and Minnesota Historical Society. A special acknowledgment is due Mrs. William Franklin Burroughs of the University of Georgia Library for kindnesses too numerous to mention here. Much of the research was made possible by grants from the American Philosophical Society. David Edwin Harrell, Jr., of the University of Alabama, Warren F. Kimball of Rutgers University, and G. Melvin Herndon of the University of Georgia were generous enough to read the manuscript and to give me the benefit of their criticisms. The editors of the *Journal of Negro History* and *American Quarterly* graciously permitted me to use material which appeared in slightly different form in these journals. Finally I am indebted to my wife, whose assistance is in no small way responsible for the completion of this volume.

Contents

THEODORE ROOSEVELT
AND THE ART OF CONTROVERSY

I

Theodore Roosevelt:
"The Soul of Controversy"

The ideal citizen of a free state must have in him the stuff ... to show himself a first-class fighting man who scorns either to endure or to inflict wrong.

One of the prime dangers of civilization has always been its tendency to cause the loss of virile fighting virtues, of the fighting edge.

I like a fight. I do like a fight.

THEODORE ROOSEVELT

In mid-January, 1898, the thirty-seven-year-old novelist Hamlin Garland dined with Theodore Roosevelt, the assistant secretary of the navy, who was three years his senior. Following this meeting, Garland recorded in his diary that Roosevelt was "a man who is likely to be much in the public eye during his life." He characterized his new acquaintance as "a man of great energy, of good impulses and of undoubted ability," who was "full of talk—always interesting talk." Roosevelt, "not unlike Kipling in some ways," he noted, was "square-headed, deep-chested and abrupt of movement." Though his preferences were strong and "his dislikes intense," he was "manly and wholesome in his impulses." [1] Shortly after Roosevelt's death in 1919, Garland wrote a eulogistic essay on his career which indicated that he had not substantially altered his original estimate of the man. For him, Roosevelt remained "the most de-

[1] Donald Pizer (ed.), *Hamlin Garland's Diaries* (San Marino, Calif.: Huntington Lib., 1968), 203.

lightful of companions" who, despite "all his simplicity and direct-
ness," never lost a certain dignity.[2] He was always the gentleman
and the scholar, even in rumpled riding clothes. Others who did not
share Garland's generous assessment frankly admitted that Roosevelt had dominated his era and that the opening years of the
twentieth century deserved to be called the "Epoch of Roosevelt." [3]

Born in 1858 in a four-story brownstone house in Manhattan,
Theodore Roosevelt was the scion of a moderately wealthy patrician
family. In his mature years he not only bore a striking physical
resemblance to his father, Theodore, after whom he was named,
but also exhibited many of his ideological commitments and personal characteristics. From him the son learned to place a premium
upon individual responsibility and moral conduct.[4] Although the
younger Roosevelt joined the Dutch Reformed Church of his father
and for a while, at least, demonstrated a rather lively interest in
religious matters, it is difficult to speak with any certainty about the
depth of his religious faith and its influence upon his life. Perhaps
it was natural for a person so rarely inclined to introspection as

[2] Hamlin Garland, "Theodore Roosevelt," *Mentor*, VII (February 2, 1920),
1–20.

[3] Judson C. Welliver, "Epoch of Roosevelt," *American Review of Reviews*,
XXXIX (1909), 338–46.

[4] The following sketch of Roosevelt's life is based essentially upon William
Henry Harbaugh, *Power and Responsibility: The Life and Times of Theodore
Roosevelt* (New York: Farrar, Straus, 1961); Henry F. Pringle, *Theodore Roose-
velt: A Biography* (New York: Harcourt, 1931); Carleton Putnam, *Theodore
Roosevelt: The Formative Years* (New York: Scribner, 1958) ; G. Wallace Chess-
man, *Theodore Roosevelt and the Politics of Power* (Boston: Little, 1969);
Howard K. Beale, *Theodore Roosevelt and America's Rise to World Power*
(Baltimore: Johns Hopkins, 1956); Elting Morison (ed.), *The Letters of Theo-
dore Roosevelt* (8 vols.; Cambridge: Harvard, 1951–54) ; Edward Wagenknecht,
The Seven Worlds of Theodore Roosevelt (New York: Longmans, 1958) ; Richard L. Watson, "Theodore Roosevelt: The Years of Preparation," *South Atlantic Quarterly*, LI (1952), 301–15; Theodore Roosevelt, *An Autobiography*
(New York: Macmillan, 1913). Among the most provocative interpretations of
Roosevelt are John M. Blum, *The Republican Roosevelt* (Cambridge: Harvard,
1954), and Lewis Einstein, *Roosevelt: His Mind in Action* (Boston: Houghton,
1930) , which have been indispensable in the preparation of this chapter. A useful bibliographic essay somewhat out of date is Dewey W. Grantham, "Theodore Roosevelt in Historical Writing, 1945–1960," *Mid-America*, XLIII (1961),
3–35.

Roosevelt to avoid or reject the mystical element in religion. He was more concerned with the "gospel of works" and with the practical application of the Ten Commandments, which served as his standard of judgment. A reference to his "atavistic Puritanism" which he once made was perhaps more appropriate than he realized.[5] Although Roosevelt was profoundly influenced both by the instruction and the example of his father, he was deeply devoted to his mother, a gentle, kind-hearted woman born and reared in Georgia. He often boasted that he was "half Southern." Commenting on his background to a friend, he once remarked, "I have not got a sectional bone in my body. I imbibed the traditions and folk lore of the South from my mother; my earliest training and principles were Southern. I sought the West of my own accord; and my manhood has largely been fought in the North." [6]

A frail child with weak eyes, Roosevelt suffered from asthma and a general state of poor health which produced in him a kind of defiance evident in his doggedly persistent effort to achieve physical fitness. His own experience in conquering the timidity and insecurity linked during childhod to his physical disabilities was a source of his later advocacy of the strenuous life. But whatever his physical frailties as a child, he possessed a precocious mind and an insatiable curiosity. His inquisitiveness was reflected in the incredible range of his reading, a habit that he retained throughout his life. During childhood his particular passion was natural history. His collection of flora and fauna, complete with annotations, classifications, and indexes, was the despair of servants in the Roosevelt household.[7]

Like other children of genteel families in the era, Roosevelt enjoyed the benefits of European travel and the best formal education. Prepared for college by private tutors, he entered Harvard College in 1876. As a student, he distinguished himself in athletics as well

[5] Chessman, *Roosevelt and the Politics of Power*, 9–17; Putnam, *Roosevelt: The Formative Years*, 34–56; George S. Viereck, *Roosevelt: A Study in Ambivalence* (New York: Jackson Press, 1920), 96.

[6] Quoted in Lawrence F. Abbott (ed.), *The Letters of Archie Butt* (Garden City, N.Y.: Doubleday, 1924), 67.

[7] Putnam, *Roosevelt: The Formative Years*, 21–33; Pringle, *Roosevelt: A Biography*, 4, 5, 16–19; Einstein, *Roosevelt: His Mind in Action*, 7–10.

as in academic fields, edited a campus newspaper, taught a Sunday school class, and acquired a host of friends who later figured prominently in his career. He also began to evidence the competitive personality and penchant for moralistic preaching which were to become trademarks of his public life. By the time of his graduation in 1880 he had abandoned his original intention of becoming a scientist and had decided to study law. In the same year he married Alice Lee of Chestnut Hill, Massachusetts, a nineteen-year-old beauty of Brahmin ancestry. Returning to New York with his bride, he began a brief tenure as a student at the Columbia Law School.[8]

In New York, Roosevelt displayed more interest in local politics than in his law studies. In 1881 he was elected to the state legislature on the Republican ticket. Perhaps, as Professor John M. Blum has noted, the most extraordinary decision that Roosevelt ever made was his choice of politics as a career.[9] The profession of politics had fallen into a state of disrepute and was generally viewed with disdain by those who belonged to Roosevelt's social class. But if a patrician entered politics, it was entirely natural that he should do so as a Republican. Although Roosevelt was identified with the reform element of his party, he came to view party regularity not as an end in itself but as the means to political power. From the outset he was distinguished from other regulars by what has been termed his "regularity with a conscience." [10] His political apprenticeship in the state legislature taught him, according to Professor G. Wallace Chessman, that "it was not enough to be moral; to be efficient the true reformer had to work *within a party* with all kinds

[8] Putnam, *Roosevelt: The Formative Years*, Chaps. 9–12.

[9] Blum, *The Republican Roosevelt*, 7. In explaining why he, "a young silkstocking" from the brownstone district, decided to enter the grubby world of politics, Roosevelt declared, "I suppose for one thing ordinary, plain, everyday duty sent me there to begin with. But more than that, I wanted to belong to the governing class, not to the governed." Jacob A. Riis, *Theodore Roosevelt: The Citizen* (New York: Outlook, 1904), 48.

[10] Blum, *The Republican Roosevelt*, 12. Lewis Einstein maintains that Roosevelt, however much he abhorred Tammany Hall, learned much from this Democratic machine. Tammany taught him the "value of the personal element in politics" and the necessity for a smooth working organization among the reform element. See *Roosevelt: His Mind in Action*, 17–19.

of men." [11] In explaining his political success, Roosevelt later declared, "I put myself in the way of things happening and they happened." [12] Such an explanation was perhaps true as far as it went, but it failed to indicate the crucial role played by the shrewd calculations not only of Roosevelt but also of his political allies in detecting and taking advantage of "things happening." Despite his reputation for impetuosity, politics was for him a cautious and questing trade aimed at acquiring the power he delighted in exercising.

In 1884 Roosevelt temporarily retired from politics. The recurrence of poor health and the Republican defeat in the presidential election of 1884 were not the only reasons for his self-imposed exile. He also suffered a double tragedy early in the same year when his mother and wife died within a few hours of each other. The death of his young wife from the complications of Bright's disease following the birth of their first child left him "a broken-hearted man." [13] Within three years, however, he married Edith Carow, a childhood acquaintance and a sensitive, intelligent woman, who not only raised Alice, the daughter by his first wife, but also bore five children of her own. During the three years between the death of Alice Lee and his second marriage, Roosevelt sought to get "away from the world" by escaping to the Dakota country, where he had earlier invested a sizable sum in the cattle business. His years in the Bad Lands, according to one Roosevelt scholar, "constituted one of the great formative experiences of his life." [14] He not only made his reputation as a cowboy and rancher here but also resumed his interest in writing and began work on several literary projects which later won for him considerable acclaim. Though far removed geo-

---

[11] Chessman, *Roosevelt and the Politics of Power*, 42. "There is a point," Roosevelt told Jacob Riis, ". . . where a man must take the isolated peak and break with all for clear principle, but until it comes he must work if he would be of use, with men as they are." And Roosevelt would always work "for the best that can be got." See Riis, *Roosevelt: The Citizen*, 60.

[12] Quoted in Watson, "Roosevelt: The Years of Preparation," 305.

[13] Pringle, *Roosevelt: A Biography*, 51.

[14] Harbaugh, *Power and Responsibility*, 48. See also Edward and Frederick Schapsmeier, "Theodore Roosevelt's Cowboy Years," *Journal of the West*, V (1966), 398–408; Mody C. Boatright, "Theodore Roosevelt, Social Darwinism, and the Cowboy," *Texas Quarterly*, VII (1964), 7–20.

graphically from eastern politics, Roosevelt nonetheless continued to maintain a lively interest in Republican affairs and kept abreast of political events through a regular correspondence with his eastern friends.

Returning to New York in 1886 to run for mayor on the Republican ticket, the young patrician-turned-cowboy placed third in the contest, behind the Democrat Abram S. Hewitt and the Single-Taxer Henry George. Despite his defeat, his "rattling canvass" contributed significantly to his political education and left him "with a better party standing than ever before." Out of politics again, Roosevelt divested himself of his Dakota interests, which had already caused him substantial losses, and concentrated for a while upon his literary labors. Although he gave up the idea of going into "a money-making business," the annual income from his inheritance made easier the fulfillment of his desire to "amount to something, either in politics or literature." [15]

Plunging into the presidential campaign of 1888, Roosevelt left his research and writing to undertake an extensive speaking tour in behalf of Benjamin Harrison. "I always genuinely enjoy it," Roosevelt wrote shortly after Harrison's triumph, "and act as target and marksman alternately with immense zest." [16] Harrison acknowledged his efforts by appointing him to the Civil Service Commission, a position which he retained under the Democrat Grover Cleveland. During his six years in Washington, Roosevelt not only widened his circle of acquaintances among patricians and intellectuals whose social standing and views were comparable to his own but also made it his business to cultivate those nearer the center of political power. As a civil service commissioner, he demonstrated his administrative ability and gained a wide reputation as an outspoken crusader for honest, efficient government service. One Roosevelt biographer characterized civil service reform as "the most confirmed and most sustained cause of Roosevelt's career" because he "read into it both the gospel of efficiency which is the

[15] Chessman, *Roosevelt and the Politics of Power,* 27–50.
[16] Theodore Roosevelt to Cecil Spring Rice, November 18, 1888, in Morison (ed.), *Roosevelt Letters,* I, 149.

conservative's creed and the open society which is the democrat's dream." [17] Though "impatient for righteousness," Roosevelt remained "a straight-out Republican" and "a great believer in practical politics." [18]

The popular image of him as a reformer which emerged from his tenure in Washington acquired a new luster as a result of his activities as a police commissioner in New York. For two tumultuous years following his appointment to the board of police commissioners in 1895, Roosevelt not only waged war on entrenched corruptionists but also attempted to modernize the police force and to achieve administrative efficiency. He inspired a generation of "reform cops" and won the enduring admiration of such young police reporters as Joseph B. Bishop, Jacob Riis, and Lincoln Steffens. Others, however, viewed his frenzied activities with something less than approval. The disruptive effect of his reform efforts upon state and local Republican politics aroused the animosity of the party leadership. By summer of 1896 he was convinced that his usefulness as a police commissioner was virtually at an end.[19]

Fully cognizant of his predicament, Roosevelt enlisted the aid of influential friends in securing a post within the new administration of William McKinley. To one of them, however, he protested: "I don't wish to appear as a suppliant for I am not a suppliant." He was certain that "somewhere or other" he could "find work to do." With no little difficulty Henry Cabot Lodge, the Bellamy Storers, and others finally prevailed upon McKinley to appoint him assistant secretary of the navy. But McKinley had serious misgivings about putting in a sensitive post such a "hot-headed," "harum-scarum" disturber of the peace. Nevertheless, Roosevelt brought to his job a long-standing interest in the navy and a strong commitment to naval preparedness. In fact, the first book he ever published was a study of the naval war of 1812, a war which impressed upon him the

[17] Harbaugh, *Power and Responsibility*, 75.

[18] Roosevelt to Henry C. Lodge, June 29, July 1, 1889, Roosevelt to Brander Mathews, July 31, 1889, in Morison (ed.), *Roosevelt Letters*, I, 167–68, 177.

[19] See Harbaugh, *Power and Responsibility*, 81–90. See also Avery D. Andrews, "Theodore Roosevelt as Police Commissioner," *New York Historical Society Quarterly*, XLII (1958), 117–41.

dangers of inadequate naval forces. Because the indulgent secretary of the navy, John D. Long, either delegated authority to him or was frequently absent from the department, Roosevelt had an extraordinary opportunity to influence policies. Though considered "a perfect dear" by Roosevelt, Secretary Long was often exasperated by the ardor and presumption of his youthful subordinate, who seemed intent upon translating the theories of Alfred T. Mahan into realities.[20]

As the nation plunged toward war with Spain, Roosevelt increasingly sounded a jingoistic note. Less circumspect than some others of his generation in expressing the war fever, he appeared on occasion to seek war for its own sake. And his former professor at Harvard, William James, believed that he regarded "one foe as good an another." Although Roosevelt persistently denied being militaristic, he was an enthusiastic advocate of military preparedness and occasionally demonstrated his proficiency as a saber-rattler. He was a "confident imperialist" who "appreciated the realities of power in foreign affairs." Roosevelt left the Navy Department in 1898 to participate directly in the Spanish-American War. The exploits of his volunteer cavalry unit, the Rough Riders, became something of a national legend and he became a conspicuous national hero. Although the Cuban campaign "brought out Roosevelt's best and some of his worst," it provided a new dimension to his public image.[21]

In 1898 Roosevelt appeared to the Republican leaders of New York as the one man capable of bailing them out of their political difficulties. A man of his reputation and popularity, they reasoned, would be able to thwart the Democratic effort to win the governorship. Backed by the "easy boss," Thomas C. Platt, Roosevelt agreed to run for governor and waged a campaign noted more for its flag-waving than for any discussion of issues or any elaboration of a program. Elected by a sizable majority, he "for the first time be-

[20] Roosevelt to Maria L. Storer, December 5, 1869, in Morison (ed.), *Roosevelt Letters,* I, 569; Pringle, *Roosevelt: A Biography,* Chap. 13.
[21] Blum, *The Republican Roosevelt,* 30–31; Harbaugh, *Power and Responsibility,* 105. For a perceptive analysis of Roosevelt's views and actions regarding imperialism, see David H. Burton, *Theodore Roosevelt: Confident Imperialist* (Philadelphia: U. of Pa., 1968).

came fully conscious of his extraordinary power to move great masses of people." [22] His term as governor of the nation's most populous state was the final, and perhaps the most important, phase of his preparation for national leadership. Never reticent to utilize his executive power, Roosevelt advanced the cause of conservation, energetically enforced the labor laws, and established a tenement-house commission. Since "the bulk of government" was, in his opinion, administration rather than legislation, it is not surprising that improvement of the state's administrative structure was one of his most notable achievements. Dedicated to the pursuit of good government, Roosevelt sought the elusive goal of honest, efficient administration by relying upon the advice of experts and by seeking the counsel of impartial investigatory commissions. With no less enthusiasm he tackled the complex of problems emerging from the socioeconomic changes of the industrial revolution. His gubernatorial experience contributed to the metamorphosis of his views regarding both labor and capital. He still detested strikes and other disturbances associated with unions because they threatened property and order. But he gradually came to appreciate some of the causes of labor's discontent and was no longer confident that force alone was the solution to strikes. In fact, by the end of his term in Albany he was well along the way toward his idea of a positive state which would insure a Square Deal to labor as well as capital.[23]

Less tangible perhaps, but no less important than some of his other achievements as governor, was the perfection of his political style and technique. He accepted the Republican Party as the vehicle for implementing his ideas and learned to thread his way among various contending interests without disrupting its basic unity. True to his promise to play fair with Boss Platt, he nonetheless sought the counsel of nonorganization Republicans. He enhanced his own independence by a skillful use of the press and by "outmaneuvering the politicians at their own game." He was in fact a professional politician adept in negotiation, adjustment, disci-

[22] Harbaugh, *Power and Responsibility*, 112.
[23] The most thorough treatment of Roosevelt as governor of New York is G. Wallace Chessman, *Governor Theodore Roosevelt: The Albany Apprenticeship, 1898–1900* (Cambridge: Harvard, 1965).

pline, and personal drama. He knew how and when to compromise and how and when to stand steadfast and alone; he also learned to restrain his own impulses and to discipline "his use of the power he pursued." [24] The personal, even aesthetic rewards of the political game itself assumed such importance that they sometimes obscured the moral goals he sincerely sought. But the moralist he remained. "When we come to . . . anything touching the Eighth Commandment and general decency," he told Platt, "I could not allow any consideration of party to come in." [25] Even if his moral courage did not equal his moral fervor, Roosevelt can scarcely be dismissed as a mere political opportunist. Despite the temptation to accept such a simple explanation, his technique was far more complicated and involved a curious blending of opportunism and altruism.

Boss Platt, always "a mite apprehensive" about the energetic young man in Albany, welcomed the opportunity to have him elevated to the vice-presidency in 1900. But various other factors figured in Roosevelt's nomination. Among these was the desire to have a Republican capable of effectively challenging the Democrat William Jennings Bryan on the hustings. The Republican victory in November placed Roosevelt in what he considered the dreary position of being the presiding officer of the Senate.[26] But less than six months after he had taken up his new duties, McKinley's assassination plummeted him into the White House. The fact that he was socially secure, well educated, and financially comfortable distinguished him from his immediate predecessors in the office. Though the youngest of Presidents, he was, by training and experience, peculiarly equipped to take the political helm of the nation at this particular juncture in its history.

Although Roosevelt "moved cautiously but steadily" during his first two and a half years in the White House, few Americans failed to detect that his administration marked "the dawn of a new era." [27]

[24] See Blum, *The Republican Roosevelt*, 15–17; Richard Lowitt, "Theodore Roosevelt," in Morton Borden (ed.), *America's Ten Greatest Presidents* (Chicago: Rand McNally, 1961), 186–87.

[25] Quoted in Blum, *The Republican Roosevelt*, 15.

[26] Roosevelt's election and brief tenure as Vice President are treated in detail in Harbaugh, *Power and Responsibility*, 131–46.

[27] "The Personality of President Roosevelt," *Century*, LXIII (1901), 276–79.

From the beginning he assumed a broad view of the presidential office and achieved some of his goals through a dramatic use of executive authority. Throughout his tenure he attracted extraordinarily able men into government service to assist him in overhauling the executive machinery. Although Roosevelt pursued a forceful foreign policy, acquired the somewhat misleading label of "trustbuster," and espoused an attitude toward labor and capital known as the Square Deal, his first months in office were devoted primarily toward capturing control of the Republican Party from McKinley's heir apparent, Marcus A. Hanna. Always "attuned to what was going on around him," Roosevelt reconciled conflicting interests and transformed the party of McKinley into his own party. He was a charismatic leader and nondoctrinaire politician who functioned as a "skillful broker of the possible." He could divide the opposition, highlight some issues and mute others, and effectively employ diversionary tactics in pursuing his own ends. Alternating between compromise and circumspection on the one hand and the high drama of inflexible determination on the other, he wrung concessions from a conservative Congress that was jealous of its prerogatives and hostile to leadership from the White House.

Roosevelt viewed himself as a practical idealist leading the nation along a just and prudent course that would avoid the excesses of both obstinate reaction and left-wing radicalism.[28] The Square Deal was predicated upon what he liked to think of as a golden mean which protected "orderly liberty" from the dangers of tyranny on the one hand and of anarchy on the other. "Rich people complain that I harass them," Roosevelt once remarked. "Maybe, but I save their children." [29] He was in the broadest sense a conservationist, interested in preserving the values and institutions of traditional America as well as the social order which he considered essential to the maintenance and improvement of a democratic society.

[28] Blum, *The Republican Roosevelt,* 5; George E. Mowry, *The Era of Theodore Roosevelt and the Birth of Modern America, 1900–1912* (New York: Harper, 1958), 113–15.
[29] Quoted in Jules J. Jusserand, *What Me Befell: Reminiscences* (Boston: Houghton, 1933), 246.

Elected by a large majority in 1904, Roosevelt was at last relieved of the burden of being President "by accident." As a sensitive politician, he responded to the obvious drift in public opinion during his second term by pressing more vigorously for domestic reforms and by pursuing a foreign policy that made the United States an active participant in international affairs. All the while, he continued to function as an efficient administrator and as a political evangelist who sermonized on an incredible range of topics. But whatever his topic, his emphasis was likely to be upon personal morality, patriotism, and civic duty. Despite the mounting opposition of old-guard Republicans, Roosevelt was remarkably successful in avoiding permanent consolidations of any one group against him, in large part because of his ability in convincing all groups of his desire to insure "a Square Deal" to each. Even those trapped in hopelessness, such as Negro Americans, were for a time seduced by his rhetoric and by the symbolism of his cautious efforts. If at the end of his term in 1909 he had accomplished relatively few of the reforms about which he preached so passionately, he at least had helped to arouse public interest in them and had paved the way for others to complete what he left unfinished.

Those of Roosevelt's own generation, whether they considered him a saint or a demon or a peculiar combination of the two, recognized that his tenure in the White House possessed a meaning and significance that transcended policies and legislative accomplishments. Many who believed that his administration marked "a new era" agreed with Mark Sullivan's assessment in 1909 that Roosevelt had "no program, no plan for reorganizing society." [30] Although Harry Thurston Peck described the record of achievement as "a very meagre one," he too was convinced that Roosevelt's accession to office had "brought in a stream of fresh, pure, bracing air." The man, his style, and his technique at once explained why he evoked such contradictory emotions and judgments among his contemporaries and why he aroused the public imagination as few Presidents have and became the dominant personality of an era.

[30] Mark Sullivan, "Roosevelt," *Collier's*, XLII (March 6, 1909), 22. In his *Autobiography* (p. 400), Roosevelt admitted that he had no grand scheme for social betterment when he came to the presidency.

Peck found the key to his "unusual and sustained popularity" in his youth. "Just as all the world loves a lover," he wrote in 1909, "so most of the world has a kindly, cordial feeling toward the extravagances of youth." Weary of the "materialism of the Hanna-McKinley era," Americans looked to their youthful President "to right a thousand wrongs in a swift, efficient way, and they were not exceedingly particular as to whether in doing so he strained a little the power of his office." [31] Although his tendency to "talk so much about what he was going to do" obscured the relative meagerness of his achievement, even his critics were not blind to his contributions in the areas of administrative and civil service reforms, conservation, railroad regulation, and pure food legislation.

The perceptive William Garrott Brown, a former lecturer in history at Harvard and an editorial writer for *Harper's Weekly*, believed that what distinguished Roosevelt from his predecessors was his introduction "into the higher walks of public life" of those characteristics associated with "city breeding and wealth and universities and foreign travel." [32] Not lost upon him was the fact that Roosevelt had been a member of the National Institute of Arts and Letters before he became a Rough Rider. He was, according to the Italian historian Guglielmo Ferrero, at once "a man of profound and delicate culture" and "a barbarian" who took a keen delight in certain forms of violence.[33] The prospect of mastering books as well as grizzly bears challenged and excited him. As a Dakota rancher he prepared for spring roundups while he was working on several literary and historical projects. Notwithstanding all his virile exploits, one of his cowhands observed that "the boss aint

[31] Harry Thurston Peck, "President Roosevelt," *Bookman,* XXIX (March, 1909), 25–31. Peck, an erudite professor of Latin at Columbia and an editor of the *Bookman,* offered one of the most penetrating portraits of Roosevelt by a contemporary in his *Twenty Years of the Republic, 1885–1905* (New York: Dodd, 1906).

[32] William Garrott Brown, "The Personality of Theodore Roosevelt," *Independent,* LV (1903), 1550.

[33] Guglielmo Ferrero, "Theodore Roosevelt: A Characterization," *South Atlantic Quarterly,* IX (1910), 286–88. Ferrero likened Roosevelt to French political leaders, whereas another writer had declared that "he seemed to belong rather to the English than to American order of public men." See "A Foreign Estimate of Mr. Roosevelt," *North American Review,* DLXXII (1904), 121.

no bronco-buster." [34] The boss was, by his own definition in 1895, "a literary man with a large family of small children." [35] A man of diverse interests, Roosevelt delighted in the company of scholars, businessmen, journalists, athletes, literary figures, politicians, and former Rough Riders. Despite a tendency to dominate conversations, he was receptive to the ideas and opinions of a wide variety of individuals ranging from the "bright young men" of his Tennis Cabinet to the Socialist Upton Sinclair.[36] Roosevelt made an effort "to know all sides of life, to learn all shades of opinion and to keep himself informed." [37] Although some disputed the depth of his knowledge, no one questioned its range. Certainly few Presidents have read so widely in so many fields or in so many languages. The scope of his learning and interests made it easy for him to shift from the plotting of an intricate political maneuver to a knowledgeable discourse on Icelandic literature or to a debate about some obscure zoological question.[38] His work as a naturalist, especially in ornithology, won wide acclaim and his achievements as a historian brought him the presidency of the American Historical Association. Roosevelt befriended artists and architects and sought their "expert judgment" in such matters as the restoration of the White House, the improvement of the coinage, and the establishment of a national gallery of art. Urged to create a council of fine arts, he told a friend: "I am going to do what these men want. It is a move for civilization.

[34] Quoted in Joseph B. Gilder, "A Man of Letters in the White House," *Critic*, XXIX (1901), 403.

[35] Roosevelt to Frederic Remington, November 29, 1895, in Morison (ed.), *Roosevelt Letters*, I, 497.

[36] Upton Sinclair, *Autobiography of Upton Sinclair* (New York: Harcourt, 1962), 118–20.

[37] Harry Thurston Peck, *Twenty Years of the Republic*, 681.

[38] For Roosevelt's interest in literary, artistic, and aesthetic matters see Willard B. Gatewood, Jr., "Theodore Roosevelt: Champion of 'Governmental Aesthetics'," *Georgia Review*, XXI (1967), 172–83; Charles Fenton, "Theodore Roosevelt as a Man of Letters," *Western Humanities Review*, XIII (1959) , 369–74; Henry A. Beers, "Roosevelt as a Man of Letters," *Yale Review*, VIII (1919), 694–709; Edwin Mims, "President Theodore Roosevelt," *South Atlantic Quarterly*, IV (1905), 49–51; Edwin S. Ranck, "What Roosevelt Did for Art in America," *Art and Archeology*, VIII (1919), 291–93; Gilder, "A Man of Letters in the White House," 401–409.

It is a good deal better than appointing third-class postmasters." [39] Although the conventions of the time and his "atavistic Puritanism" severely restricted his appreciation of literature, novelists and poets received encouragement from the White House throughout his tenure. "For once in our history," his friend Owen Wister remarked, "we had an American *salon*." [40] Grudgingly H. L. Mencken later admitted that "only one President since the birth of the Republic has ever welcomed men of letters at the White House," but added that "that one, the sainted Roosevelt, judged them by their theological orthodoxy and the hair on their chests." [41]

For many who knew Roosevelt intimately the key to understanding his peculiar hold upon the American people was his temperament. In political campaigns, Roosevelt himself rather than his accomplishments or the Square Deal was likely to be the principal issue. After talking with him for five hours on his second day in the White House, Richard Watson Gilder, editor of the *Century*, wrote, "He rings true! He is a noble fellow. He has an excess of temperament but a serviceable conscience as well." [42] Ida Tarbell, the muckraker, recalled that as she sat near the President during a White House musicale she was suddenly seized with alarm lest he burst out of his clothes. "I felt his clothes might not contain him," she declared, "he was so steamed up, so ready to go, to attack anything, anywhere." [43] David S. Barry, the veteran Washington correspondent of the New York *Sun*, insisted that Roosevelt's "per-

[39] Quoted in Cass Gilbert, "Roosevelt and the Fine Arts: A Foreword," *American Architect*, CXVI (1919), 710. Despite the breadth of Roosevelt's learning and interests, he was not oblivious to his shortcomings. In a conversation with Madame Jusserand, the wife of the French ambassador, he declared, "I am not learned. I know about some subjects which have interested me and which I have studied. Between them are immense gaps. Mrs. Roosevelt is much more literary than I am; she can read Spenser, which is for me impossible." Such references to his "immense gaps" appeared often in his conversations with artists. Jusserand,*What Me Befell*, 222.

[40] Owen Wister, *Roosevelt: The Story of a Friendship, 1880–1919* (New York: Macmillan, 1930), 124.

[41] H. L. Mencken, *Prejudices: Fifth Series* (New York: Knopf, 1926), 184–85.

[42] Quoted in Rosamond Gilder (ed.), *The Letters of Richard Watson Gilder* (Boston: Houghton, 1916), 341.

[43] Ida Tarbell, *All in a Day's Work: An Autobiography* (New York: Macmillan, 1939), 211.

sonality was so fascinating, so appealing to popular fancy, so over-powering, so alive, and altogether so unique that, in a way, it overshadowed his public acts; that is, the public was more inter-ested in him, and the way he did things and in seeing him do them than they were about what he did." Roosevelt received enthusi-astic approval for behavior which "if followed by any other man would have been criticized and condemned." [44] Highly vocal critics existed, to be sure; but many were like Henry Adams, who, in spite of complaints about "Theodore's vanity, ambition, dogmatic tem-per, and cephalopodic brain," was irresistibly attracted to "the fiend with tusks and eyeglasses across the way." [45] William Allen White, an unabashed admirer of this "gorgeous, fighting, loving, hating, robust man," conceded that he occasionally "gave voice loudest to convince himself." [46]

The perpetual motion of Roosevelt—whether he was delivering a homily on "malefactors of wealth," crusading against Nature-Fakers,[47] or exhausting generals and foreign ambassadors in some type of physical exercise—was a constant source of popular fascina-tion. But his was not merely a facility for action—it was action en-dowed with intense moral conviction and drama. Without any intention of disparagement Lord John Morley described Roosevelt as "an interesting combination of St. Vitus and St. Paul" and placed him alongside the "Niagara Rapids" as the most impressive phe-nomenon in America.[48] In the words of one acquaintance, Roosevelt displayed "the force and energy of two strong men combined." [49]

[44] David S. Barry, *Forty Years in Washington* (Boston: Little, 1924), 263.

[45] Henry Adams to Elizabeth Cameron, March 2, 1902, Adams to Margaret Chanler, January 27, 1905, in Worthington C. Ford (ed.), *Letters of Henry Adams* (2 vols.; Boston: Houghton, 1938), II, 376, 445.

[46] William Allen White, *Masks in a Pageant* (New York: Macmillan, 1928), 286–87.

[47] For an account of the Nature-Fakers episode see Broadus F. Farrar, "John Burroughs, Theodore Roosevelt and the Nature-Fakers," *Tennessee Studies in Literature*, IV (1959), 121–30.

[48] Peck, *Twenty Years of the Republic*, 669; John Morley, *Recollections* (New York: Macmillan, 1917), 107–108.

[49] Lyman Gage, *Memoirs of Lyman Gage* (New York: House of Field, 1937), 142.

Another suggested that action was a drug for him.[50] His frenzied pace undoubtedly contributed to the spread of rumors charging that he was continually under the influence of alcohol. Finally, in 1913, he laid these rumors to rest and established his sobriety by a successful libel suit against a Michigan editor.[51]

As many of his contemporaries discerned, Roosevelt's "actions often failed to square with his spoken word." [52] For all his "wild talk," Henry Adams observed, Roosevelt was "exceedingly conservative." [53] Imbued with a profound respect for traditional institutions and for "orderly liberty," he opposed radical alterations likely to produce disruptive effects. "The reform that counts," he declared in 1906, "is that which comes through steady, continuous growth." [54] Writing as a progressive disillusioned with the Progressive Era, John Chamberlain claimed that "all the chopping and changing, the roaring invocations to morality and the sudden descents to political bargaining" only proved that Roosevelt was "a perfect *representative*" of the confused middle class, which "had delusions about rising into the plutocracy and yet it feared being forced into the ranks of labor." The result was equivocation on virtually all vital issues.[55] Nearer the verdict of historians who have attempted to account for the disparity between Roosevelt's words and actions was the analysis in 1905 by Harry Thurston Peck, who claimed that "he was amenable to pressure" and frequently took "the line of least resistance, rather than fight doggedly against a stubborn opposition." [56]

Roosevelt may not have been the "complete rationalizer" that some claimed he was, but his profession made him a great compromiser and his moral code compelled him to justify every ac-

---

[50] John Chamberlain, *Farewell to Reform* (New York: Liveright, 1932), 236.

[51] See Melvin G. Holli and C. Davis Tompkins, "Roosevelt vs. Newett: The Politics of Libel," *Michigan History*, XLVII (1963), 338–56.

[52] Peck, *Twenty Years of the Republic*, 674.

[53] Adams to Charles Milnes Gaskell, April 23, 1906, in Ford (ed.), *Henry Adams Letters*, II, 469.

[54] A. B. Hart and H. R. Ferleger (eds.), *Theodore Roosevelt Cyclopedia* (New York: Roosevelt Memorial Assn., 1941), 514.

[55] Chamberlain, *Farewell to Reform*, 269.

[56] Peck, *Twenty Years of the Republic*, 674.

tion. That the truth sometimes became blurred in the process allowed critics to raise questions about his integrity. Oliver Wendell Holmes, Jr., whom Roosevelt appointed to the Supreme Court in 1902, interpreted his behavior as that of a shrewd and "pretty unscrupulous politician." [57] But the fact that Roosevelt acted at all in crucial areas, regardless of whether he compromised more than was necessary or promised more than he delivered, provided the stimulus essential to reform. Astute observers like Peck predicted that in time Roosevelt's name would justifiably become "linked with a great series of social and political movements to which he gave, at times, the initial impulse." [58]

In 1903 William Garrott Brown suggested that posterity would view Roosevelt as "a representative of his time rather than the creator of new national ideals." [59] His concern was the restoration of the moral and ethical values of the older mercantile community in which he had been reared. Although Roosevelt often gave expression to the deterministic philosophy so much in vogue in the late nineteenth century, he did not altogether reject the assumption of certain reformers that man could direct his own destiny. For him the human condition was determined partly by "great blind forces" and partly by the individual.[60] "We, ourselves," Roosevelt wrote in 1894, "are not certain that progress is assured; we only assert that it may be assured if we live wise, brave, and upright lives." [61] His emphasis was always upon individual responsibility and the development of what he called character. On one occasion he declared that character was composed of two sets of traits: one included "clean living, decency, morality, virtue, the desire and power to deal fairly by his neighbor, each by his friends, each toward the state"; the other set was made up of "hardihood, resolution, courage,

[57] Mark DeWolfe Howe (ed.), *Holmes–Pollock Letters: Correspondence of Mr. Justice Holmes and Sir Frederick Pollock, 1874–1932* (2 vols.; Cambridge: Harvard, 1941), II, 63–64.

[58] Peck, "President Roosevelt," 30.

[59] Brown, "The Personality of Theodore Roosevelt," 1551.

[60] Mowry, *Era of Roosevelt*, 112.

[61] Theodore Roosevelt, "National Life and Character," *Sewanee Review*, II (1894), 375.

the power to do, the power to dare, the power to endure." [62] To-gether these qualities constituted the "sum of social efficiency," which was "the prime factor in the preservation of a race." [63] Hence, Roosevelt claimed that he was "neither for the rich man nor the poor man as such," but "for the upright man, rich or poor." For him the real need in America was "the *fundamental* fight for morality," a fight in which he assumed the leadership.[64] No one, Henry Cabot Lodge asserted, could read his speeches without realizing his "striving for righteousness." [65]

Embodying the bad as well as the good of America, Roosevelt was admired by his countrymen almost as much for his failings as for his "finer qualities." If he gave voice to the nobler aspirations of the nation, his defects were those of a majority of the people. Harry Thurston Peck noted that "the self-consciousness, the touch of the swagger, the love of applause and of publicity, the occasional lapse of official dignity, even the reckless speech, the unnecessary frankness, and the disregard of form" which characterized Roosevelt were in reality "traits that . . . were national." [66] One of Roosevelt's bitterest critics wrote, "Roosevelt is popular—as popular as any President in our history. America has a hysterical element. Official hysterics appeal to them. With some of our people physical size means greatness. In them Roosevelt touches a responsive chord. Many of our people are boastful and self-assertive. Roosevelt is their ideal. Fulmination, bluster, clamorousness appeal to some of us. Roosevelt satisfies us. Millions of us love Roosevelt for what he is not, but what we think him; for what we think he has done, not for what he has actually done." [67] Because many Americans saw in

62 Quoted in Hart and Ferleger (eds.) , *Theodore Roosevelt Cyclopedia*, 69.

63 Theodore Roosevelt, *American Ideals and Other Essays* (2 vols.; New York: Putnam, 1903), II, 263.

64 Quoted in Richard Hofstadter, *The American Political Tradition and the Men Who Made It* (New York: Vintage, 1960), 229.

65 Henry C. Lodge, "Theodore Roosevelt," *Critic*, XLIV (1904) , 312–14.

66 Peck, *Twenty Years of the Republic*, 678. Lewis Einstein said of Roosevelt, "In his tastes as in his origin he regarded himself as a kind of synthesis of the United States and deliberately shaped his life in that direction." *Roosevelt: His Mind in Action*, 243.

67 John W. Bennett, *Roosevelt and the Republic* (New York: Broadway Publishing Co., 1908), 401.

Roosevelt a reflection of themselves, "his most obvious faults commended him to the multitude and made for a popularity that never quite deserted him." [68] Perhaps, as H. G. Wells observed in 1906, the President was "America for the first time vocal to herself." [69]

Roosevelt was a man whose impulses were as contradictory as they were strong. He was many things to many people, as Professor George Mowry has noted, "because he was also many things to himself." [70] At one time or another he was likened to Tiberius Gracchus, Andrew Jackson, Napoleon, William II of Germany, and "a school boy." [71] George S. Viereck, an apologist for Germany who was the focus of Roosevelt's ire during World War I, maintained that because the President was a typical example of the bipolar personality, his whole career was "a study in ambivalence." Roosevelt "was at once the Progressive and the Reactionary," Viereck wrote. "He was sophist and Rough Rider, Simple Simon and Machiavelli, rolled into one." [72] It is not surprising in view of this bipolarity that his contemporaries rendered conflicting judgments on his character and personality. Partisans extolled his virtues and claimed for him a degree of greatness that he never attained. Critics, all the while, employed such adjectives as *cunning, selfish, vindictive, melodramatic, dishonest, shallow,* and *cynical* to describe a President who in their opinion managed to gloss over his glaring defects by a skillful use of publicity and a well-organized press service. [73] And if

[68] Henry Watterson, *"Marse Henry": An Autobiography* (2 vols.; New York: Doran, 1919), II, 158.

[69] H. G. Wells, *The Future of America* (New York: Harper, 1906), 249–50.

[70] Mowry, *Era of Roosevelt*, 110.

[71] Charles Dana, "Theodore Roosevelt and Tiberius Gracchus," *North American Review*, DLXXX (1905), 327–34; A. Maurice Low, "Theodore Roosevelt," *Forum*, XXXII (1901), 259–67; George Harvey, "Jackson and Roosevelt: A Parallel," *North American Review*, DCXII (1907), 742–54.

[72] Viereck, *Roosevelt: A Study in Ambivalence*, 56.

[73] See Bennett, *Roosevelt and the Republic*, 401–11. Various writers discussed the special relationship between Roosevelt and the press and referred to the President's talents as a "publicity agent." J. J. Dickinson considered him "the greatest publicity promoter among the sons of man today," and Mrs. Annie Riley Hale referred to his "manipulation of the press" and to his appointment of so many newspapermen to government offices. Oswald Garrison Villard of the New York *Evening Post* maintained that Roosevelt "did more to corrupt the press than anyone else." See Dickinson, "Theodore Roosevelt: Press Agent,"

Roosevelt's friends claimed he "had more genuine sympathy with more classes of people than any other man in the public life of the country," [74] his critics were equally certain that he was disdainful of the masses and transformed the White House into "a kingly court." [75]

Contemporary opinion also sharply divided over the question of Roosevelt's "open-mindedness." Several of those who were intimately acquainted with him fully agreed with Henry L. Stoddard's declaration: "I recall none more ready to listen to the views of others, more willing when convinced to put aside his own ideas, more ready to accept group judgment in preference to his own than Theodore Roosevelt." [76] Others interpreted such a characterization as evidence that he was a cynical, self-seeking politician willing to accommodate "group judgment" for purely selfish reasons. For them his "case of incipient megalomania" [77] precluded the placing of too much stress upon his "open-mindedness," and suggested instead that he was inclined toward self-hypnosis or self-deceit. "His mind," according to Henry Watterson, who had known him since childhood, "was of the order which is prone to believe what it wants to believe." [78] And, convinced that he was always on the side of righteousness, he was determined "to have his own way." [79] Because Roosevelt was "self-centered to an extreme," one knowledgeable acquaintance observed, he was blind to "glaring exceptions in his applications of the Square Deal." [80] Among those who corroborated

Harper's Weekly, LI (1907), 1410, 1428; Hale, *Rooseveltian Fact and Fable* (New York: Broadway Publishing Co., 1908), 86–95; Villard, *Fighting Years: Memoirs of a Liberal Editor* (New York: Harcourt, 1939), 151–52.

[74] Charles G. Washburn, *Theodore Roosevelt: The Logic of His Career* (Boston: Houghton, 1916), 202.

[75] Bennett, *Roosevelt and the Republic,* 352.

[76] Henry L. Stoddard, *As I Knew Them* (New York: Harper, 1927), 293. See also L. Abbott, "Theodore Roosevelt: A Personal Sketch," *Outlook,* LXXVIII (1904), 523–26; Albert Shaw, "Theodore Roosevelt," *American Review of Reviews,* LIX (1919), 156–60; Day A. Willey, "The Personality of Theodore Roosevelt," *Munsey's Magazine,* XXI (1904), 161–69.

[77] Peck, "President Roosevelt," 29.

[78] Watterson, *"Marse Henry,"* II, 167.

[79] John D. Works, "A Glance at President Roosevelt's Administration and Personality," *Arena,* XXXIX (1908), 157.

[80] Solomon B. Griffin, *People and Politics* (Boston: Little, 1923), 397–98.

this view from personal experience was Joseph L. Bristow, a trouble-shooter for the Roosevelt administration and a principal investigator during the exposure of the postal scandals in 1903. Bristow, convinced that he had been treated shabbily, believed that "in his personal friendships and personal relations" Roosevelt was "insincere, subordinating all matters of personal loyalty or the rights of an individual . . . to his own ambitions and interests." In his opinion Roosevelt's insatiable lust for public applause transcended any desire he had to "give a weak man a square deal." [81] By his own admission the President consciously sought popular approval. "I love it," he declared, "for the power it gives." [82] Because Roosevelt possessed a strain of ruthlessness often linked to the competitive personality, he broke his own rules of justice and fairness. He condemned individuals without first giving them a hearing, rarely admitted the possibility of error, and occasionally employed the dangerous tactic of guilt by association. Opponents who could not be won over were likely to be dismissed as traitors or mollycoddles.

Another persistent source of disagreement among contemporaries who ventured judgments on Roosevelt concerned his penchant for impulsive behavior and rash speech. On one occasion Henry Adams remarked that "mind in the technical sense, he has not" because "his mind is impulse." The result, Adams insisted, was utter confusion which was "none the less confused" because Roosevelt "rides on it." [83] In a similar vein Henry Watterson attributed "the inconsistencies and quarrels" in which Roosevelt became involved to the fact that "he did not take much time to think" and "leaped to conclusions." These quarrels and inconsistencies were, according to John Chamberlain, related to Roosevelt's most obvious characteristic—his "inability to think things through." [84] Others less temperate in their estimates described him as "an erratic and irresponsible force," as a disruptive factor in American life, who had proved to

[81] Quoted in Charles G. Dawes, *A Journal of the McKinley Years* (Chicago: Lakeside Press, 1950), 405–406.

[82] Quoted in Jusserand, *What Me Befell*, 346.

[83] Ernest Samuels, *Henry Adams: The Major Phase* (Cambridge: Harvard, 1964), 252; Adams to Cameron, June 6, 1905, in Ford (ed.), *Henry Adams Letters*, II, 454.

[84] Watterson, *"Marse Henry,"* 167; Chamberlain, *Farewell to Reform*, 265.

be the madman that Mark Hanna had said he was in 1900 when he protested Roosevelt's nomination for the vice-presidency. In their view, virtually every act by Roosevelt, whether it concerned taking "In God We Trust" off coins or closing the post office in Indianola, Mississippi, was credited to his impulsiveness. His lack of restraint, coupled with what was termed his taste for "monarchial forms," prompted some to consider him a menace to republican institutions.[85]

The testimony of a vast majority of those on intimate terms with Roosevelt forthrightly contradicted the allegations regarding his impetuosity. In noting the most impressive qualities of Roosevelt, Lawrence Abbott placed "caution" first in a list that included courage, gentleness, and humor.[86] To corroborate this view others emphasized that the President had "in his veins the blood of a long line of Dutch ancestors, a race noted rather for their phlegm than for their impetuosity." [87] Convinced that Roosevelt "rarely spoke hastily" and "never acted tardily," William Allen White declared, "Out of his countenance two men were wont to gaze at the world: one was a primitive—impetuous, imperious, splashing in a reservoir of vigor; the other was sophisticated, never quite furtive, but often feline." [88] The "substratum of Dutch caution" could, so the argument ran, be counted upon to restrain the strong and vivid impulses. "No man," Henry Cabot Lodge asserted in 1904, "has been in the White House for many years who is so ready to take advice, who has made up his mind more slowly, more deliberately and after more consultation." [89] In a series of perceptive lectures at Amherst College in 1924, Professor Charles E. Merriam maintained that Roosevelt's courage "seldom led him into rashness." He observed, "There was an element of canniness and prudence in his temperament that held him back from enterprises that were foolhardy. His life was not all San Juans and Armageddons. In the main

85 See especially Bennett, *Roosevelt and the Republic*, 298–312; Hale, *Rooseveltian Fact and Fable*, 190.

86 Lawrence Abbott, *Impressions of Theodore Roosevelt* (Garden City, N.Y.: Doubleday, 1919), 267–73.

87 Seth Low, "Theodore Roosevelt," *Forum*, XXXII (1901), 264.

88 White, *Masks in a Pageant*, 285.

89 Henry Cabot Lodge, "Roosevelt," *McClure's*, XXIV (November, 1904), 10.

he succeeded in selecting strategic points where the chances for success were an insurable political risk." [90] A host of Roosevelt's acquaintances claimed that his reputation for impulsiveness was the mischievous work of those who underestimated "the quickness of his mind," which was conservatively estimated to be "about ten times that of the ordinary man." [91] Booker T. Washington, crediting the President with qualities which he himself possessed in abundance, insisted that Roosevelt was at all times master of himself and of his surroundings because "he not only thinks quickly, but he plans and thinks a long distance ahead." [92] Perhaps, as Henry L. Stoddard suggested, those "impulsive phrases which his opponents made popular by their denunciation, were the most deliberately thought out phrases of all, and usually got the reaction he wanted." [93] It may well have been that many of Roosevelt's so-called indiscretions were not so much the product of sudden impulse as they were of calculated efforts to score a point by employing his talent for dramatic effect.

Whatever the differences regarding Roosevelt's impulsiveness, both friend and foe agreed on another facet of his personality—his affinity for controversy. Combative by instinct and early training, Roosevelt throughout his career was a storm center of controversy. His term as President opened with a disturbance caused by his dinner with Booker T. Washington and ended amid a bitter quarrel with Congress over the Secret Service. Jules Jusserand, the French ambassador, declared, "Until the end of his presidency Mr. Roosevelt remained *qualis ab incepte*: same ideal, same means, for better for worse, for reaching such an ideal. That means was to give battle." [94] Commenting on his penchant for controversy, one Roosevelt scholar has written, "He created it, he fell into it, and he

[90] Charles E. Merriam, *Four American Party Leaders* (Freeport, N.Y.: Bks. for Libs., 1967), 41.

[91] L. Abbott, "Theodore Roosevelt: A Personal Sketch," 524. See also L. F. Abbott (ed.), *Archie Butt Letters*, 112; Joseph B. Bishop, *Notes and Anecdotes of Many Years* (New York: Scribner, 1925), 128–29.

[92] Booker T. Washington, *My Larger Education: Being Chapters from My Experience* (Garden City, N.Y.: Doubleday, 1911), 169.

[93] Stoddard, *As I Knew Them*, 311–12.

[94] Jusserand, *What Me Befell*, 342.

searched it out. When he was not rebuking his once trusted friends, he was taunting his long-sworn enemies, and if he was fleetingly at peace with both, as occasionally he was, it was rarely the peace that passeth understanding." [95] Some controversies erupted as a result of his battle in behalf of a long-standing commitment to an important principle, as in the case of his campaign for the conservation of natural resources; others were largely tactical as when he used the case of William A. Miller, a foreman in the Government Printing Office, to establish the open shop in government service; and on rare occasions Roosevelt provoked controversy by espousing a quixotic cause like spelling reform.[96] Never hesitant to put the Ananias badge on both the quick and the dead, Roosevelt was always "the soul of controversy." [97] Early in 1902, Henry Adams wrote a friend that Roosevelt was thriving on "at least one fight a week" and that he himself had come to "dread the daily bread of battle." [98] William Roscoe Thayer agreed that Roosevelt's dominant trait was his combativeness but insisted that "the idea that he was truculent or pugnacious, that he went about with a chip on his shoulder, that he loved fighting for the sake of fighting" was a mistake.[99] Although historians have often explained this trait largely as a result of compensation for his physical inferiority as a youth, Richard Hofstadter contends that Roosevelt "was fleeing from some more persistent sense of deficiency than that induced by the obvious traumatic experiences of his childhood." [100] There can be no doubt that the Roosevelt style was rooted in his personal past; but, as Harry Thurston Peck suggested in 1909, Roosevelt "is not easy to explain except in a psychological laboratory." [101] Perhaps more important

[95] Harbaugh, *Power and Responsibility*, 303.

[96] A brief treatment of Roosevelt's involvement in spelling reform is found in C. H. Dornbusch, "American Spelling Simplified by Presidential Edict," *American Speech*, XXXVI (1961), 236–38.

[97] Watterson, *"Marse Henry,"* II, 158.

[98] Adams to Cameron, March 2, 1902, in Ford (ed.), *Henry Adams Letters*, II, 376.

[99] William Roscoe Thayer, *Theodore Roosevelt: An Intimate Biography* (Boston: Houghton, 1919), 201.

[100] Hofstadter, *American Political Tradition*, 210.

[101] Peck, "President Roosevelt," 29.

than the unique Roosevelt psyche was his uncanny ability to use his pugnacity.

In retrospect, some of the combat upon which Roosevelt lavished so much passion and energy appears to have been merely the "childish pirouetting over a void" that one contemporary said it was.[102] On occasion such effort was largely a source of popular entertainment. Even Roosevelt himself appreciated the humorous aspect of his highly publicized quarrel with Mrs. Bellamy Storer, the wife of the American ambassador to Austria, who involved the White House in her intrigues at the Vatican. But many of the controversies which "he created, fell into or searched out" served more significant functions. Not the least among these was an opportunity to dramatize an issue and to focus public attention upon it. Whatever his deficiencies as an orator, he performed superbly as a preacher[103] and press agent capable of endowing the commonplace with sufficient moral conviction or bellicose emotion to give it "pith and point." Such a talent enabled him to transform a relatively minor incident into a *cause célèbre*. In the process he not only educated public opinion but also attended his own interests and justified the correctness of his position in a voice loud enough to convince himself as well as others.

Controversy, whether small or large, was a vehicle for indulging his talent for preaching. "Wherever he goes," one caustic critic remarked in 1908, "he sets up an impromptu pulpit, and his pious enunciations fall—like the rain and the sunshine, upon the just and the unjust—accompanied with a timely warning to the latter to look sharp!" [104] Indeed, the White House was to Roosevelt a "bully pulpit," [105] from which he preached "partly by instinct, partly by design," for seven and a half years. He capitalized even on his defects and "learned how to make the most effective use of the falsetto

[102] Chamberlain, *Farewell to Reform*, 236.
[103] Reference to Roosevelt as a preacher appeared often in contemporary estimates of him. See White, *Masks in a Pageant*, 318–20; "Our Preacher President," *Independent*, LXI (1906), 1431–32; "Roosevelt as Preacher," *Living Age*, CCLXVIII (1911), 555–58.
[104] Hale, *Rooseveltian Fact and Fable*, 73.
[105] See Mark Sullivan, *Our Times* (6 vols.; New York: Scribner, 1926–35), III, 74.

in his voice, of his well-known teeth, and of his pile-driving manner." [106] William James described his homilies as "just the ordinary street-level talk of fairness and courage, and down with molly-coddles, meaning by them all the men with courage enough to oppose him." For others Rooseveltian oratory conveyed the impression of "a sturdy Dutch statesman with a dash of *élan*." [107] "I am not an orator," Roosevelt explained. "I can't talk anything but platitudes. But platitudes and iteration are necessary in order to hammer the truths and principles I advocate into people's heads." [108] And when Henry Cabot Lodge once suggested that he was preaching too much, Roosevelt retorted: "They like it, don't they?" [109] To be sure, the moralistic tone of his rhetoric sometimes obscured the more mundane objectives of his exhortations. But there is reason to suspect that it was intended that way.

As Roosevelt prepared to take leave of the White House in 1909, Americans inclined to reflect upon his tenure generally agreed that it possessed a distinctive quality. Mark Twain, while fascinated by the Rooseveltian personality, was critical of his administration. For all his "ferocious attacks" upon trusts, Twain concluded, he had "merely indulged in wordy bluster about what he was going to do." But more serious, in his view, was Roosevelt's contribution to the creation of a monarchy in the United States. Other critics likened his departure to "Caesar laying down his crown." By "perverting democratic ideals and centralizing governmental power," they argued, Roosevelt bequeathed to his successor, William Howard Taft, a bureaucratic government "as personal as that of a Czar." [110] Implicit in such diatribes was a recognition of his chief contribution, namely the revitalization of the presidential office and the improve-

---

[106] Blum, *The Republican Roosevelt*, 60; Merriam, *Four American Party Leaders*, 38.

[107] Quoted in Perry Bliss, *Life and Letters of Henry Lee Higginson* (Boston: Atlantic Monthly Press, 1921), 362. Despite James's criticism, he declared, "At the same time I believe his [Roosevelt's] influence on our public life and on our people's feeling about public life has been of enormous value." *Ibid*; Merriam, *Four American Party Leaders*, 38.

[108] Bishop, *Notes and Anecdotes of Many Years*, 117.

[109] Quoted in Griffin, *People and Politics*, 395.

[110] Mark Twain, *Mark Twain in Eruption*, ed. Bernard De Voto (New York: Harper, 1922), 1–4; Bennett, *Roosevelt and the Republic*, 422.

ment in the quality and morale of civil servants. Some analysts attempted to explain the meaning of the Roosevelt administration by citing its specific accomplishments. But as most of them recognized, neither descriptions of Roosevelt's foreign policies nor references to trust-busting, railroad and pure food regulation, conservation, administrative efficiency, the Great White Fleet, the Nobel Peace Prize, and the Panama Canal captured the essence of the "Epoch of Roosevelt." The essence was Roosevelt himself, the "vital radiance" and inspirational quality of the man.[111] The *Nation*, whose editors had often exchanged insults with the President, interpreted his administration in terms of his "salient personality" and consummate skill as a politician. "For knowing when to seize the occasion; for understanding perfectly how to hit popular feeling between wind and water," the *Nation* declared editorially, "and above all, for ability to impress and handle men, not singly but by the millions, we have not looked upon his like." [112] Equally perceptive was another frequent critic of Roosevelt, Senator Robert La Follette, who predicted in March, 1909, that historians were "likely to say he did many notable things," but the most notable, though one for which Roosevelt was loath to take credit, was his success in making reform respectable. "The task of making reform respectable," La Follette concluded, ". . . is greater than the man who performed it is likely to think." [113] For Henry Adams, who appeared never to take Roosevelt seriously, the "last vision of fun and gaiety" would vanish with his departure from office. Past complaints and criticisms notwithstanding, Adams confessed, "never can we replace him." [114]

On March 4, 1909, the "many-sided Roosevelt"—preacher, politician, man of letters, diplomat, soldier, hunter, naturalist, "the eternal human," who for seven and a half years had inspired, amazed, delighted, and infuriated the American people—left the White House. Until his death almost a decade later, he remained

---

[111] See Mrs. Winthrop Chanler, *Roman Spring: Memoirs* (Boston: Little, 1934), 195.

[112] "A Parting Glance at Roosevelt," *Nation*, LXXXVIII (1909), 241.

[113] *La Follette's Magazine*, I (March 13, 1909), 4.

[114] Adams to Sir Ronald Lindsay, January 16, 1909, in Ford (ed.), *Henry Adams Letters*, II, 515.

an active and a highly visible force in the life of the nation. His postpresidential years were spent as a contributing editor of the *Outlook,* an advocate of the New Nationalism, the Progressive Party's unsuccessful presidential candidate in 1912, and a persistent critic of the domestic and foreign policies of Woodrow Wilson. On renewing his acquaintance with the former President in 1910, Rudyard Kipling wrote an American friend: "Take care of him. He is scarce and valuable." [115] In the words of Guglielmo Ferrero, Roosevelt personified Young America, which, though wedded to the past in many respects, looked confidently to the future.[116] To understand him was to appreciate the complexities and incongruities of American life.

---

[115] Quoted in James Ford Rhodes, *The McKinley and Roosevelt Administrations, 1897–1909* (New York: Macmillan, 1923), 399.
[116] Ferrero, "Theodore Roosevelt," 286–87.

II

The Roosevelt–Washington Dinner:
The Accretion of Folklore

*When I asked Booker T. Washington to dinner I did not
devote very much thought to the matter . . . . I respect
him greatly and believe in the work he has done. I have
consulted so much with him it seemed to me that it was
natural to ask him to dinner to talk over this work, and the
very fact that I felt a moment's qualm on inviting him because of his color made me ashamed of myself and made
me hasten to send the invitation. I did not think of its
bearing one way or the other, either on my own future or
on anything else.*

THEODORE ROOSEVELT

Several days before the inauguration of Theodore Roosevelt in
March, 1905, an incident occurred in a District of Columbia school
which called attention to a controversial act committed by him
more than three years earlier. The students in an English class at
Western High School were writing sentences on the blackboard to
illustrate the meaning of various words. The word *debased* fell to a
student by the name of Reginald Hodgson, who used it in the following sentence: "Roosevelt debased himself by eating with a nigger." The school principal immediately demanded his expulsion,
but her superiors hesitated to take such drastic action for fear that
it would have an "adverse effect upon student morale." Instead,
Hodgson was punished by being deprived of marching with the
school band in the inauguration parade to honor the President
guilty of such self-debasement.[1] Young Hodgson's vivid expression
of an attitude prevalent among white Americans early in the twen-

[1] New York *Times*, March 11, 1905.

tieth century referred to a meal that became a *cause célèbre* in American history. It was Roosevelt's dinner at the White House on October 16, 1901, with the famous Negro educator Booker T. Washington.[2]

A relationship of respect and admiration had developed between Roosevelt and Washington during their acquaintance of several years before the fateful meal. Roosevelt, assuming that Washington was the spokesman for Negro America and impressed by his conservative approach to racial problems, placed much faith in his judgment and reckoned him a useful ally. Washington, a complex and often devious individual, likewise recognized the advantages of his intimacy with Roosevelt, whom he later described as "the highest type of all-round man that I have ever met." In the summer of 1901, Roosevelt made plans for a visit to Tuskegee Institute, the Negro school in Alabama headed by Washington. But the assassination of President William McKinley interrupted these plans.[3]

On September 14, 1901, the day that Roosevelt took the oath of office, he wrote Washington to notify him that his visit to Tuskegee would have to be postponed and to urge him to come to the White House "as soon as possible." The President wrote, "I want to talk over the question of possible future appointments in the South exactly on the lines of our last conversation together." [4] Shortly afterward, Washington conferred with Roosevelt at the White House without attracting any publicity. Upon returning to Alabama, he learned that a federal judgeship in the state had become vacant as a result of the death of Judge John Bruce on October 1, 1901. Unable to make another trip to the capital at the time, Wash-

[2] The most detailed treatment of the dinner is found in Dewey W. Grantham, Jr., "Dinner at the White House: Theodore Roosevelt, Booker T. Washington and the South," *Tennessee Historical Quarterly*, XVII (1958), 112–30. Grantham, however, does not touch upon the conflicting versions of the incident.

[3] Booker T. Washington, *My Larger Education: Being Chapters from My Experience* (Garden City, N.Y.: Doubleday, 1911), 168–76; Theodore Roosevelt to Booker T. Washington, March 21, July 9, 1901, in Elting Morison (ed.), *The Letters of Theodore Roosevelt* (8 vols.; Cambridge: Harvard, 1951–54), III, 24, 113.

[4] Roosevelt to Washington, September 14, 1901, in Morison (ed.), *Roosevelt Letters*, III, 149.

ington sent his trusted secretary, Emmett J. Scott, to plead the cause of Thomas G. Jones, a conservative Democrat and former governor of Alabama, who vigorously opposed lynching and other crude manifestations of racial prejudice. When pressed by newspapermen to disclose the nature of his mission, Scott adroitly explained that he had merely stopped at the White House on his way to Buffalo in order to invite the President to Tuskegee. He had interviews with Roosevelt on October 4 and 5. Two days after their second conference, the President announced the appointment of Jones to the federal bench, an act that marked the beginning of Washington's role as an arbiter of southern appointments. Fully aware of Washington's role in the selection of Jones, southern Democrats nonetheless greeted the appointment with unrestrained enthusiasm.[5]

Within a few days after Scott's visits to the White House, Roosevelt again felt the need to consult Washington about party affairs in the South. The intraparty struggle among South Carolina Republicans and the "utterly rotten" Republican organization in Mississippi were sources of particular concern to him. Washington was on a tour of Mississippi when he "received word to the effect that the President would like to have a conference" with him. Despite some misgivings about assuming the responsibilities of a political adviser to the President, he decided to go to Washington as soon as he completed his work in Mississippi. He had already scheduled business appointments in New York and had accepted an invitation to represent Tuskegee at the bicentennial celebration at Yale University on October 23, so apparently he planned to stop in Washington for a conference with the President on his way north. Arriving in the capital city early in the afternoon of October 16, Washington went to the home of Whitefield McKinlay, a Negro real-estate dealer and his most trusted ally in the District of Columbia, with whom he customarily stayed when visiting in the city.[6] Waiting for him at McKinlay's house was an invitation from the President to dine at

[5] Emmett J. Scott and Lyman B. Stowe, *Booker T. Washington: Builder of a Civilization* (Garden City, N.Y.: Doubleday, 1916), 49–54; Washington *Evening Star*, October 4, 1901; New York *Daily Tribune*, October 8, 1901.

[6] Washington, *My Larger Education*, 174–75; New York *Daily Tribune*, October 23, 24, 1901.

the White House at 7:30 that evening. Washington accepted and at the appointed hour had dinner with the Roosevelt family and another guest, Philip B. Stewart, a wealthy mining and utility executive long active in Republican politics in Colorado. Following the dinner, Roosevelt conferred with Washington about southern affairs and with Stewart about the muddled political situation in Colorado. Upon leaving the White House, Washington immediately boarded a train for New York.[7]

In spite of Washington's precautions to avoid publicity, news of the dinner almost inadvertently found its way into the press. In checking the White House guest register, a reporter noticed Washington's name, and as a result a routine item, which merely recorded the fact of his presence at a White House dinner, appeared in the city's newspapers on October 17, 1901.[8] Within a few days, however, the event had provoked a storm of controversy. Although the Negro educator might be tolerated as a presidential adviser, the act of breaking bread with the Chief Executive and his family appeared to many, especially in the South, as a gross violation of the racial code. Negroes, on the other hand, seized upon the dinner as a fragment of hope amidst a rising tide of discrimination and disfranchisement. Some whites, notably William Lloyd Garrison, Moorfield Storey, Thomas Wentworth Higginson, and others identified with the abolitionist tradition, applauded the President's act. The American Missionary Association passed a resolution at its annual meeting endorsing the dinner as an appropriate gesture of recognition for an eminent Negro citizen.[9]

Because the so-called Booker Washington incident coincided with a frenzied wave of racism in the South, it touched off an orgy of

[7] Washington, *My Larger Education*, 175–76; Washington to Roosevelt, October 16, 1901, in Theodore Roosevelt Papers, Manuscript Division, Library of Congress; Washington *Evening Star*, October 16, 17, 1901; Roosevelt to P. B. Stewart, October 25, 1901, in Morison (ed.), *Roosevelt Letters*, III, 182.

[8] Washington *Evening Star*, October 17, 1901. In view of the South's violent reaction to Washington's dinner at the White House, Whitefield McKinlay thought it appropriate to make public the fact that a prominent white southerner invited Washington to dine with him on the evening of October 16 and was "greatly disappointed" to learn that he had already accepted an invitation from the President. See Washington *Evening Star*, October 21, 1901.

[9] New York *Daily Tribune*, October 19, 23, 1901.

hysteria there. The dinner, so the southern argument ran, was an act of social equality between the races which implied Roosevelt's tacit approval of miscegenation. The southern press emphasized that Mrs. Roosevelt had been present at the dinner and that the invitation to Washington was a deliberate, premeditated gesture of social equality. A cartoonist depicted Mrs. Roosevelt serving a hideous black monster while the President smiled broadly. In his syndicated columns that appeared in rural weeklies throughout the South, Bill Arp (Charles Henry Smith) suggested that Booker T. Washington's daughter, Portia, who was a student at Wellesley College, might spend the Christmas holidays at the White House, where the President's son could "fall in love with her and marry her without having to elope." [10] One southern editor, bent upon placing the worst possible interpretation upon the incident, telegraphed his Washington representative, "Ascertain if Washington's wife accompanied him to the White House. If so, see if Roosevelt escorted her in to dinner on his arm." [11]

For several years after 1901, riots, lynchings, and racial disturbances in general were traced to the President's dinner with Booker T. Washington on the grounds that it had created restlessness and discontent among Negroes. Much to the dismay of Roosevelt his "act of social equality" was blamed for a wide variety of problems in the South, ranging from the shortage of domestic servants to the burning of four Negroes at the stake in Statesboro, Georgia, in 1904. Demagogues such as Benjamin R. Tillman of South Carolina and James K. Vardaman of Mississippi, not to mention a host of lesser luminaries, persisted in exploiting the theme of "our coon-flavored president" for the sake of promoting their own political careers. Crudest of all was Vardaman, who claimed that the White House had become "so saturated with the odor of the nigger that the rats

[10] For southern reaction to the incident see Grantham, "Dinner at the White House," 115–23, and the Atlanta *Journal*, October 21, 23, 29, 1901. Shortly after the dinner, Henry Watterson accurately predicted, "It was a sensation. Already it rises to the dignity of a 'cause celebre.' Presently we shall begin to speak of 'the Booker Washington incident.'" See Louisville *Courier-Journal*, October 22, 1901; Thomas D. Clark, *The Southern Country Editor* (Indianapolis: Bobbs, 1948), 311.

[11] New York *Daily Tribune*, October 19, 1901.

have taken refuge in the stable." [12] Such exercises in vulgarity almost invariably contained dire warnings that Roosevelt would restore "nigger supremacy" in the South even more thoroughly than in the days of Reconstruction. A well-known Episcopal clergyman in the South expressed a common view when he declared that Roosevelt "could never atone to the Southern people for the one act of eating with a Negro." In 1908, a critic of the President declared that the Booker Washington incident tinged "for the South every subsequent act of his in which the Negro was involved." [13]

It was ironic that Theodore Roosevelt should have suffered such a fate, because his racial views were in many respects similar to the attitudes of those whom he labeled the "best people" in the South. His concept of these "best people" and of the region in general owed much to the influence of his mother, who was a Georgia aristocrat. "My earliest training and principles were Southern," Roosevelt once remarked. He often spoke warmly of his Confederate uncles and occasionally fancied himself a southern gentleman with a taste for mint juleps. When he was elevated to the presidency in 1901, southerners familiar with his books were happy to find so many laudatory references to the fighting qualities of those who wore the gray.[14]

But even though Roosevelt admired the gallantry of certain Confederate military leaders and sympathized with the plight of the South at the opening of the twentieth century, his attitude was scarcely as prosouthern as some editors made it seem at the time of his inauguration. Actually he believed that the predicament of the South was largely of its own making. For him the presence of Negroes in the region was the basic source of the so-called southern

[12] Greenwood (Miss.) *Commonwealth*, January 31, 1903. As late as 1904 Vardaman was still expounding on the Booker Washington incident. He blamed Roosevelt for issuing the invitation and Washington for accepting it. "Booker is a good negro," Vardaman argued. "He is all right if he only keeps in his place." See Jackson (Miss.) *Daily Clarion-Ledger*, April 17, 1904.

[13] *How to Solve the Race Problem: Proceedings of the Washington Conference on the Race Problem in the United States* (Washington: Beresford Printer, 1904), 159; Alfred H. Stone, *Studies in the American Race Problem* (Garden City, N.Y.: Doubleday, 1908), 315.

[14] Lawrence F. Abbott (ed.), *The Letters of Archie Butt* (Garden City, N.Y.: Doubleday, 1924), 18–19, 67.

problem. Although he abhorred slavery and idolized Lincoln, he conceded that the establishment of Negro suffrage by Radical Republicans was a serious mistake. But whatever the excesses of Radical Reconstruction, he argued, "the initial folly" lay with the South, which had embraced a morally indefensible system of slavery and nearly destroyed the Union by attempting to extend that wicked system into free territories. "Every step which followed, from freeing the slave to enfranchising him," was due, he insisted, "only to the North being slowly and reluctantly forced to act by the South's persistence in its wickedness and folly." In his opinion the Fourteenth Amendment was wholly commendable, and even if the Fifteenth Amendment was less desirable, he was unwilling to entertain southern proposals that it be abolished. Convinced that active enforcement of these amendments would create more problems than it would solve, he nonetheless considered their existence necessary as a restraint against the more extreme manifestations of prejudice against black citizens. He occasionally expressed concern about the South's disproportionate representation in Congress as a result of disfranchisement of Negroes, but he consistently refused to take a strong stand against the legal contrivances by which black citizens were denied the vote.[15]

The contradictory nature of his attitude toward these black citizens resulted in part from the constant war between his social consciousness and his commitment to Anglo-Saxon superiority. Like most white Americans of the time, he believed that Negroes as a race were inferior. Yet he conceded that there were individual Negroes of ability who were entitled to recognition and reward. And while the race in general might be considered inferior, its masses were not to be subjected to abuse and degradation at the hands of the superior Anglo-Saxons. Lynching and mob violence were in his view more damaging to the white man than to the black, because they led to disorder and lawlessness, which threatened the very underpinnings of society. Taking a paternalistic view of the Negro

[15] Roosevelt dealt with the southern problem at length in his correspondence. References abound throughout the eight volumes of his published correspondence. The quotation above is from Roosevelt to James Ford Rhodes, February 20, 1905, in Morison (ed.), *Roosevelt Letters*, IV, 1125.

masses, he prescribed for them the self-help formula of Booker T. Washington, which coincided with his own emphasis upon individual responsibility. In brief, Roosevelt sought for the black man what he termed decent treatment rather than the full rights of citizenship. His quarrel with white southerners was not directed at their concept of Anglo-Saxon supremacy but rather at their method of asserting it. That Negro Americans came to view him as a "worthy successor to the Great Emancipator" was more a commentary on the desperate nature of their plight in the Progressive Era than on the magnitude of his cautious efforts to extend the Square Deal to black people.[16]

Roosevelt was both surprised and chagrined by the violent reaction of white southerners to his dinner with Booker T. Washington. He was all the more "melancholy" because the "best people" upon whom he relied for moderation and reason participated in the agitation. In time he came to view the emotional outburst against him as evidence of the South's utter irrationality on the race question. In fact, the reaction to his dinner with Washington made him aware of certain developments in the racial attitudes of the South that he had not previously comprehended. He came to understand that one reason for the clamor in the South against his "act of social equality" was the fact that his administration coincided with the climax of rabidly racist campaigns that accompanied and followed the movement in the region to disfranchise Negroes. But despite his increasing awareness of the perplexities of the "color question," he never fully comprehended the nuances of southern racism. He continued to be baffled and appalled by what he considered the white southerner's talent for wholly inconsistent behavior on matters of race. Perhaps most difficult for him to appreciate were the complex subtleties of the racial caste system.[17]

[16] See Roosevelt to L. J. Moore, February 5, 1900, Roosevelt to Robert J. Fleming, May 21, 1900, in Morison (ed.), *Roosevelt Letters*, II, 1169, 1304–1306; Roosevelt to Owen Wister, April 27, 1906, in Owen Wister, *Roosevelt: The Story of a Friendship, 1880–1919* (New York: Macmillan, 1930), 253.

[17] "Ugh," Roosevelt once remarked, "There is no more puzzling problem in this country today than the problem of color." Quoted in George E. Mowry, "The South and the Progressive Lily White Party of 1912," *Journal of Southern History*, VI (1940), 246.

Interestingly enough, neither Roosevelt nor Washington at the time issued any public statements regarding their dinner. Although Washington repeatedly denied that he granted any interviews concerning the incident, the Indianapolis *Freeman*, a Negro newspaper edited by one of his acquaintances, published what purported to be his comments on it. According to Washington, his first explanation of the episode appeared in print in 1911 with the publication of his autobiographical *My Larger Education*. Roosevelt, significantly perhaps, omitted any mention of the dinner in his autobiography published two years later.[18] Although Roosevelt and Washington refused to elaborate publicly upon the incident at the time, versions of it which were at considerable variance with the actual facts began to circulate shortly afterward. Embellishments appeared occasionally as long as contemporaries of Roosevelt and Washington continued to publish their recollections. Some of these errors, which in time achieved the sanctity of facts, have been incorporated into historical treatments of the incident. One significant aspect of the episode, however, has rarely been disputed in the different versions: Roosevelt invited Washington to the White House because he desired to consult him about southern appointments. Such agreement is understandable since Washington's presence at the White House table with the nation's first family, rather than his role as a presidential adviser, was the primary source of controversy.[19]

At one time or another during the first third of the twentieth century, almost every other facet of the famous meal, ranging from minor details and dates to questions as to whether it was a dinner at all, became a part of a virtual folklore enshrouding the incident. Undoubtedly, some of the errors were the results of faulty memories which attempted to reconstruct an event of the distant past; others appear to have been rationalizations prompted by racial prejudices on the part of individuals whose admiration of Roosevelt would not

[18] New York *Daily Tribune*, October 23, 1901; Washington, *My Larger Education*, 175; Herbert Aptheker (ed.), *A Documentary History of the Negro People in the United States* (2 vols.; New York: Citadel, 1951), II, 863–64; Arna Bontemps, *100 Years of Freedom* (New York: Dodd, 1962), 208–209; Theodore Roosevelt, *An Autobiography* (New York: Macmillan, 1913).

[19] John M. Blum, *The Republican Roosevelt* (Cambridge: Harvard, 1954), 44–45.

allow them to believe that he would invite a Negro to dine at his table. But the timing and progression of the distortions suggest that other factors were involved in transforming the Booker Washington incident from a dinner to which Washington was invited some time in advance into a lunch which he shared with the President alone merely because the latter did not wish to terminate their discussion when lunch was served.

Notwithstanding the fact that the news accounts appearing immediately after the Washington-Roosevelt dinner rather accurately described the details of the affair, slight alterations in the facts began to find their way into print before the end of 1901. A biography of President Roosevelt, written by Charles E. Banks and Leroy Armstrong and published late that year, probably deserves to be classified as the first contribution to the folklore of the Booker Washington incident. Although Washington customarily stayed with his friend Whitefield McKinlay, whose guest he was on the occasion of the famous dinner, Banks and Armstrong insisted that he always stayed at "a small hotel kept for Negroes, named the Southern" because "all the more pretentious hotels . . . were closed to Negroes." To this hotel the President "sent a summons" for Washington to come to the White House. Without specifying what type of meal the Negro leader ate at the White House, Banks and Armstrong claimed that when he left the President's office "he bore in his hand an invitation for Thomas G. Jones to accept appointment as district judge." [20] Others, including Roosevelt himself, committed a similar error when they implied that the decision to select Jones had been the principal topic of the after-dinner conversation between him and Washington.[21] Such a decision could scarcely have been reached at that time since the appointment of Jones had been officially announced on October 7, nine days prior to the White House dinner.

Undoubtedly one topic discussed by the President and Washington was the appointment of William D. Crum, a Negro physician, to a federal post in South Carolina. Washington suggested Crum as

[20] Charles E. Banks and Leroy Armstrong, *Theodore Roosevelt* (Philadelphia: Keeler-Raleigh, 1901), 381–82, 386.

[21] Roosevelt to C. G. Washburn, November 15, 1915, in Morison (ed.), *Roosevelt Letters*, VIII, 981.

collector of internal revenue, a position left vacant on September 17, 1901, by the death of Eugene A. Webster, the white Republican "boss" in the state for many years. By securing positions for Crum and Jones, Washington hoped that "the President could thereby announce at the same time the appointment of a first-grade Southern white Democrat and a first-class colored man." Unfortunately for his plans, a white Republican had already been slated for the revenue post, but the President promised to "consider Crum for any other place" that Washington suggested.[22] Almost a year later, on September 11, 1902, the collector of the Port of Charleston died. Upon Washington's recommendation, Roosevelt appointed Crum to the position. The appointment set off a barrage of criticism in the North as well as the South and revived interest in the Washington-Roosevelt dinner since both incidents were viewed as evidence of the President's heresy regarding the race issue. The critics, however, failed to indicate that they were aware that Crum's appointment might well have been a topic of conversation at that dinner. At any rate, the President released for publication a letter that he had written on November 26, 1902, to the Charleston mayor in defense of his appointment of a Negro as port collector.[23]

This letter largely overshadowed another item pertinent to Roosevelt's so-called Negro policy, which appeared in the press at the same time. It was a report of an interview with Marcus J. Wright, a former Confederate officer employed in the records and pensions division of the War Department since 1878, who provided a wholly new version of the meal which Booker T. Washington had eaten at the White House. An admirer of the President, Wright apparently hoped to quiet fears among his fellow southerners regarding Roosevelt's attitude toward Negroes. While visiting relatives in Memphis, he told a reporter, "Washington did not dine at the White House table, did not break bread with the President's wife and daughters, and was in no sense a guest upon terms of social

[22] Scott and Stowe, *Booker T. Washington*, 53–54; Washington to E. J. Scott (Telegram), October 4, 1901, in Roosevelt Papers.

[23] Roosevelt to J. A. Smyth, November 26, 1902, in Morison (ed.), *Roosevelt Letters*, III, 383–85; Atlanta *Constitution*, November 28, 1902; Washington *Evening Star*, November 27, 1902.

equality." He explained that at Roosevelt's request Washington had come to the White House to discuss southern affairs. They began their conference in the executive office but numerous interruptions forced them to move to an adjoining room. In the midst of this private conference the President's lunch was brought in on a tray. Roosevelt immediately ordered another tray for Washington so that their conference might proceed without further interruption. Wright placed particular emphasis on one point: "no one but the two were present." In reply to a question as to why the President had never denied the dinner version of the incident, Wright declared that such a denial would have been beneath the dignity of a man like Roosevelt, who "was an aristocrat to his finger tips." Some southerners conceded that Wright's account of the affair, "though late," was "important if true." [24]

But for the next three years it apparently caused little change in the hostile attitude of the South toward Roosevelt. The fateful dinner continued to be mentioned in connection with the prolonged agitation over Crum, whose appointment was not finally confirmed until 1905, as well as the new controversy provoked by the President's closing of the post office in Indianola, Mississippi, in 1903, when the white citizens intimidated the Negro postmistress. Early in 1904, two peddlers from Chicago were arrested in Indianola for distributing "obscene photographs" among Negroes. The illicit items were actually pictures of "President Roosevelt and Booker Washington dining together" amid banners boldly proclaiming EQUALITY.[25] The dinner also figured in the Maryland political campaign of 1903. The Democrats used campaign buttons showing Roosevelt and Washington at dinner.[26] Voicing a sentiment preva-

[24] Macon (Ga.) *News*, November 27, 1902; Augusta (Ga.) *Chronicle*, November 27, 1902.

[25] "Southern Press on the Indianola Incident," *Literary Digest*, XXVI (1903), 71–72; *Congressional Record*, 57th Cong., 2nd Sess., 853–54.

[26] Washington *Evening Star*, October 28, 1901; Roosevelt to L. Abbott, October 29, 1903, in Morison (ed.), *Roosevelt Letters*, III, 639. The Booker Washington incident not only figured in the Maryland campaigns of 1901 and 1903, but was also used by the advocates of Negro disfranchisement in Virginia and Alabama in 1901 and by James K. Vardaman of Mississippi on numerous occasions between 1901 and 1909.

lent among southern Democrats, the Richmond *Times-Dispatch*, in 1904, insisted that "the President's entertainment of Booker T. Washington . . . is still a live subject" which, the paper said hopefully, would "figure in the forthcoming presidential campaign." [27]

Evidence that the Democrats would attempt to capitalize on the subject in the campaign of 1904 apparently prompted considerable anxiety among Republicans, especially in the border states. Their efforts to preclude Democratic use of the episode for campaign purposes resulted both in new revelations and new distortions. In the fall of 1903, the Boston *Herald*, a Republican newspaper, printed a story stating that Roosevelt's invitation to Washington "was not preconceived" but was issued "out of consideration for the Negro leader" only when official duties made it impossible for the President to keep his original appointment with him.[28] Then, several months later, in February, 1904, Francis E. Leupp, a journalist and close friend of the President, published *The Man Roosevelt*, a book that served as a campaign biography. The work included a detailed description of the circumstances under which Washington dined at the White House. Desirous of making his "call at the White House without meeting any reporters," Washington had enlisted the assistance of Leupp, who "suggested a plan which worked admirably as far as it went, but failed at its final stage because we could not make the president a party to it." Leupp did not elaborate upon the nature of the plan but did explain that it failed because of the guest list kept for the local press by the doorkeepers. In analyzing the disturbance occasioned by the dinner, Leupp touched upon the basic reason for the bitterness of the reaction when he quoted a young southerner as saying, "I don't know that I should have had any feeling about the President's asking him [Washington] to a lunch or dinner by themselves. But to invite him to a table with ladies—that is what no Southerner can brook!" Although *The Man Roosevelt* furnished the most comprehensive statement of the Booker Washington incident to that date, it was obviously a partisan work designed to create an image of Roosevelt acceptable to a ma-

[27] Richmond *Times-Dispatch*, May 21, 1904.
[28] Boston *Herald* quoted in Charleston *News and Courier*, October 30, 1903.

jority of white Americans. Leupp admitted that Roosevelt and Washington met "on terms of frank equality," but he was careful to describe the President as "a Caucasian to the tips of his fingers," whose high regard for the "personal character and civic virtue" of the Negro leader induced him to seek his advice in an attempt to secure more reputable and efficient federal officeholders in the South. In an effort to absolve Roosevelt of the charge that his dinner with Washington had set a dangerous precedent, Leupp declared that Washington was not the first Negro who had "enjoyed the hospitalities of the White House." [29]

The question of whether Washington had been the first Negro entertained in the White House became the subject of lively debate in Congress during the early months of 1904. Congressman George G. Gilbert, a Democrat from Kentucky, raised the issue in the course of a discussion of the District of Columbia appropriation bill on February 29, 1904. His account purported to show how Booker T. Washington happened to have dinner with the Roosevelt family rather than a private lunch with the President:

> Still another instance of freedom and equality of all men was perhaps shown when a certain other darkey by the name of Booker T. Washington came to lunch at the White House and the President expressed his regrets that his family were away and insisted that Mr. Washington return to dinner. So this Negro did return to dinner, with the President of the United States at one end of the table, Mrs. Roosevelt at the other, Miss Alice and Theodore Jr. on either side, and Booker Washington seated at the seat of honor at the right hand of the President, eating out of the same dish and "sopping" out of the same bowl.[30]

Though obviously facetious, Gilbert's account of the affair nonetheless prompted replies from Republicans bent upon emphasizing two points in particular: precedents for the entertainment of a Negro had been established by Roosevelt's Democratic predecessors

[29] Francis E. Leupp, *The Man Roosevelt: A Portrait Sketch* (New York: Appleton, 1904), 217–30. Another Roosevelt biography of the campaign type, also published early in 1904, alluded to the Booker Washington incident without specifying whether it was a dinner or a lunch. See Jacob A. Riis, *Theodore Roosevelt: The Citizen* (New York: Outlook, 1904), 368–70.

[30] *Congressional Record*, 58th Cong., 2nd Sess., 2562.

in the White House; the meal in question had actually been a "hurried, informal luncheon" rather than a prearranged dinner.

The first Republican to respond to Gilbert was Congressman Charles F. Scott of Kansas, who maintained that C. H. J. Taylor, editor of the Kansas City *World* and a "negro as black as you ever saw," had dined at the White House during Grover Cleveland's first term. In the meantime, others such as Thomas E. Watson of Georgia, a Populist, accused Cleveland of inviting Frederick Douglass to his wedding reception. In several letters to prominent Democrats in the House, Cleveland emphatically denied that he had ever invited a Negro to a meal in the White House and suggested that Scott's reference to Taylor as a "black negro" was sufficient evidence that the Kansas congressman did "not know what he is talking about." Scott ultimately abandoned the fight when confronted by the direct testimony of the former President himself.[31]

Another Republican, Congressman Richard Bartholdt of Missouri, avoided the possibility of such contradiction by charging Thomas Jefferson with an act far more inimical to white supremacy than Roosevelt's informal luncheon with Washington. According to Bartholdt, a scholarly Negro by the name of Julius Melbourn had been a guest for several days at Monticello, the home of the "father of the Democratic Party," where a formal dinner was arranged in his honor. Hence, Bartholdt insisted that the Democrats' agitation over the Booker Washington incident was wholly inconsistent with the practices of their most revered leader. To point up the relatively innocuous nature of Roosevelt's breach of the racial code, he contrasted it with Jefferson's treatment of Melbourn: "In one case we have a president [Roosevelt] who, in the unparalleled rush of business, makes the suggestion to Mr. Washington that they might as well talk politics and business while partaking of a hurried meal. In the other case, we have Mr. Jefferson formally inviting a negro by card to dinner . . . In the one case, a hurried, informal luncheon in a room adjoining the business office; in the other case, a well-arranged banquet-like . . . affair at the famous Monticello." [32]

[31] *Ibid.*, 2565, 2742, 4708–16; Charleston *News and Courier*, March 3, 4, April 13, 1904; New York *Times*, March 1, 1904.
[32] *Congressional Record*, 58th Cong., 2nd Sess., 4709.

John Sharp Williams of Mississippi, the Democratic leader of the House, assured his colleagues that if "the nigger ate at Monticello, he ate in Mr. Jefferson's kitchen." [33] Nevertheless, Bartholdt's description of the Booker Washington incident as an unpremeditated luncheon at which only the President and Washington were present gained wide acceptance in Republican circles on the eve of the election of 1904.

Shortly after the congressional debate, Lew Dockstadter, a minstrel famous for his political monologues, unwittingly precipitated further discussion of the Washington dinner. As a part of a new act, Dockstadter arranged for the Edison Company to make a short motion picture of a skit in which his troupe did a "take off" on Roosevelt's relationship with Booker T. Washington. The skit, filmed on May 19, 1904, in front of the Capitol steps, quickly assumed sinister political overtones as rumors circulated to the effect that the Democratic Party had paid the minstrel four million dollars for the use of the film in the presidential campaign. Dockstadter became the object of an elaborate search by the Secret Service and the police of various cities. Although he denied any political plot, his film was confiscated and destroyed with the approval of the President. The Dockstadter case provided editors with another opportunity to assess the implications of the Roosevelt-Washington dinner.[34] But obviously by this time they were less certain whether it was a luncheon or a dinner; some simply avoided the issue by referring to "Roosevelt's entertainment of Washington" or to "Washington's meal at the White House." [35] Interestingly enough, the

[33] Charleston *News and Courier*, April 13, 1904.

[34] See Willard B. Gatewood, Jr., "Theodore Roosevelt and the 'Kinetoscope Fakes': An Incident in the Campaign of 1904," *Mid-America*, XLIX (1967), 190–99.

[35] For the views of a Virginia-born Republican see John S. Wise, *Recollections of Thirteen Presidents* (Garden City, N.Y.: Doubleday, 1906), 265–70. Senator Joseph B. Foraker claimed to be the first public official to defend the President's invitation to Booker T. Washington in a speech at the opening of the 1901 Republican campaign in Ohio. In that speech he referred to the meal as a dinner, but interestingly he labeled it a luncheon in his memoirs. See Joseph B. Foraker, *Notes on a Busy Life* (2 vols.; Cincinnati: Stewart and Kidd, 1916), II, 105–106. The text of his speech is found in the New York *Daily Tribune*, October 20, 1901.

New York *Age*, a Negro newspaper closely allied with Washington's so-called Tuskegee machine, specifically described the meal as a luncheon and harshly criticized Republican leaders for "dodging and apologizing about it ever since it occurred." [36]

Even in the South, where the dinner version continued to prevail, the idea of an offhand invitation to lunch in time gained wide acceptance.[37] Following Roosevelt's triumphant tour of the South in October, 1905—the visit which he had promised Booker T. Washington four years earlier—southerners generally became more magnanimous in their treatment of his past actions.[38] Obviously an unplanned lunch with the President alone was far more acceptable than a dinner at which white ladies were present. The transformation was perhaps all the easier for southerners because they often referred to the noon meal as either dinner or lunch, and to the evening meal as supper. One Republican candidate for Congress in the South managed to appease his audiences by giving them a grotesque version of the incident in which Roosevelt was supposed to have told Washington, "Go around to the back door. . . . Mandy will give you the best in the house." [39]

In view of the initial reaction to the affair by southerners, their acceptance of the modified luncheon version may possibly be considered an example of what some have termed the regional gift for self-deception. If so, it would also appear to confirm the view of others who have interpreted such regional characteristics merely as dramatic manifestations of national traits. White Americans, in general, readily embraced the idea of a busy President impulsively inviting the spokesman for Negro Americans to share lunch with him, either on separate (and presumably equal) trays or in a private

[36] New York *Age*, May 26, 1904.

[37] Examples of southerners who accepted the luncheon version included a Roosevelt partisan, Edwin Mims ["President Theodore Roosevelt," *South Atlantic Quarterly*, IV (1905), 61]; and a Roosevelt critic, Annie Riley Hale [*Rooseveltian Fact and Fable* (New York: Broadway Publishing Co., 1908), 136–37].

[38] Professor C. Vann Woodward noted that southern folklore transformed Washington's meal at the White House from a dinner into a luncheon "after Roosevelt regained his popularity" in the region. See his *Origins of the New South, 1877–1913* (Baton Rouge: La. State, 1951), 464n.

[39] Mark Sullivan, *Our Times* (6 vols.; New York: Scribner, 1926–35), III, 146.

dining room, while they continued their conference. After all, the luncheon version was largely the handiwork of nonsoutherners. And so widespread was it by 1911 that Booker T. Washington's rather full account of the dinner incident in his autobiography had little effect as a corrective.[40]

The death of Washington in October, 1915, followed by that of Roosevelt a little more than three years later, rekindled interest in what had become one of the most celebrated meals in American history. Within a month after Washington's death, the Boston *Transcript* published an article entitled "True Story of the Luncheon." This account claimed that Washington, having been entrusted with a mission by the President, came to the White House to report. Alone in the dining room having lunch when Washington arrived, Roosevelt had him ushered in and insisted that he have a "bite to eat with him." Reluctantly, Washington agreed.[41] This latest explanation of the incident prompted Charles G. Washburn, who at the time was preparing a book about Roosevelt's career, to write the former President directly for clarification. Roosevelt's reply was the most complete commentary that he ever made on the incident. He assured Washburn that the *Transcript* article was "fifty per cent false," and explained why he came to consider his dinner with Washington a mistake:

> It is true that he [Washington] came in to speak to me about the Judge. It is not true that I said I would appoint Judge Jones solely on Wash-

---

[40] References to the Booker Washington incident appeared frequently during the election year of 1912. Roosevelt, as the presidential candidate of the Progressive Party, was plagued throughout the campaign by his decision to adopt a Lily White attitude toward Southern Negroes. Fearful lest such an approach erode its grip on the South, the Democratic Party treated the voters in the region to a full review of his racial heresies as President. Among those the most frequently cited was his meal with Booker T. Washington which, whether described as a lunch or a dinner, was offered as evidence of the insincerity of his Lily White policy. See George E. Mowry, "The South and the Progressive Lily White Party of 1912," 237–47; "Roosevelt's Plea to the South," *Literary Digest*, LXV (1912), 608.

[41] Boston *Transcript* quoted in James E. Amos, *Theodore Roosevelt: Hero to Valet* (New York: Day, 1927), 52–53. See also Washburn's comments before the Massachusetts Historical Society on February 13, 1919, in the *Proceedings, October, 1918, June, 1919* (Boston: Massachusetts Historical Society, 1919), 119.

ington's recommendation. President Cleveland had written me very warmly for Jones. I had heard very well of him. I was anxious, however, as I was in the case of every Southern judge, to be sure that the judge was a man who on matters like peonage could be trusted to stand absolutely for the rights of the black man and the white man alike. Booker Washington called to see me about the Judge; I went into this branch of the matter with him; and he spoke most highly of Judge Jones. I was not at luncheon. I asked him to come and take dinner with me that night. When I was Governor, I had one colored man take dinner with me in the Executive Mansion. I had had [William H.] Lewis . . . spend the night here in my own house. On any rational theory of public and social life my action was absolutely proper. All the tomfool mugwumps of the land . . . hysterically applauded what I did. Yet as a matter of fact what I did was a mistake. It was misinterpreted by the white men of the South and by the black men of the South; and in the North it had no effect, either good or bad. It was one of those cases where the application of a lofty and proper code of social observance to conditions which in actual fact were certain to cause the action to be misunderstood resulted badly.[42]

But Roosevelt advised Washburn merely to "recite the facts as I have given them" in the forthcoming book and to omit any reference to the dinner being a mistake. To make such an admission, Roosevelt argued, was as surely to be misinterpreted as the meal itself had been.[43]

In 1916, Roosevelt wrote a preface for *Booker T. Washington: Builder of a Civilization*, an admiring account by Washington's secretary Emmett J. Scott and Lyman Beecher Stowe. The authors discussed the dinner episode in some detail in an effort to clarify what had been the subject of "so many imaginary versions." Scott and Stowe maintained that the popular approval of Thomas G. Jones's appointment, made largely on Washington's recommendation, had prompted Roosevelt to request the Negro leader to come to the White House again to discuss other appointments. Washington, according to their version, conferred with the President on the morning of October 16, 1901, but because other commitments did

[42] Roosevelt to Washburn, November 20, 1915, in Morison (ed.), *Roosevelt Letters*, VIII, 981–82.

[43] *Ibid.* See also Charles G. Washburn, *Theodore Roosevelt: The Logic of His Career* (Boston: Houghton, 1916).

not allow them to conclude their discussion, Roosevelt invited him to return for dinner that evening. Washington "went to the White House at the appointed time, dined with the President and his family and two other guests, and after dinner discussed with the President the character of individual colored officeholders and applicants for office." [44] Although this account could be construed as harmonious with that in Roosevelt's letter to Washburn, it differed in several respects from the version in Washington's autobiography. Washington clearly indicated that a *written* invitation to dinner was waiting for him at McKinlay's house and implied that he had not conferred with Roosevelt during the morning prior to the dinner.[45]

A version of the meal in even greater conflict with Washington's autobiographical account was included in Benjamin F. Riley's *Life and Times of Booker T. Washington*, which also was published in 1916. Riley, a Baptist clergyman and educator in the South, was an admirer of Washington and his approach to race relations. He denied the story of a White House dinner at which Roosevelt and Washington had discussed politics and described it as the work of "some omnivorous correspondent" eager "to make a scoop." Riley insisted that Washington actually went to the White House to discuss with the President some matters pertaining to Tuskegee Institute. Unable "to give him the required attention," Roosevelt suggested that he return at the noon hour. "Washington returned at the time named," Riley wrote, "and while the conversation was in progress the president's luncheon was brought to his office on a large waiter. Remarking that there was sufficient for both, Mr. Roosevelt offered to share with his caller, who could not have declined and be polite. While they went through the business they ate the limited luncheon, after which Mr. Washington left." [46] Rufus N. Rhodes of

44 Scott and Stowe, *Booker T. Washington*, 116.

45 For some reason Mark Sullivan seems to have misread Washington's autobiography. He claimed that Washington did not make clear whether the invitation to the White House "was to take a meal, or merely to call." Washington actually wrote, "When I reached Mr. McKinlay's house, I found an invitation from President Roosevelt, asking me to dine with him at the White House at eight o'clock." See Sullivan, *Our Times*, III, 146; Washington, *My Larger Education*, 175.

46 Benjamin F. Riley, *The Life and Times of Booker T. Washington* (New

the Birmingham *News*, a friend of Washington, claimed that the Negro leader himself had confided to him a somewhat similar version. Washington, he said, told him that it was Roosevelt's custom to have his lunch served in his office and to order a separate tray for anyone with whom he happened to be conferring at the time. On the contrary, Mark Sullivan testified of his own knowledge that Roosevelt never lunched in this manner.[47]

During the four years following Roosevelt's death in 1919, various writers, some of whom had been his close friends, further clouded the details of the meal. William R. Thayer, in his "intimate biography" of Roosevelt (1919), described it as an unpremeditated luncheon.[48] The memoirs of the well-known journalist Arthur Wallace Dunn, published in 1922, corroborated Thayer's account by citing Roosevelt's response to the news that Maryland Democrats were making political capital out of his meal with Washington. Dunn quoted Roosevelt as saying, "I am sorry if the good people of Maryland are disturbed by the affair. I'll tell you how it happened. The man [Washington] was here talking with me when luncheon was announced, and I told him to come in and have lunch with me while we continued to talk. That was all there was to it." [49] Despite this evidence, Roosevelt biographers such as Joseph B. Bishop, William Draper Lewis, and Bradley Gilman insisted that the President invited Washington to dinner well in advance.[50] Bishop, the more or less official biographer, recalled that he had spent the night

---

York: Revell, 1916), 86–87. For other works published in 1915 and 1916 which also subscribed to the luncheon version, see Edward Stanwood, *A History of the Presidency from 1897 to 1916* (Boston: Houghton, 1916), 86–87; Frederick E. Drinker, *Booker T. Washington: The Mastermind of a Child of Slavery* (n.p., 1915), 129–30.

[47] Sullivan, *Our Times*, III, 146–47.

[48] William Roscoe Thayer, *Theodore Roosevelt: An Intimate Biography* (Boston: Houghton, 1919), 283–84.

[49] Arthur Wallace Dunn, *From Harrison to Harding: A Personal Narrative Covering a Third of a Century, 1881–1921* (2 vols.; New York: Putnam, 1922), I, 358–59.

[50] Joseph B. Bishop, *Theodore Roosevelt and His Time* (2 vols.; New York: Scribner, 1920), I, 165–70; William Draper Lewis, *The Life of Theodore Roosevelt* (n.p.: United Publishers, 1919), 195–96; Bradley Gilman, *Roosevelt: The Happy Warrior* (Boston: Little, 1923), 203–209.

prior to the dinner (which he incorrectly dated October 18) at the White House, and that Roosevelt had urged him to stay over in order to dine with Washington. Though he was unable to be present at the dinner, he was certain that Roosevelt had anticipated "no such outburst of disapproval" as it occasioned.[51] In his book *The McKinley and Roosevelt Administrations* (1923), James Ford Rhodes relied heavily upon Bishop's work for his account of the dinner but quoted a statement made by Roosevelt in which he admitted "that he had made a mistake in asking Booker Washington to dinner." [52] The issues raised by Bishop and Rhodes—namely, whether Roosevelt anticipated any adverse criticism of his dinner with Washington and whether upon reflection he considered the dinner a mistake—joined a host of other questions which by 1925 tended to involve the incident in a plethora of contradictions.

To complicate matters, an account of the meal was provided in the following year by James E. Amos, Roosevelt's Negro valet, who claimed that he had been an eyewitness. In his recollections of his "beloved boss" published in *Collier's* in the summer of 1926, Amos directly challenged Thayer's explanation of the invitation to Washington as "a purely thoughtless one imposed by circumstances" and asserted that Roosevelt himself "never tried to hide behind such explanation." But Amos insisted that the invitation was to a luncheon, not a dinner. "I was in attendance at that luncheon," he wrote. Apparently, he meant that he had served the meal. Shortly after the appearance of the account in *Collier's*, Charles G. Washburn explained in a letter to Amos his desire to ascertain the actual facts of the affair, which had puzzled him more than a decade earlier. He assured Amos that in 1915 Roosevelt had told him the meal was a dinner. The book edition of Amos' recollections, published in 1927, included Washburn's letter. Though still convinced that Washington had had lunch at the White House, Amos appeared more

---

[51] Bishop, *Roosevelt*, I, 165.

[52] James Ford Rhodes, *The McKinley and Roosevelt Administrations, 1897–1909* (New York: Macmillan, 1923), 227–30. Another historian who apparently relied on Bishop's work and, like Rhodes, gave the date of the dinner as October 18, 1901, was John Spencer Bassett. See his *Expansion and Reform, 1889–1926* (New York: Longmans, 1926), 98–99.

interested in proving that Roosevelt's invitation was deliberate rather than impulsive. His account might well be more convincing if there were not certain textual discrepancies regarding his initial meeting with Roosevelt which raise questions as to whether he could have been present at the controversial meal on October 16, 1901.[53] Undoubtedly, Amos saw Washington in conference with the President on later occasions and heard much gossip about the famous meal. Conceivably, fact and hearsay became confused in his memory after a quarter of a century.

Whatever the validity of Amos' account, it called attention again to the widely disparate versions of the Booker Washington incident. In 1926, when Mark Sullivan published the first volume of *Our Times*, he gave October 18, 1901, as the date of the meal and referred to it as "one of the most talked-of luncheons ever eaten in America." [54] In the third volume, published four years later, he wrote less confidently about the matter and, in fact, included a lengthy note to explain a "baffling detail"—whether it was a lunch or dinner. After citing various conflicting sources, Sullivan concluded it was impossible "to be certain, either from memories of living witnesses . . . or from available records, whether a certain famous meal was a lunch or a dinner." [55] Several biographies of Roosevelt published a year later, in 1931, tended to confirm Sullivan's observation. Contrary to all other versions, Clifford Smyth's brief volume in the "Builders of America" series described the controversial meal as a breakfast. Although a breakfast might well have had more disturbing implications than either a lunch or a dinner, Smyth failed to reveal any new evidence in support of his version.[56] Two other Roosevelt biographies, by William F. McCaleb[57] and Henry F. Pringle, also published in 1931, accepted the dinner ver-

[53] See especially James E. Amos and John T. Flynn, "Beloved Boss," *Collier's*, LXXVIII (July 31, 1926), 13–14, 33; Amos, *Roosevelt: Hero to Valet*, 3, 7, 51–54.

[54] Sullivan, *Our Times*, I, 562.

[55] *Ibid.*, III, 145–47.

[56] Clifford Smyth, *Theodore Roosevelt, Who Fought for a Square Deal and a New Nationalism* (New York: Funk, 1931), 140–41.

[57] William F. McCaleb, *Theodore Roosevelt* (New York: Albert and Charles Boni, 1931), 132.

sion. In fact, Pringle's biography, which was one of the first such works based upon extensive research in manuscript sources, seemed to achieve that degree of certainty that Sullivan found so elusive. Fully aware of the conflicting versions of the Booker Washington incident, Pringle insisted that it involved "a dinner, not a luncheon" and supported his contention by citing a note to Roosevelt, dated October 16, 1901, and written in Washington's own hand, which read, "I shall be glad to accept your invitation to dinner this evening at 7:30." [58]

Either unaware of such evidence or unconvinced by it, contemporaries of Roosevelt continued to insist that Washington's meal at the White House had been an impromptu lunch. One of these was Warrington Dawson, a minor literary figure and native of South Carolina, who was the source of at least three versions of the affair. Dawson accompanied Roosevelt to Africa in 1909, and the former President presumably talked freely to him at that time about various controversies during his administration. Though an expatriate living in Paris, Dawson was cognizant of the enduring hostility of his fellow Charlestonians toward Roosevelt as a result of the Crum appointment. His first account of the Booker Washington incident appeared in 1912 in his *Le Negre aux États-Unis,* a discourse on the "Negro problem" in the United States addressed to a European audience. According to this version, Roosevelt informed Washington of his desire to consult him about matters affecting his race. Washington then arranged to visit the President while on his way to New York. During a two-hour interval between trains in the capital, he called at the White House and, as it happened, arrived there during the dinner hour. "The President invited him to have dinner in order not to miss the opportunity to consult him." Dawson insisted that the invitation was "a spontaneous gesture" which, in the President's view, "involved no question of principle," least of all that of social equality.[59]

[58] Henry F. Pringle, *Theodore Roosevelt: A Biography* (New York: Harcourt, 1931), 248–49. See also Henry F. Pringle, "Theodore Roosevelt and the South," *Virginia Quarterly Review,* IX (1933), 14–25.

[59] Warrington Dawson, *Le Negre aux États-Unis* (Paris: E. Guilmoto, 1912), 201–202. Dawson wrote ten years later that among the questions he discussed

More than three decades later, a different version of the affair originating with Dawson was made public for the first time by Major Daniel L. Sinkler of Charleston in a newspaper article published in the fall of 1934. In this version the meal was a lunch rather than a dinner: Roosevelt and Washington were in conference when a servant announced lunch, whereupon the President, "without thinking," invited the Negro leader to join him. Dawson quoted Roosevelt as saying, "Washington accepted immediately and it was too late to back out." [60] Dawson not only fully approved of Sinkler's article but also hastened to provide him with "additional details" about the episode which, in effect, constituted yet another version of it. "As for the Booker Washington lunch," Dawson wrote,

> Colonel Roosevelt laid particular stress on one point when telling me what happened. It was that, contrary to the numerous reports published at the time, he had not invited Booker Washington to sit at the White House table with his family and himself. A conversation which he was holding with Booker Washington in his office having been prolonged past the luncheon hour, a servant brought in his lunch on a tray, expecting to find the President alone. The President, not wishing to break off the conversation, ordered another tray to be brought in to Booker Washington.
>
> I asked Colonel Roosevelt why he had not made this important fact public since what shocked the South was the idea of the family lunch at the White House table. He replied: "It was for Booker Washington to make the correction. Anything I might have made public on the subject at the time would have been a discourtesy to a man who, after all, was my guest." [61]

In both of Dawson's luncheon versions there were strong implications that Roosevelt himself held Washington responsible for the incident. Although a few southerners in 1901 had criticized Washington for accepting the presidential invitation, Dawson was apparently the first to suggest that Roosevelt himself shared their view.

---

with Roosevelt during the African trip was "the Booker Washington lunch (which was not a lunch) and the Crum appointment (a test case)." See Dawson, *Opportunity and Theodore Roosevelt* (Chicago: Honest Truth, 1923), 52.

[60] Charleston *News and Courier*, October 22, 1934.

[61] Warrington Dawson to Daniel L. Sinkler, November 14, 1934, in Warrington Dawson II Papers, Duke University Library, Durham, N.C.

In view of the conflicting evidence, it is understandable that historians and biographers have displayed considerable disparity in their estimates of the Booker Washington incident. The idea of a luncheon has generally been more useful to those who viewed it as merely "an impulsive foray" by Roosevelt against racial discrimination. The treatment of the incident in the two biographies of Washington published since World War II indicates that even those with access to the extensive correspondence of Washington and Roosevelt have interpreted the meal as an example of Rooseveltian impulsiveness.[62] In some instances, historians have unwittingly reflected the existing confusion over the episode by using the terms *dinner,* *luncheon,* and *meal* interchangeably.[63] And even those who have probed the incident in some depth have, with one exception, failed to offer any explanation for the emergence of the luncheon version.[64] In view of the historiographical vicissitudes of the celebrated affair, a recent biographer of Roosevelt perhaps displayed more wisdom than he realized when he avoided labeling Washington's meal as either a dinner or luncheon and instead referred to it as the first instance in which an American Negro was invited "to break bread in the White House." [65]

[62] Basil Mathews, *Booker T. Washington: Educator and Interracial Interpreter* (Cambridge: Harvard, 1948), 233–34; Samuel R. Spencer, Jr., *Booker T. Washington and the Negro's Place in American Life* (Boston: Little, 1955), 133–34.

[63] Clark, *Southern Country Editor,* 309–11, 314, 319; John Hope Franklin, *From Slavery to Freedom: A History of American Negroes* (New York: Knopf, 1948), 386, 427, 430. A curious instance of using the terms *lunch* and *dinner* interchangeably appears in John P. Davis (ed.), *The American Negro Reference Book* (Englewood Cliffs, N. J.: Prentice-Hall, 1966), 58, 965. The text reads that Roosevelt invited Booker T. Washington "to dine at the White House," but entries in the index refer only to a lunch.

[64] The works by Grantham, Pringle, and Sullivan, cited above, treated the Roosevelt-Washington dinner at length but none of them suggested any explanation for the rise and persistence of the luncheon version. Only C. Vann Woodward (*Origins of the New South,* p. 464) has hinted at the reason why southerners might have found the luncheon version more plausible.

[65] William Henry Harbaugh, *Power and Responsibility: The Life and Times of Theodore Roosevelt* (New York: Farrar, Straus, 1961), 219. Among the notable works which refer to the meal as a luncheon are Gunnar Myrdal, *An American Dilemma: The Negro Problem and Modern Democracy* (2 vols.; New York: Harper, 1944), I, 662; Samuel Eliot Morison and Henry S. Commager, *The*

The historical record appears to be irrefutable on at least one point: the White House meal which provoked a storm of controversy in October, 1901, was a *dinner*. The evidence strongly suggests that Roosevelt's dinner invitation to Washington was not an offhand, impulsive gesture occasioned by their failure to finish a conference earlier in the day. But obviously a discussion of whether the invitation to Washington was premeditated or impromptu may well lead to an impasse in semantics. Perhaps more instructive would be a consideration of other questions: Was there any basis in fact for the luncheon version? Or was it merely a fabrication, in the face of the public record, designed to mitigate what many considered Roosevelt's breach of the racial code? And was Roosevelt himself in any way responsible for the luncheon versions?

It seems possible at first glance that the luncheon version may have originated with those who confused Washington's second conference with Roosevelt on October 16, 1901, with his first conference held sometime between September 14, when the President first requested him to come to the capital, and the death of Judge John Bruce on October 1. Washington was so successful in escaping newspaper notice on his first visit that the precise date is difficult to determine. In his own account he simply stated, "Shortly after Mr. Roosevelt became established in the White House, I went there to see him and we spent the greater part of an evening in talk concerning the South." [66] But it is not clear whether he was referring to his first or second visit. Even so, the fact that newspapermen were so quick to take notice of Scott's daytime visit to the White House on October 4 suggests that a morning visit by Washington would have at least warranted mention in the daily columns listing "presidential callers." [67] The absence of such mention, coupled with

---

Growth of the American Republic (4th ed.; 2 vols.; New York: Oxford U.P., 1958), II, 420; Saunders Redding, *The Lonesome Road: The Story of the Negro's Part in America* (Garden City, N.Y.: Doubleday, 1958), 174–75.

[66] Washington, *My Larger Education*, 169.

[67] Lists of "presidential callers," which appeared daily in the Washington *Evening Star* and the New York *Daily Tribune* from September 15 to October 15, 1901, did not include Washington's name. Nor was it included in the lists of White House appointments for the same date published as an appendix in Morison (ed.), *Roosevelt Letters*, IV, 1346. However, the *Tribune*'s story of

Washington's rather general statement, indicates that his first visit also involved an evening conference, which scarcely provided any basis for the luncheon version.

Yet various individuals quoted both Washington and Roosevelt to the effect that the meal was a luncheon. Confronted with the claim by Rufus N. Rhodes that Washington told him it was an impromptu lunch, Mark Sullivan plausibly argued that "it would have been like the man Washington was . . . to tell a version, which . . . would do the least harm to the white man, the President who was his friend." [68] More difficult to explain are the claims by several friends and acquaintances of Roosevelt that he, too, described the affair as a luncheon "imposed by circumstances." Such quotations to this effect stand in sharp contrast to the descriptions of the affair that he committed to paper. In his correspondence immediately following the event,[69] as well as in his letter to Washburn in 1915, Roosevelt consistently referred to the affair as a dinner. Only in the latter was there anything to suggest that it may have been hastily arranged and the invitation sent "at the last minute," as some have indicated.[70] Moreover, on other occasions Roosevelt had invited prominent Negroes to his home. In fact, Booker T. Washington himself had previously been a guest of the Roosevelt family.[71] But Roosevelt apparently realized that such invitations to the White House might cause trouble. He admitted in a letter to Albion W. Tourgée in November, 1901, that the "very fact that I felt a moment's qualm in inviting him [Washington] because of his color made me ashamed of myself and made me hasten the invitation." [72] Later, Roosevelt

---

Judge Jones's appointment, published on October 8, 1901, included a reference to Washington's visit to the White House "a week ago." This may pertain either to Washington's first visit or possibly to Emmett Scott's visit on October 4, 1901.

[68] Sullivan, *Our Times,* III, 146.

[69] See Roosevelt's letters to Lucius N. Littauer, October 24, 1901, to Stewart, October 25, 1901, and to Henry Cabot Lodge, October 28, 1901, in Morison (ed.), *Roosevelt Letters,* III, 181, 182, 184–85.

[70] Seth Scheiner, "President Theodore Roosevelt and the Negro, 1901–1908," *Journal of Negro History,* XLVII (1962), 171.

[71] Pringle, "Roosevelt and the South," 19.

[72] Roosevelt to A. W. Tourgée, November 8, 1901, in Morison (ed.), *Roosevelt Letters,* III, 190.

conceded that the dinner was a mistake.[73] Whatever his reason for this interpretation, he did not invite Washington to dine at the White House again, although the two men continued to confer regularly.[74]

The President's qualms both before and after the dinner seem at first glance to strengthen the possibility that he himself may have been responsible for the luncheon version in an effort to mitigate any adverse repercussions of the incident. Certainly, he displayed extraordinary caution in avoiding anything likely to interfere with his nomination and election in 1904. He well may have been disturbed about the effect of the dinner upon southern Republicans, whose role in the nomination of the party's presidential candidate was far more significant than their influence at the polls. And he was only too well aware of the Lily White tendencies among Republicans in the South, especially those identified with Senator Mark Hanna, a potential rival for the nomination. Furthermore, Roosevelt, who so often boasted that he was "half Southern," obviously desired to regain favor in the region of his maternal ancestors. If he was a "weather-wise politician" eager to be popular with all the people, he was also a man of strong and contradictory impulses whose facility for self-hypnosis helps to explain his occasional carelessness with the truth. Although Roosevelt may have been as much of a rationalizer as John Chamberlain said he was, it is clear that he was not primarily responsible for transforming his prearranged dinner with Booker T. Washington into an impromptu lunch.[75] Rather

[73] M. A. DeWolfe Howe, *George von Lengerke Meyer: His Life and Public Services* (New York: Dodd, 1920), 416; Wister, *Roosevelt*, 254–55.

[74] The British biographer of Roosevelt, Lord Charnwood, commented, "Perhaps it should be confessed that the greatest shock which Roosevelt ever gave his English admirers was when, having invited Mr. Booker Washington to meet his wife and family at luncheon, and having set the South in a blaze by so doing, he failed to repeat his offense." See Lord Charnwood [Godfrey Rathbone Benson, 1st Baron of Charnwood], *Theodore Roosevelt* (Boston: Atlantic Monthly Press, 1923), 104.

[75] John Chamberlain, *Farewell to Reform* (New York: Liveright, 1932), 264–66. More generous than Chamberlain was Lewis Einstein, who commented that the Booker Washington incident revealed that "the aristocrat in Roosevelt was too convinced of his own standing to care about distinctions in others, but the politician in him understood the tactlessness of uselessly offending the preju-

it was the work of others, notably Republican congressmen and Roosevelt apologists, who distorted the facts of the incident in an effort to lessen the seriousness of what they considered his breach of racial etiquette. But regardless of the sources of the folklore, the historiography of the incident seems to justify Mark Sullivan's concern lest the distortions of a comparatively trivial detail also "be characteristic of the picture."

---

dices of a great section of the country." See Einstein, *Roosevelt: His Mind in Action* (Boston: Houghton, 1930), 106–107.

III

The Indianola
Post Office Affair

*. . . the mob then notified the colored postmistress that she
must at once resign her office. The "best citizens" of the
town did what throughout the South the "best citizens" . . .
almost always do in such emergencies . . . that is they
"deprecated" the conduct of the mob and said it was "not
representative of the real Southern feeling"; and then
added that to save trouble the woman must go! She went.
The mayor and the sheriff notified her and me that they
would not protect her if she came back. I shut up the office
for the remainder of her term. It was all I could do and
the least I could do.*

THEODORE ROOSEVELT

Few problems so severely tested the presidential leadership of
Theodore Roosevelt throughout his term of office as the so-called
Negro question. His administration began in 1901 with a controversy over a dinner with the noted Negro leader Booker T. Washington and ended in 1909 in the midst of investigations prompted
by his dismissal of a battalion of Negro troops accused of being involved in the Brownsville affray.[1] Negroes themselves were "alter-

[1] Negro soldiers of the Twenty-fifth United States Infantry stationed near
Brownsville, Texas, were accused of shooting up the town on the night of
August 3, 1906, presumably as an expression of their resentment at the discriminatory practices of the white citizens. When no soldier in the three Negro
companies at Brownsville admitted any connection with the affray, Roosevelt
ordered the discharge of all three companies. The President's order precipitated
a long and acrimonious controversy in which Senator Joseph B. Foraker of
Ohio acted as the champion of the discharged troops. No other action by the
President prompted such hostile reaction among Negroes as his discharge of
the troops. See James A. Tinsley, "Roosevelt, Foraker and the Brownsville
Affray," *Journal of Negro History*, XLI (1956), 43–65; Emma Lou Thorn-

nately pleased and angered by his actions." [2] But of the controversies prompted by Roosevelt's handling of the Negro question none revealed more clearly the explosive nature of the issue than the so-called Indianola affair, which involved his closing of the post office in Indianola, Mississippi, early in 1903 after the town's white citizens had forced the resignation of the Negro postmaster. Because the incident coincided with his reorganization of the Republican Party in Mississippi and his search for convention delegates, it not only raised questions about the motives that prompted his action but also made him and his policies significant issues in the state's political campaigns of 1903. The closing of the post office provided a convenient focus for the racist demagoguery employed by James K. Vardaman in his rise to power. Indeed, the whole course of the Indianola affair—from the events that led to the resignation of the postmaster to the settlement of the dispute in 1904—pointed up the intricate connection between local and national politics.

Indianola, the county seat of Sunflower County, was a town of approximately 1,000 people located in the rich delta lands of the Yazoo River. Negroes constituted an overwhelming majority of the population in both the town and the county. As the center of a large agricultural district, Indianola had the appearance of a bustling business community. The two weekly newspapers often boasted of its electric light plant, modern water works, two banks, ice-manufacturing establishment, cottonseed oil mill, and several cotton gins. The Brooklyn Bridge Store, owned by D. Cohn, "the oldest merchant in Indianola," included among its merchandise the latest in feminine fashions imported directly from Memphis and

---

brough, "The Brownsville Episode and the Negro Vote," *Mississippi Valley Historical Review*, XLIV (1957), 469–83. For assessments of Roosevelt's handling of the Negro question in general, see especially Seth M. Scheiner, "President Theodore Roosevelt and the Negro, 1901–1908," *Journal of Negro History*, XLVII (1962), 169–82; Dewey W. Grantham, Jr., "Dinner at the White House: Theodore Roosevelt, Booker T. Washington, and the South," *Tennessee Historical Quarterly*, XVII (1958), 112–30; Henry F. Pringle, "Theodore Roosevelt and the South," *Virginia Quarterly Review*, IX (1933), 14–25; Kelly Miller, *Roosevelt and the Negro* (Washington: n.p., 1907), 2–21.

[2] August Meier, *Negro Thought in America, 1880–1915: Racial Ideologies in the Age of Booker T. Washington* (Ann Arbor: U. of Mich., 1963), 164.

New Orleans. The Sunflower Pharmacy and the Indianola Drug Company enticed customers with fountain delicacies such as Sappho and Dr Pepper. Not the least among the businesses was the post office, which served over 3,000 patrons. The scope of postal operations, as well as the salary of $1,100 paid the postmaster, made the position one of the most responsible and lucrative public offices in the area.[3]

For years Mrs. Minnie M. Cox, a quiet, sophisticated Negro woman, had been postmaster at Indianola. She and her husband, Wayne W. Cox, a postal employee in the railway mail service, enjoyed a privileged status in the community. Their extensive landholdings, as well as their interests in several banks, placed them among Indianola's most prosperous citizens. Both of the Coxes had attended college: she held a teacher's certificate from Fisk University; he was a graduate of Alcorn University. Their educational qualifications and steadfast allegiance to the Republican Party largely accounted for their positions in government service. It was not extraordinary for Negroes to occupy fourth-class postmasterships in Mississippi early in the twentieth century, but Mrs. Cox was one of only five Negroes in the state who held a presidential third-class office. She was first put into office by Benjamin Harrison when no white Republican in the area qualified for the job. After the Democratic interlude under Grover Cleveland, she was reappointed by William McKinley in 1897. On January 25, 1900, McKinley raised the rank of her position from fourth-class to third-class and appointed her for a full four-year term. Both senators from Mississippi approved her appointment and three prominent white citizens of Indianola served as her bondsmen.[4]

The manner in which Mrs. Cox conducted her office won the

[3] Indianola (Miss.) *Enterprise*, January 1, 1902–December 31, 1903; New York *Herald*, June 29, 1903; New York *Sun*, March 29, 1903.

[4] Cleveland *Gazette*, February 7, 1903; Edgar S. Wilson to Theodore Roosevelt, October 26, 1902, in Theodore Roosevelt Papers, Manuscript Division, Library of Congress; *Outlook*, LXXIII (1903), 188; Joseph B. Bishop, "The Negro and Public Office," *International Quarterly*, VII (1903), 231–32; Charles Fitzgerald to Joe P. Johnston, December 11, 1902, in "Resignation of the Postmaster," *House Documents*, 57th Cong., 2nd Sess., No. 422, pp. 21–22, hereinafter cited as "Resignation of the Postmaster."

universal praise of patrons and postal officials. Charles Fitzgerald, the postal inspector for the area, who was a native Mississippian and a "rockribbed Democrat," regularly reported to his superiors that Mrs. Cox's office was a model of efficiency, tidiness, and good service.[5] Fitzgerald was much impressed by an incident that occurred during one of his inspection tours. A little white girl ran into the post office. "Minnie, mamma says is there any mail for us today?" she asked. "No, honey," Mrs. Cox replied, "there is no mail today but your bonnet is on crooked. Let me straighten it." [6] But the postmaster's consideration of her patrons extended far beyond such pleasantries. For example, she had a telephone installed at her own expense so that patrons would be able to ascertain whether they had any mail without a trip to the post office. And every quarter she personally covered delinquent box rents with her own funds "in order to avoid any friction with the white patrons." [7]

In spite of the efficiency and tact displayed by Mrs. Cox, her relationship with the white citizens of Indianola deteriorated markedly in 1902. The reasons for this change involved a subtle interaction of various factors. But it is apparent that Indianola's sudden concern that its postmaster was a Negro and a Republican was related to President Roosevelt's efforts to reorganize the Republican Party in the South, particularly in Mississippi. Although the President desired to rejuvenate the party in the region in such a way that it would contribute to his nomination in 1904, he was also intent upon replacing venal Republican officeholders with qualified, respectable personnel. In fact, the topic discussed by the President and Booker T. Washington at their controversial dinner in October, 1901, was the making of federal appointments in the South. It appears that Mississippi figured in their deliberations even then. Indeed, the Republican Party there was so "utterly rotten" that Roosevelt thought it impossible of reconstruction on the basis of its

[5] For the reports of Inspector Charles Fitzgerald see "Resignation of the Postmaster," 5–6.

[6] Edgar S. Wilson, "Memoirs," Chap. 77, p. 3, in Edgar S. Wilson Papers, Mississippi State Department of Archives and History, Jackson.

[7] Fitzgerald to Johnston, December 15, 1902, in "Resignation of the Postmaster," 6.

existing leadership. On Booker T. Washington's recommendation, he entrusted the rebuilding of the state organization to a Democrat, Edgar S. Wilson, whom he appointed marshal of the Southern District of Mississippi in January, 1902.[8] Even Senator Hanna, presumably Roosevelt's chief rival for the Republican nomination in 1904, was enthusiastic about Wilson's appointment. When the President had consulted him about it earlier, Hanna disclosed that shortly before his assassination McKinley had also expressed a desire to appoint Wilson to some federal post.[9]

That two Republican Presidents reached the same conclusion quite independently indicated the unusual nature of Wilson's political position. He was, in brief, a maverick in Mississippi politics.[10] A journalist of ability, he edited several newspapers and for a dozen years before 1903 served as Mississippi correspondent of the New Orleans *Daily Picayune*. As a young man he had been private secretary to Senator L. Q. C. Lamar, whose political philosophy served as a model for his own conduct. Though a lifelong Democrat, Wilson refused to follow the leadership of William Jennings Bryan and joined the ranks of dissident Gold Democrats who supported the Palmer–Buckner ticket in 1896. In 1899 he assisted his brother-in-law Andrew H. Longino in waging a successful campaign for governor of Mississippi. During the next four years, when Wilson's influence was at its peak in state politics, Governor Longino achieved a national reputation for his efforts to curb the outbursts of violence and intimidation directed against Negroes. The record of Wilson and that of his brother-in-law appealed to President Roosevelt and his principal adviser on southern affairs, Booker T. Washington. In time a rather intimate friendship developed between the President

[8] Mary Floyd Sumners, "Edgar Stewart Wilson: The Mississippi Eagle, Journalist of the New South" (Ph.D. dissertation, Mississippi State University, 1962), 149–51; Booker T. Washington to Roosevelt, December 24, 1902, in Roosevelt Papers; Roosevelt to Wilson, January 4, 1902, in Elting Morison (ed.), *The Letters of Theodore Roosevelt* (8 vols.; Cambridge: Harvard, 1951–54), III, 216; New York *Times*, January 10, 1902.

[9] Roosevelt to Wilson, January 4, 1902, in Morison (ed.), *Roosevelt Letters*, III, 216.

[10] For a detailed account of Wilson's career see Sumners, "Edgar S. Wilson: Mississippi Eagle."

and his Mississippi "referee," [11] but Washington was the liaison between Wilson and the White House in the initial months of their association. Though Wilson shared many of the regional prejudices against Negroes, he appears to have been genuinely committed to the idea that "there is no color in the Constitution and the enforcement of laws." [12] Wilson and Washington made an effective team; they met often, usually outside Mississippi, and planned their strategy with painstaking care. Washington assured the President, "Mr. Wilson is not only keeping in mind the putting of first class men in office but also . . . the bringing about of such conditions as will not injure the party and the support which you should have from Mississippi. The more I see of him the more I am convinced of his wisdom and unselfishness and his great power for good." [13] By the end of his first year in office Wilson himself, optimistic about the progress of reorganizing Mississippi Republicanism, reported to Roosevelt that his friends were in control of the state executive committee. At the same time he remained in close contact with the Democratic administration of his brother-in-law and carefully avoided any political entanglement with the forces of James K. Vardaman, whose rank racism he abhorred.[14]

The selection of Edgar Wilson, a "gold" Democrat, as the Republican referee in Mississippi elicited a mixed reaction. The *Nation* voiced a common sentiment when it praised the appointment as a sign of Roosevelt's intention to reject unfit Republican officeholders in the South.[15] An opposite view was expressed by various Negro spokesmen, who interpreted Wilson's appointment to mean that Roosevelt was turning a deaf ear to the claims of black Republicans. Those disenchanted with Booker T. Washington were inclined to

[11] The term *referee* was applied to individuals in certain states to whom Roosevelt referred matters of federal patronage relating to those states. Roosevelt himself apparently preferred the term *endorser*. See Alfred H. Stone, *Studies in the American Race Problem* (Garden City, N.Y.: Doubleday, 1908), 341–44; Roosevelt to John Graham Brooks, November 13, 1908, in Morison (ed.), *Roosevelt Letters*, VI, 1344–45.

[12] Wilson to Roosevelt, January 17, 1903, in Roosevelt Papers.

[13] Washington to Roosevelt, December 24, 1901, in Roosevelt Papers.

[14] Wilson to Roosevelt, October 26, 1902, Washington to Roosevelt, November 6, 1902, in Roosevelt Papers.

[15] *Nation*, LXXIV (January 23, 1902), 59.

hold him responsible for the selection of such a "well known Negro hater" as Wilson.[16] In Mississippi the most prominent Negro Republican to oppose the appointment was James Hill, who became a conspicuous casualty of Wilson's new order. For years he had occupied various federal offices, from which he exerted a powerful influence over Republican affairs in the state. But Roosevelt failed to reappoint him to any office and Wilson pre-empted his party functions. Failing to block Wilson's confirmation by the Senate, Hill launched an anti-Roosevelt movement among Mississippi Republicans in the hope of securing a delegation to the national convention in 1904 which would oppose the President's nomination.[17] But even James S. Clarkson, a patronage adviser to Roosevelt skilled in corralling Negro delegates from the South, believed that Hill's "usefulness to the party had gone for good." Despite reservations about the President's "interesting experiment in Mississippi," Clarkson considered Edgar Wilson a "man of great intelligence and quick discernment" who was likely to improve the party's position in Mississippi.[18]

The appointment of a white Democrat as referee, coupled with the removal of so prominent a Negro Republican as Hill, led many white Mississippians to the erroneous conclusion that Roosevelt would acquiesce in the elimination of Negro officeholders and look with favor on white Democratic applicants for such posts. It was under such a misconception that the movement began in Indianola to oust Mrs. Cox. In the spring of 1902, individuals who desired the office either for themselves or for relatives started to agitate the question of "nigger domination" and to call attention to Mrs. Cox's presence as a "menace to white civilization." The purpose of their agitation was to create a vacancy in the post office.[19] The most persistent candidate for the position was A. B. Weeks, the impoverished brother-in-law of Indianola's mayor, J. L. Davis, who possessed close

16 Cleveland *Gazette*, February 1, 15, 1902.

17 *Ibid.*; Thomas Richardson to Roosevelt, January 22, 1903, in Roosevelt Papers; Chicago *Broad Ax*, February 21, 1903.

18 James S. Clarkson to George B. Cortelyou, January 21, 1903, in Roosevelt Papers.

19 Fitzgerald to Johnston, December 11, 1902, in "Resignation of the Postmaster," 21–22.

ties with the local power structure in general. In April, 1902, Weeks began what was to become a barrage of sycophantic letters to President Roosevelt and Postmaster General Henry C. Payne. His chief claims to the office were his poverty, race, and shift to the Republican Party in 1896. He also argued that it was unfair for such a wealthy couple as the Coxes to hold two federal offices.[20] The persistence of this theme throughout the agitation lent credence to the observation that the "prosperity of the Coxes was their undoing." [21]

During the summer and early fall of 1902 the quickening tempo of Democratic politics in the state served to increase the racial strife in Indianola. As the election of 1903 approached, political leaders aligned themselves with the various candidates for governor and senator. Backed by Senator Anselm J. McLaurin's "machine" and the influence of his brother-in-law Edgar Wilson, Governor Longino opened his campaign for the Senate against the incumbent, Hernando DeSoto Money. Allied with Money was his cousin James K. Vardaman, editor of the Greenwood *Commonwealth*, who announced his intention to run for governor a third time. Though defeated in 1895 by McLaurin and in 1899 by Longino, Vardaman had nonetheless kept himself in the limelight as an ardent champion of white supremacy. His theme in 1902–1903 was the same that it had been earlier: the Negro was "a lazy, lying lustful animal which no conceivable amount of training can transform into a tolerable citizen." Hence, the keynote of his campaign was a scheme which would have virtually abolished Negro education.[22]

Social and political developments that had occurred in Mississippi since Vardaman's previous attempts to win the gubernatorial nom-

[20] Copies of the eighteen letters sent by Weeks to the President and the Post Office Department between April 7, 1902, and January 10, 1903, appear *ibid.*, 7–13.

[21] Cleveland *Gazette*, February 7, 1903.

[22] Albert D. Kirwan, *Revolt of the Rednecks: Mississippi Politics, 1876–1925* (Lexington: U. of Ky., 1951), 146–51. The other three candidates for the Democratic nomination for governor in 1903 were Edmund F. Noel, author of the primary law; Judge Frank A. Critz, a former state senator; and Andrew F. Fox, a congressman. Described by Vardaman as the candidate of the Wilson-Longino faction, Fox entered the primary contest late and withdrew after the closing of the Indianola post office intensified racial antagonism to such a degree that his "rational policy" no longer had any appeal.

ination enhanced the prospects for the success of his racist themes in 1904. Despite Longino's efforts to maintain racial harmony, lynchings and "whitecapping" had steadily multiplied during his administration. The passage of a primary law in 1902 created the means by which Vardaman was able to exploit and intensify the existing racial tensions. The primary not only solidified the disfranchisement of the Negro but also revolutionized campaigning techniques. The selection of the party's nominees by voters rather than convention delegates meant that the personality and oratory of the candidates became crucial factors in political contests. More than any of the other three gubernatorial candidates, all of whom opposed any radical change in Negro education, Vardaman was endowed with a flamboyant personality and a gift for incendiary rhetoric.[23]

Early in the campaign Vardaman began to relate the "negro menace" in Mississippi with the "social equality policies" of President Roosevelt. Despite the fact that white Democrats constituted an overwhelming majority of those recommended by Edgar Wilson for federal appointments, the President's referee was described as a political and racial Judas Iscariot bent upon destroying white supremacy. And because Governor Longino was Wilson's brother-in-law and political ally, he too was depicted as a participant in a Roosevelt-Wilson conspiracy to prevent Vardaman's election.[24] As proof that such a cabal actually existed, Vardaman cited two incidents in particular: one was Longino's invitation to the President, issued through Wilson, to hunt bear in Mississippi in the fall of 1902; the other was a fistfight that occurred in August in front of a Jackson hotel between Wilson and Congressman John Sharp Williams, who was supporting Vardaman's candidacy. Vardaman somehow transformed these events into proof of a plot being waged against him and white supremacy by the "coon-flavored miscegenationist in the White House" and his Mississippi representatives, Longino and

[23] *Ibid.*, 132. See also Clara Lopez, "James K. Vardaman and the Negro: The Foundation of Mississippi's Racial Policy," *Southern Quarterly*, III (1965), 168–71; Eugene E. White, "Anti-Racial Agitation in Politics: James Kimble Vardaman in the Mississippi Gubernatorial Campaign of 1903," *Journal of Mississippi History*, VII (1945), 91–101.

[24] Greenwood (Miss.) *Commonwealth*, October 17, 24, 31, 1902.

Wilson.[25] The President's forthcoming visit prompted Vardaman to post an advertisement in his paper which read, "Wanted sixteen 'coons' to sleep with Roosevelt when he comes down to go bear hunting with Mississippi's onliest governor Longy." [26]

In the autumn of 1902 Vardaman delivered several speeches in Indianola, where the presence of a Negro Republican officeholder prompted him to achieve new heights of racist oratory. He chided the people for "tolerating a negro wench as postmaster" and left the impression that Mrs. Cox owed her position to Roosevelt and Wilson.[27] His references to the Negro postmaster played directly into the hands of those seeking to obtain her position. When such individuals came to realize that neither Roosevelt nor his referee sympathized with their cause, they seized upon the anti-Negro agitation involved in the political campaign as a means of achieving their aims. In mid-September, 1902, A. B. Weeks assured the Post Office Department that the people of Indianola were more than ever determined "to make the present postmistress resign or give up the office in some way." "They only do this," he concluded, "because she is colored." [28] Shortly after Weeks posted his letter, Indianola was the scene of an incident involving a Negro which brought to a climax the movement to oust Mrs. Cox.

Late in September, 1902, the white townspeople became excited over rumors that a Negro porter in Cohn's Brooklyn Bridge Store had been "habitually discourteous" to a white salesgirl employed there. They concluded that the time had come "to stop the whole Negro business." A public meeting was convened to determine a course of action, and approximately fifty white citizens attended. They not only voted to banish the porter immediately, but also notified Dr. J. C. Fulton, a Negro physician with a lucrative practice among members of his own race, that he would be given until January 1, 1903, to leave town. Fulton, like the Coxes, had appar-

[25] Indianola *Enterprise*, August 22, 1902; Greenwood *Commonwealth*, October 31, 1902; George C. Osborn, *John Sharp Williams: Planter-Statesman of the Deep South* (Baton Rouge: La. State, 1943), 103–104.

[26] Greenwood *Commonwealth*, October 31, 1902.

[27] Wilson, "Memoirs," Chap. 77, p. 1, in Wilson Papers.

[28] A. B. Weeks to the Fourth Assistant Postmaster General, September 19, 1902, in "Resignation of the Postmaster," 10.

ently become too prosperous. Disturbed by the decision to get rid of the doctor, certain white citizens of the town convened a second public meeting, which was attended by almost a hundred people. Although this group rescinded the earlier action regarding Dr. Fulton by a narrow margin of votes, he decided to leave anyway for fear of retaliation by the "positive minority." [29]

These meetings provided the opportunity for a showdown on the question of the Negro postmaster. Clearly the issue was secondary to the excitement created when "a young lady clerking in a Jew store was insulted by a negro." Nevertheless, a majority of those attending the second mass meeting voted to order Mrs. Cox to vacate her office by January 1, 1903. The action was not unexpected. In fact, a petition requesting her resignation by November 1, 1902, had been circulated earlier. Aware that a vote would probably be taken at the public gathering, Mrs. Cox made it known that she would not be a candidate for reappointment if she were allowed to complete her term of office. It is interesting to note that neither the petition nor a formal statement of the action by the assembled citizens was ever presented to her.[30] Evidently those responsible for the movement to oust Mrs. Cox were careful to leave no documentary record of their activities which might arouse publicity. Their precautions resulted in a kind of conspiracy of silence. Even the Indianola *Enterprise*, usually quick to publish local news items, omitted any mention of the mass meetings. As if to convince itself and its readers that all was well in Indianola, the *Enterprise* editorialized, "Our people enjoy the best of relations and have no feuds to settle. They live in peace with the world and have plenty of the necessities of life." [31]

At the very time the local paper was extolling the town's blissful

[29] Report of Inspector Charles Fitzgerald, December 15, 1902, *ibid.*, 22–25; Wilson, "Memoirs," Chap. 77, pp. 1–5, in Wilson Papers; *Congressional Record*, 57th Cong., 2nd Sess., 853–54, 1187–89; *Independent*, LV (1903), 518–19; "The Nation vs. Indianola," *Nation*, LXXVI (January 29, 1903), 86–87; New York *Sun*, March 29, 1903; Roosevelt to Brooks, November 13, 1908, in Morison (ed.), *Roosevelt Letters*, IV, 1346–48.

[30] Report of Inspector Fitzgerald, December 15, 1902, in "Resignation of the Postmaster," 22–25; *Congressional Record*, 57th Cong., 2nd Sess., 853–54.

[31] Indianola *Enterprise*, November 7, 1902.

condition, the attempt to force Mrs. Cox's resignation was the subject of negotiation and investigation. Her husband, Wayne Cox, who knew "how to handle the typical Southern white man," was attempting to work out some arrangement so that she could retain her post until the expiration of her commission in 1904. He visited Edgar Wilson in Jackson and urged him to intercede in her behalf, explaining that the crisis had been precipitated by those interested in the office for themselves. Rather incredibly, Wilson wrote in his memoirs that he first learned that Indianola's postmaster was a Negro when he read in the newspapers of Vardaman's reference to a "negro wench" holding the position. Whatever the validity of his claim, he did heed the request of Wayne Cox. He investigated the matter and attempted to avert a public controversy which might result in the closing of the post office. His plan was to maintain Mrs. Cox in office until 1904, then recommend for the job a white Democrat who had in no way been connected with the movement to depose her.[32] While Wilson was searching for a solution, his friend Postal Inspector Charles Fitzgerald had undertaken an investigation at the direction of the Post Office Department. His findings corroborated Wayne Cox's view that the whole situation had resulted from the agitation of a few Democrats eager to obtain the office. "These people," Fitzgerald reported, "publicly deprecate the lawlessness of the case but privately connive at it." He denied that the mass meeting which demanded Mrs. Cox's resignation had been composed of riffraff. It was, he said, "a mob of gentlemen but a mob nevertheless."[33]

At first Fitzgerald thought he and Wilson "could adjust matters and remove the friction" without aid from Washington authorities. Fitzgerald enlisted the aid of B. G. Humphreys, the congressman-elect from the Indianola district, while Wilson urged his old friend, state Senator J. Holmes Baker, who was one of Mrs. Cox's bondsmen, to assist in finding a way to continue her in office until 1904. Both efforts were futile. Humphreys reported that in Indianola

[32] Wilson, "Memoirs," Chap. 77, p. 1, in Wilson Papers; Wayne Cox to Fitzgerald, November 18, 1902, in "Resignation of the Postmaster," 19.

[33] Report of Inspector Fitzgerald, December 15, 1902, in "Resignation of the Postmaster," 24.

"race prejudice . . . is running too high just now to be checked by a simple resort to reason." [34] Fitzgerald himself was disturbed by the "unreasonable talk" occasioned by the Indianola crisis. In fact, he was utterly alarmed to hear reputable citizens publicly assert that "the very presence of these negroes in the post offices was a constant incitant to the less responsible negro men to rape." A few citizens suggested that unless Mrs. Cox's resignation were forthcoming she would be in physical danger. Both the mayor and the sheriff refused to accept responsibility for her safety if she attempted to retain the office.[35] Early in December, Mrs. Cox wrote Inspector Fitzgerald, "It is my opinion that if I don't resign there will be trouble and cause the town to lose [its] post-office facilities. This is my home, and I feel a deep interest in the town and its people." A few days later, on December 4, 1902, she tendered her resignation "to take effect January 1, 1903, or as soon thereafter as my successor can be appointed." [36]

Inflammatory diatribes by Vardaman had seriously complicated the task of mediating the Indianola impasse. Seizing upon the incident for campaign purposes, he had returned to Indianola twice in November for speaking engagements in which he congratulated the citizens on their action toward the "negro wench." He explained in his newspaper that the town had suffered the affront of "receiving mail from the hands of a coon" for so long rather than incur the wrath of "the azure boweled bigots of the Roosevelt variety" or risk bringing down upon itself all "the horrors dormant in the fourteenth and fifteenth amendments." Vardaman commended the white people of Indianola for the courage which they had belatedly shown by serving notice on the Roosevelt administration that Mississippians were *not going to let niggers hold office.*[37] Such rhetoric merely served to strengthen the determination of Indianola's white citizenry to stand firm in their opposition to Mrs. Cox even if it meant losing the post office.

Precisely at what point President Roosevelt was first apprised of

[34] B. G. Humphreys to Fitzgerald, December 22, 1902, *ibid.*, 26–27.
[35] Report of Inspector Fitzgerald, November 15, 1902, *ibid.*, 23–25.
[36] Minnie M. Cox to Fitzgerald, December 7, December 4, 1902, *ibid.*, 20.
[37] Greenwood *Commonwealth*, November 28, 1902. Italics in original.

the Indianola crisis is not altogether clear. Edgar Wilson may have mentioned it to him during his bear-hunting expedition to Mississippi of November 13–18, 1902. But at the time Wilson and Fitzgerald still thought that they would be able to effect "a proper adjustment of the matter." Furthermore, Wilson appeared to be primarily concerned with convincing the President that pro-Roosevelt forces controlled the Republican Party in Mississippi. At any rate, not until December 30, 1902, did he advise Roosevelt in writing of the Indianola situation; and the later fanfare about a famous letter in which Wilson urged the President to "stand by Minnie Cox" apparently referred to his letter of that date.[38] Regardless of the extent to which Wilson informed the White House of developments in Indianola, the President undoubtedly learned of the situation from reports and recommendations made by Inspector Fitzgerald to the Post Office Department. On December 15, 1902, ten days after receiving Mrs. Cox's resignation, Fitzgerald rendered his own decision in the case. Frustrated in his efforts to find a solution and convinced that Mrs. Cox would be in danger if she refused to heed the demand of the mass meeting, he recommended the closing of the post office at Indianola. Among the precedents for such action was a similar situation in Pickens, Mississippi, which had prompted him to recommend the closing of its post office during McKinley's administration. In his report on the Indianola crisis he pointed out:

> And thus is the issue joined between the forces of law and order on the one side and of lawlessness and disorder on the other. Here we have a citizen of the United States of America legally commissioned by the President to exercise the functions of an office. No objection has been filed . . . as to the honesty, fidelity and capacity and courtesy of the incumbent; but a mob sits in solemn conclave in the town of Indianola, Miss., and deliberately nullifies a commission issued to a citizen by the President in the discharge of his sworn duty. The people of this section of the state say the President is forcing Negro domination on them, whereas in various counties of the Delta region white Democratic voters elect negro justices of the peace and negro constables.
>
> Imagine the mighty howl that would reecho through canebrakes, lagoons, and cotton fields and forests of the Mississippi Delta if the

---

[38] Sumners, "Edgar S. Wilson: Mississippi Eagle," 163–64; Wilson to Roosevelt, December 30, 1902, in Roosevelt Papers.

office of justice of the peace or constable were within the gift of the President of the United States and he should appoint a negro constable to arrest white people or a negro magistrate to pass upon questions affecting the liberty and property of the white people. But this is precisely what Mississippians do, without it in the least menacing white civilization.

It is within conservative bounds to say that there are as many negro magistrates and constables in the Mississippi Delta as there are negro postmasters in that section to-day, and no one will say that the holding of the offices of constable and magistrate by the negroes, elected by a white Democratic constituency, has ever incited a negro to a single act of lawlessness. Yet we are gravely informed that a 'nigger' in a post office incites negroes to crime and is a perpetual menace to Anglo-Saxon civilization. Verily these good people are not hampered with that foolish consistency which, we are told, is the hobgoblin of little minds.[39]

Fitzgerald concluded that if the Roosevelt administration yielded to local pressure in the Indianola case it would "be the beginning of interminable trouble." [40]

The President conferred regularly with his cabinet and especially with Postmaster General Payne on the proper course to pursue in the Indianola matter. Payne favored action which would vigorously assert "the majesty of the Federal Government" and suggested that as a bona fide federal officer Mrs. Cox should be protected, by federal troops if necessary, in the discharge of her duties.[41] Roosevelt dismissed this possibility as quickly as he had that of surrendering to the will of the local mass meeting. Although he was "hunting for delegates" at the time, political considerations apparently did not influence his handling of the Indianola crisis. The evidence fails to support the interpretation that he viewed the incident as an opportunity to appeal to the northern Negro vote or to thwart James Hill's anti-Roosevelt movement among Negro Republicans in Mississippi. Instead, he looked upon the incident as an unfortunate one

[39] Report of Inspector Fitzgerald, December 15, 1902, in "Resignation of the Postmaster," 24.

[40] *Ibid.*, 25.

[41] Appendix, Morison (ed.), *Roosevelt Letters*, IV, 1356; Francis E. Leupp, *The Man Roosevelt: A Portrait Sketch* (New York: Appleton, 1904), 95; William Draper Lewis, *The Life of Theodore Roosevelt* (n. p., 1919), 197; New York *Times*, January 3, 1903.

in which the rights of an individual as well as the authority of the federal government had been seriously compromised. Convinced that the offense demanded action, he decided to follow the simple expedient recommended by Postal Inspector Fitzgerald rather than risk the consequences of Payne's suggestion.[42] Thus, the President refused to accept Mrs. Cox's resignation and ordered the post office at Indianola closed on January 2, 1903. The post office was suspended, not abolished, because legally every seat of county government was entitled to postal facilities. Roosevelt emphasized that Indianola still had a post office and a postmaster who would continue to draw her salary and that whenever Mrs. Cox could resume her duties, normal postal service would be restored. In the meantime, all mail destined for Indianola was to be routed to Greenville, a town located thirty miles away, and the attorney general was to proceed against those citizens who had threatened Mrs. Cox with violence if she refused to vacate the office. In announcing his decision Roosevelt was careful to point out that a "brutal and lawless element" had perpetuated the outrage at Indianola but only with the acquiescence of the "reputable people." [43]

Indianola greeted the President's announcement with characteristic intransigence. The white citizens were convinced that Senators McLaurin and Money would have the postal service restored quickly, but if not, they were quite willing to allow the post office "to remain closed until doomsday" in order to get rid of the Negro postmaster.[44] When Inspector Fitzgerald visited Indianola on January 4, 1903, in order to transfer the funds of the closed post office, he "found the populace deeply stirred, yet on the surface everything was quiet and orderly." His curious encounter with the sheriff and mayor revealed much about the prevailing mood. These officials

[42] Roosevelt later described the closing of the Indianola post office as "all I could do and the least I could do." See Roosevelt to Owen Wister, April 27, 1906, in Owen Wister, *Roosevelt: The Story of a Friendship, 1880–1919* (New York: Macmillan, 1930), 256.

[43] New York *Sun*, January 3, 1903; H. C. Payne to J. Holmes Baker, January 3, 1903, Payne to Postmaster, Greenville, Miss., January 3, 1903, in Letters of the Postmaster General, National Archives.

[44] Jackson (Miss.) *Evening News*, January 5, 1903; Indianola *Enterprise*, January 16, 30, 1903.

were disturbed by the publicity given Fitzgerald's reports regarding their refusal to guarantee Mrs. Cox's safety if she attempted to reopen the post office. Aided by the mayor's brother-in-law, A. B. Weeks, who still hoped to obtain the position, these two men lured Fitzgerald to the sheriff's home with the intention of forcing him to retract certain statements that had appeared in the press. Their plan misfired because J. A. Richardson, editor of the Indianola *Toscin,* who had opposed the whole movement to oust the postmaster, insisted upon accompanying Fitzgerald to the sheriff's house.[45] No less than the postal inspector, newspaper reporters were impressed by the "undercurrent of excitement" in Indianola and the surrounding area. Some detected a "hint of race war in the air" as twenty deputies patrolled streets crowded with strangers. The atmosphere finally became so menacing that Mrs. Cox left Indianola on the night of January 5, 1903, for what was described as an extended visit with friends in Birmingham. Shortly after her departure, citizens openly boasted that if she returned to the post office "she would get her neck broken inside of two hours." Lest retaliation be wreaked upon Mrs. Cox and her family, Inspector Fitzgerald advised the President to postpone any court action in the case. Apparently, the idea of bringing her tormentors to justice was abandoned altogether.[46]

Although the townspeople of Indianola expressed a willingness to forgo postal facilities as the price of ridding themselves of Negro officials, they were unwilling to suffer in silence. They complained loudly that the closing of the post office was detrimental to both their business and their image. They pleaded with their congressman to have the post office reopened in order to avert economic disaster. Virtually all the public officials issued statements denying the existence of racial animosities in the community and protesting the "cheap advertisement and notoriety that we did not seek and

[45] Fitzgerald to Johnston, January 6, 1903, in "Resignation of the Postmaster," 27–28. See also Indianola *Toscin* quoted in Greenwood (Miss.) *Enterprise,* January 23, 1903.

[46] Washington *Evening Star,* January 5, 6, 7, 1903; Atlanta *Constitution,* January 5, 6, 7, 1903; Fitzgerald to Johnston, January 8, 1903, in "Resignation of the Postmaster," 27–30.

did not want." [47] At the same time these spokesmen not only admitted that Mrs. Cox's race was the sole consideration in the movement to depose her but also were quick to blame the plight of their community upon the President and his pro-Negro policies, which had "inflamed racial antipathies." Not content with denying the town its legal right to a post office and slandering the "good name of its citizens," the argument ran, Roosevelt had "just for spite" ordered the mail routed to Greenville rather than to Heathman, a flag station only four miles away. In time most white citizens of Indianola had their mail addressed to Heathman, and both local newspapers were posted from there.[48] A so-called McLaurin post office financed by private subscriptions was established in the courthouse for the purpose of distributing mail hauled from Heathman and Greenville by a Confederate veteran and a Negro, respectively. A favorite theme of the Indianola *Enterprise* was that Roosevelt's closing of the post office "punished the very people that he wants to serve" because Negroes lacked the means of transporting their mail, much of which piled up in the Greenville post office.[49]

In Washington Senator McLaurin became the champion of Indianola's cause. He conferred regularly with Roosevelt and Payne in an effort to have the post office reopened under a white postmaster. Failure to win any concessions from them prompted him to take his fight to Congress.[50] Rising to a question of privilege on January 15, 1903, he attempted to dispel the notion that Mrs. Cox had been forced to resign or that any threats had been made against her. Hence, the President's public statement explaining his reasons for closing the post office was a slur upon the "high-toned, chivalrous, industrious . . . and law-abiding people" of Indianola.[51] True to his earlier promise, Republican Senator John C. Spooner of Wisconsin

[47] P. C. Chapman to A. J. McLaurin, January 6, 1903, D. M. Quinn to McLaurin, January 10, 1903, in *Congressional Record*, 57th Cong., 2nd Sess., 853–54; Indianola *Enterprise*, January 16, 1903.

[48] Jackson *Evening News*, January 6, 7, 1903; Indianola *Enterprise*, January 30, 1903; New York *World*, February 7, 1903.

[49] Indianola *Enterprise*, January 30, February 13, 27, 1903.

[50] New York *Times*, January 6, 1903; Washington *Evening Star*, January 15, 16, 1903.

[51] *Congressional Record*, 57th Cong., 2nd Sess., 853–54.

rose in the Senate on January 24, 1903, to defend Roosevelt's handling of the Indianola affair. He denied the validity of McLaurin's claim that the citizens of Indianola were guilty of no other crime than that of exercising their right to assemble peacefully and to petition for the redress of what they considered to be a grievance. "It is as idle as the wind," Spooner declared, "to cavil upon the proposition that this was not a forced resignation. It is altogether evasive to dwell upon the 'politeness' of the request for her resignation. It was the power behind it which constituted the duress; it was the fact that that power was executed by white citizens of that county, and that this person against whom it was directed was colored." [52] But Spooner preferred to emphasize the constitutional, rather than the racial, aspects of the incident. The President, he argued, had acted on the sound principle that the federal government must exercise its constitutional authority and administer its affairs "without obstruction and without local duress applied to its officials." [53] Before the Indianola affair had been exhausted as a subject of congressional debate, Senators Edward W. Carmack of Tennessee and Benjamin R. Tillman of South Carolina added their voices to the chorus denouncing the President for his "tyrannical and unconstitutional act" in closing the post office.[54] By direction of a resolution introduced by Congressman Edgar D. Crumpacker of Indiana, the postmaster general transmitted to Congress on March 2, 1903, all documents in his possession relating to the Indianola affair.[55] Even the most hostile critics of the President could scarcely have failed to be impressed by the evidence supporting the propriety of his action.

No less spirited than the congressional deliberations were the discussions of the Indianola affair in the press. That it coincided with Roosevelt's appointment of a Negro, William D. Crum, as

[52] *Ibid.,* 1178.

[53] See Spooner's remarks as well as those of other senators who participated in the debate on the Indianola post office affair on January 24, 1903, *ibid.,* 1174–90.

[54] *Ibid.,* 2511–15; Francis B. Simkins, *Pitchfork Ben Tillman: South Carolinian* (Baton Rouge: La. State, 1944), 415–16.

[55] *Congressional Record,* 57th Cong., 2nd Sess., 1266; New York *Times,* January 20, March 3, 1903.

collector of the Port of Charleston, only intensified the agitation.[56] Many editors saw the President's actions in both instances as part of his strategy to secure the Republican nomination in 1904. They argued that his support of Mrs. Cox was motivated solely by his desire to win black votes in the North and to counter the growing threat posed by the Lily White Republicans in the South, who supported Mark Hanna for the nomination. Following a theme pursued by Senator McLaurin, editorialists representing both parties criticized Roosevelt's suspension of the post office on the grounds that it punished the innocent as well as the guilty.[57] William Jennings Bryan reminded the readers of his *Commoner* that the Indianola affair pointed up the feasibility of his plan to have postmasters popularly elected by local constituents.[58] Although the President received support from such journals as the New York *Tribune* and the Washington *Evening Star*,[59] a substantial segment of the press inclined to agree that he had committed "a highly impolitic act" which would only stir up racial animosities. According to the New York *Times,* the South had "carried the question of negro equality far toward a settlement in which practically the whole country acquiesced. There was no other possible settlement." [60] Even the Negro press was not unanimous in its endorsement of the President's solution to the Indianola crisis. Although the *Colored American* considered it an appropriate act to commemorate the fortieth anniversary of the Emancipation Proclamation, other influential Negro journals were suspicious of the President's motives.[61]

[56] Thomas R. Waring to R. G. Rhett, November 5, 1902, in Roosevelt Papers; Roosevelt to Rhett, November 10, 1902, in Morison (ed.), *Roosevelt Letters,* III, 375–76; "Negro Appointments in the South," *Literary Digest,* XXV (1902), 737.

[57] See New York *Times,* January 6, 1903; *Harper's Weekly,* XLVIII (1903), 140; "Negro Officials in the South," *Public Opinion,* XXXIV (January 15, 1903), 68–69.

[58] *Commoner,* III (January 30, 1903), 4; *ibid.,* IV (August 5, 1904), 3.

[59] New York *Daily Tribune,* January 6, 1903; Washington *Evening Star,* January 6, 8, 17, 31, February 17, 1903. See also *Outlook,* LXXIII (January 24, 1903), 188–89; *Independent,* LV (1903), 60–61.

[60] New York *Times,* January 6, 1903.

[61] Washington *Colored American,* January 10, 17, 1903; Cleveland *Gazette,* January 18, 31, 1903.

In the South the suspension of the post office sparked an emotional outburst against Roosevelt comparable to that which followed his famous dinner with Booker T. Washington in 1901. Roosevelt was, in the eyes of white southerners, a "cynical Negrophile" whose theories of social and political equality were responsible for a long list of problems ranging from "the outbreak of Negro outrages" to the "servant problem" in the South.[62] The Louisville *Courier-Journal* maintained that the extremist method used by the Indianola citizens to get rid of the postmaster was merely a response to the "extremism of the President" regarding the race question. Furthermore, there would have been no crisis over Indianola if the President had abided by the wishes of the majority of the white people.[63] "To make a person postmaster who is objectionable to the community . . . ," the Savannah *Morning News* declared, "is not in keeping with republican institutions, . . . the rule of the majority, [or] . . . the principles of local self-government." [64] For more than a year the southern press lavished special attention upon every development in the Indianola crisis, which came increasingly to be described as the mischievous work of Roosevelt's referee Edgar Wilson. On the one hand, Wilson was denounced for advising the President to "stand by Minnie" and on the other for conspiring to oust her in order to name his own candidate to the post.[65] In time, too, southerners discovered what they believed to be the real cause of the trouble in Indianola: the congregation of "crap-shooting darkies" in the lobby of the post office "where white women and children had to pass and repass." [66]

[62] "Southern Press on the Indianola Incident," *Literary Digest*, XXVI (1903), 71–72; Atlanta *News*, January 3, 4, 26, 27, 1903; Louisville *Courier-Journal*, January 4, 1903; Thomas D. Clark, *The Southern Country Editor* (Indianapolis: Bobbs, 1948), 314–15. For a view of the Indianola affair by a "southern lady," see Annie Riley Hale, *Rooseveltian Fact and Fable* (New York: Broadway Publishing Co., 1908), 139–41.

[63] Louisville *Courier-Journal*, January 9, 1903.

[64] Savannah (Ga.) *Morning News*, January 6, 1903. For the expression of a similar view see John W. Bennett's anti-Roosevelt tract *Roosevelt and the Republic* (New York: Broadway Publishing Co., 1908), 152.

[65] Atlanta *Constitution*, February 2, 1903; Atlanta *News*, January 4, February 2, 14, 1903; Greenwood *Commonwealth*, January 10, February 28, 1903.

[66] Atlanta *Journal*, August 13, 1903. Senator Money even suggested that the

In Mississippi virtually all white citizens rallied to the defense of the beleaguered people of Indianola. But few embraced their cause with more enthusiasm than Senator Money during his campaign for reelection. Illness had prevented his presence in the Senate during the debates on Indianola; but upon his return early in March, he delivered a ringing speech on the subject which was obviously designed as much for his constituents as for his Senate colleagues. His defense of the Indianola citizenry was at times eclipsed by his lengthy excursions into such topics as the general inferiority of the Negro, the implications of Roosevelt's dinner with Booker T. Washington in 1901, and the plight of Haiti under Negro rule.[67] When ten thousand copies of his "Indianola address" ordered from the Government Printing Office failed to arrive at the senator's campaign headquarters on schedule, rumors circulated that the delay had been caused by Roosevelt partisans. Either Roosevelt himself had ordered the printing office to postpone shipment or a Negro mail clerk, probably Wayne Cox, had disposed of the material.[68] In addition to this speech—which ultimately arrived and was widely circulated—other campaign documents issued by Money's headquarters used the Indianola affair to point up the relationship between the senator's opponent, Longino, and the Roosevelt-Wilson "social equality forces." [69] Taking up this theme, pro-Money newspapers claimed that Longino disqualified himself as a serious contender in the Senate race because of his close political alliance with his brother-in-law, Edgar Wilson, "that miserable republican referee" who "would place black heels on white necks if he could." [70]

---

lobby of Mrs. Cox's post office was the place in which the Negro porter employed at Cohn's store had insulted the white salesgirl. See *Congressional Record*, 58th Cong., 1st Sess., 128.

[67] *Congressional Record*, 58th Cong., 1st Sess., 125–35.

[68] *The Indianola, Miss., Post-Office Incident to the Race Question: Speech of Hon. H. D. Money of Mississippi in the Senate of the United States* (Washington: Government Printing Office, 1903); Jackson *Evening News*, April 15, 1903; Indianola *Enterprise*, April 3, 1903; Greenwood *Commonwealth*, April 11, 1903.

[69] See *As to the Nigger* (Pamphlet issued by the Money Campaign Committee, 1903).

[70] Yazoo *Sentinel* and Biloxi *Review* quoted in Indianola *Enterprise*, April 24, June 5, 1903, respectively.

At first Longino attempted to soft-pedal the Negro issue and to disregard the personal attacks. He urged politicians to refrain from exploiting the race question and to recognize the Negro as a permanent factor in southern life. "It is our duty," he declared, "to teach him to become a better man and a more intelligent farmer." [71] But when Senator Money's partisans demanded that Longino take a stand on the President's closing of the Indianola post office, he replied that it was "a high-handed proceeding and was not warranted by the circumstances." In his turn, the governor demanded to know why Senator Money, who found Edgar Wilson so objectionable, had voted to confirm his appointment as federal marshal. The senator explained his vote on humanitarian grounds: Wilson had "told him he had a sick child at home." [72]

Senator Money's exploitation of the Indianola incident paled beside that of Vardaman. No sooner had the President ordered the suspension of the post office than Vardaman seized upon the act as a major theme in his campaign for governor. He surpassed all previous records for verbal crudity in his descriptions of "the low down, dirty and contemptible conduct of President Roosevelt regarding the Indianola Post Office." Like much of the anti-Roosevelt press outside Mississippi, he made it appear as though the Indianola crisis had been caused by Roosevelt's "appointment of Minnie Cox." Although Vardaman enthralled his audiences by referring to the President as a "human coyote" and a "political boll weevil pregnant with evil," [73] his most vulgar description was in an editorial on the Indianola affair which appeared in his newspaper. "It is said," he wrote, "that men follow the bent of their genius and that prenatal influences are often potent in shaping thoughts and ideas of after life. Probably old lady Roosevelt, during the period of gestation, was frightened by a dog and that fact may account for the qualities of the male pup which are so prominent in Teddy. . . . I am disposed

[71] Atlanta *Constitution*, June 29, 1903.
[72] Indianola *Enterprise*, April 24, May 8, June 5, 19, July 3, 17, 24, 31, 1903; Greenwood *Enterprise*, April 24, 1903.
[73] Greenwood *Commonwealth*, January 10, 17, 31, 1903.

to apologize to the dog for mentioning it." [74] Scarcely less lurid were Vardaman's references to Edgar Wilson, who was held responsible for the Indianola crisis because he urged Roosevelt to "stand by Minnie Cox." Taking his stand on an "anti-Minnie Cox platform," Vardaman appealed to the passions and prejudices of white voters with his own inimitable concoction of political fiction. The details varied from time to time but the essential ingredients remained the same: Roosevelt's "nigger loving gang in Washington" and its counterpart in Mississippi, the Longino-Wilson "Jackson gang," were united in a mighty effort to defeat Vardaman. The whole conspiracy was being financed by the Union League Club of New York. Hence, to vote for any of Vardaman's opponents in the Democratic primary was to invite more "nigger postmasters" and more troubles of the Indianola variety. [75]

Both Money and Vardaman achieved victories in the Democratic primary in Mississippi, which were tantamount to election. [76] Political observers emphasized the critical role of the Indianola incident in their campaigns. Some even claimed that if Roosevelt had handled the crisis differently—presumably if he had acquiesced in the actions of the white citizens—Vardaman would have been as unsuccessful in his campaign for governor in 1903 as he had been on two previous occasions. [77] Perhaps Edgar Wilson was more correct

[74] Quoted in Kirwan, *Revolt of the Rednecks*, 153. See also Wilson, "Memoirs," Chap. 77, p. 2, in Wilson Papers.

[75] See Greenwood *Commonwealth*, January 24, 31, February 28, March 14, April 18, May 10, June 27, July 18, August 22, 1903. Vardaman summarized the "facts in the case": "Roosevelt is against Vardaman. His referee Edgar Wilson is against Vardaman. All the appointees of these two men are against Vardaman . . . . A vote for Vardaman emphasizes white supremacy and will be a rebuke to Roosevelt."

[76] In the primary held on August 6, 1903, Vardaman failed to win a majority and thus was forced into a run-off against Judge Frank Critz, whom he defeated. Money defeated Longino in the Senate rate without a second primary. Interestingly enough, Sunflower County (Indianola) voted heavily in favor of Money, but in the second gubernatorial primary the county gave Critz 379 votes and Vardaman 350 votes. New Orleans *Daily Picayune*, August 29, 1903.

[77] Atlanta *Constitution*, August 13, 29, 1903; New Orleans *Daily Picayune*, August 29, 30, 1903; Chattanooga *News*, September 5, 1903; Greenwood *Commonwealth*, August 22, 1903.

in his contention that the primary, unlike the convention method of nomination, created a situation which allowed Vardaman to ride to power by exploiting the Indianola post office affair.[78] Roosevelt himself was fully aware of the role ascribed to him and his policies in bringing about the political triumph of one whose program and technique he loathed. Although the Indianola incident might well be considered to be related more specifically to the emergence of demagogic racism than either his dinner with Booker T. Washington or his appointment of Crum, Roosevelt was never plagued by misgivings about his support of Mrs. Cox as he was about his actions in the other two instances.[79] Perhaps, like Inspector Fitzgerald, the President believed that the closing of the post office at Indianola had prevented a wholesale crusade against Negro postmasters elsewhere in Mississippi.[80]

But if Roosevelt was convinced of the propriety of his action in the Indianola crisis, the question arises as to why he allowed the post office to be reopened in 1904 under a white postmaster. The answer is more complicated than it appears on the surface. From the beginning Roosevelt had intended to keep the post office closed only so long as the white citizens of Indianola refused to accept Mrs. Cox as postmaster during her term; a change in circumstances might dictate another course at the expiration of her commission in 1904. Late in 1903, all reports, including those of Inspector Fitzgerald, indicated that Vardaman's victory had merely solidified the determination of Indianola's citizens to prevent Mrs. Cox or any other Negro from holding the office. Further evidence of the prevailing mood was a resolution passed by the Mississippi legislature in Jan-

[78] Wilson, "Memoirs," Chap. 77, p. 5, in Wilson Papers.

[79] Roosevelt to Wister, April 27, 1906, in Wister, *Roosevelt*, 254–56; Roosevelt to Brooks, November 13, 1908, in Morison (ed.), *Roosevelt Letters*, IV, 1146–48.

[80] Inspector Fitzgerald was convinced that "a crusade against the few negro postmasters in this state has been effectively checked" by Roosevelt's prompt action in the Indianola case. His action apparently stifled efforts by the white citizens of Goza, Miss., to force their Negro postmaster out of office in May, 1903. See Fitzgerald to Johnston, January 6, 1903, in "Resignation of the Postmaster," 27–28; Atlanta *Constitution*, May 26, 1903.

uary, 1904, which severely arraigned Roosevelt for his "wilful nulli-fication of the Constitution . . . and the laws of Congress" in closing the Indianola post office.[81] Fully aware of the atmosphere, Mrs. Cox informed the President that under no circumstances would she be a candidate for reappointment. The same fears which motivated her decision precluded applications from other Negroes who might have qualified for the position.[82] The choices left for the President were either to keep the post office closed indefinitely or to open it under a white postmaster. Indefinite suspension, which could easily be interpreted as abolition, risked legal complications arising from the statutes requiring postal facilities in all seats of county govern-ment. Even Negro editors who abhorred the prospect of reopening the post office under a white postmaster conceded that "there was nothing else to be done." [83]

When Roosevelt announced his decision to restore postal facil-ities in the town, the southern press rejoiced that "the white people of Indianola have won their cause: namely the appointment of a white postmaster." [84] But their victory was less than complete, be-cause Roosevelt had refused to consider any applicant for the posi-tion who had "been in sympathy with, or had anything to do, di-rectly or indirectly," with the movement to compel the resignation of Mrs. Cox.[85] Following the recommendations of Edgar Wilson and Inspector Fitzgerald, the President appointed as postmaster William B. Martin, the chairman of the local Democratic executive committee, who had served as one of Mrs. Cox's bondsmen and remained "her staunch friend throughout the whole trouble." [86] Then, as a final stroke, the postmaster general reduced the rank of

81 New Orleans *Daily Picayune*, January 19, 1904.

82 Wilson, "Memoirs," Chap. 77, pp. 2–3, in Wilson Papers; Cleveland *Ga-zette*, February 13, 1904.

83 Cleveland *Gazette*, February 13, 1904; Chicago *Broad Ax*, February 20, 1904; New York *Age*, February 11, 1904.

84 Atlanta *Journal*, January 28, 1904.

85 Payne to J. L. Bristow, January 19, 1904, in Letters of the Postmaster General.

86 New York *Times*, January 28, 1904; New Orleans *Daily Picayune*, January 28, 1904.

the postal facility at Indianola from third-class to fourth-class on the grounds that its receipts for 1903–1904 did not warrant presidential status.[87]

Shortly after the reopening of the post office in Indianola, another incident in the town attracted attention briefly. On March 10, 1904, two peddlers from Chicago were arrested there for selling "obscene photographs" to Negroes. Reports by the Associated Press described the offensive merchandise as pictures of "President Roosevelt and Booker Washington dining together." [88] Publicity of the incident prompted a lengthy explanation from Senator McLaurin, who claimed that the press had again grossly "misrepresented the good people of Indianola." He informed the Senate that although the peddlers had indeed distributed pictures of the Washington-Roosevelt dinner to Negroes in the Indianola area, they had actually been arrested for selling stereoscopic slides of Adolphe Bouguereau's *Birth of Venus* in which the male figure had been colored black. The incident, he argued, offered a perfect example of the northern white man inciting the "inferior race" to commit "a nameless crime against the white women" of Mississippi. Because the pictures had been manufactured by the Whiteside View Company of Cincinnati, Senator Joseph B. Foraker of Ohio apologized to McLaurin and assured the Senate that the company was not a "representative enterprise" of that fair Ohio city.[89] During its session of 1904 the Mississippi legislature, no less than the United States Senate, expressed an interest in Indianola. Although the legislators defeated a bill to "reimburse the people of Indianola for money spent in maintaining their post office," they were quick to enact a law which prohibited "selling or giving away indecent books, writing paper, drawings, photographs, etc." Representative Percy Bell, the sponsor of the latter act, made clear that it had been prompted by the "dirty pictures" incident in Indianola. It was obviously designed as a measure of racial control, and the label *indecent* applied to

[87] New York *Daily Tribune,* August 16, 1904.
[88] New York *Times,* March 11, 13, 1904; Washington *Evening Star,* March 11, 1904.
[89] *Congressional Record,* 58th Cong., 2nd Sess., 3170–71.

"social equality pictures" as well as to "pictures of nude women." [90] Although Indianola disappeared from the headlines following this aftermath of the post office affair, the "good people" of the town continued to hold Roosevelt responsible for disturbing their racial harmony. Not until thirty-five years later, when their community was the focus of two famous studies on race relations, did it again enjoy the limelight, and then only as an anonymous southern town.[91]

Several weeks before the row over the obscene pictures, Mrs. Cox returned to Indianola from Birmingham, where she had remained during the agitation over the post office. The Cox home, located in the white residential district of the town, was repainted and "put in first class order within and without." Shortly after their return, she and her husband, who remained an employee of the railway mail division of the Post Office Department, organized the Delta Penny Savings Bank of Indianola and purchased additional farm land in Sunflower County. No other people of color were held in such esteem by the white business community.[92] Through Booker T. Washington, the President was kept informed of the fate of the Coxes following the decline of the post office disturbance. He expressed pride in their educational and economic attainments, which he cited as characteristic of the "new Negroes of the generation that has grown up since the war." [93] But like Washington, he noted the irony of their situation: the same white citizens who objected to Mrs. Cox as postmaster on the grounds of her color deposited their money in her husband's bank.[94]

[90] Jackson *Clarion-Ledger,* March 22, April 25, 1904; *Journal of the House of Representatives of the State of Mississippi, 1904,* pp. 625, 774, 801, 803, 961, 968.

[91] See John Dollard, *Caste and Class in a Southern Town* (New Haven: Yale, 1937); Hortense Powdermaker, *After Freedom: A Cultural Study of the Deep South* (New York: Viking, 1939).

[92] New York *Sun,* February 6, 1904; Washington to Roosevelt, June 19, 1906, in Emmett J. Scott and Lyman B. Stowe, *Booker T. Washington: Builder of a Civilization* (Garden City, N.Y.: Doubleday, 1916), 120–21.

[93] Roosevelt to Wister, June 21, 1906, in Wister, *Roosevelt,* 261.

[94] *Ibid.,* 261–62.

IV

Square Deal for Dr. Crum

*I cannot consent by my action to take the position that
the door of hope—the door of opportunity—is to be shut
upon all men, no matter how worthy, purely on the
grounds of color. Such an attitude would according to my
convictions be fundamentally wrong.*

THEODORE ROOSEVELT

Early in 1903 veteran observers of the American scene noted that
agitation of the Negro question appeared to be at "a high water
mark." In the midst of the debate over the Indianola incident
Roosevelt again waded into "the deep waters of the race problem"
by appointing William D. Crum, a Negro physician, as collector of
the Port of Charleston, South Carolina.[1] Critics of the President
interpreted both matters as new evidence of a heretical racial policy. In some respects, the two had much in common, but their differences outweighed whatever similarities they may have had. The role
of party politics was more obvious in the appointment of Crum.
The reopening of the Indianola post office in 1904 largely terminated the agitation over the affair within a year, but the presence of

[1] Henry Litchfield West, "American Politics," *Forum*, XXXIV (1903), 494–
97; Joseph B. Bishop, "The Negro and Public Office," *International Quarterly*,
VII (1903), 231–35; "Deep Waters of the Race Problem," *World's Work*, V
(1903), 2935.

a Negro in the Charleston customs house for six years beginning in 1903 meant that the Crum appointment was a durable topic of debate throughout the remainder of Roosevelt's administration.

The circumstances which originally led to the controversial appointment involved both Roosevelt's bid to become "president in his own right" in 1904 and the peculiar political situation existing in South Carolina. No sooner had Roosevelt occupied the White House in September, 1901, than he set out to strengthen his influence in the Republican Party in order to insure his nomination three years hence. His efforts were primarily directed toward thwarting the challenge posed by Senator Hanna of Ohio. Chairman of the national committee and an architect of McKinley Republicanism, Hanna obviously was in a strong position to make a successful bid for the presidential nomination in 1904. Among the means Roosevelt employed to overcome any threat that Hanna may have posed was his skillful distribution of patronage. To an extraordinary degree the President succeeded in combining his search for convention delegates with his search for efficient, honest federal officeholders.[2] Transforming the party of McKinley and Hanna into the party of Roosevelt involved a series of intricate maneuvers among Republicans in the South whose influence lay in the role they played in the nomination of the presidential candidate rather than in their ability to deliver any electoral votes. In few states, in the South or elsewhere, did Roosevelt encounter so many vexing problems as in South Carolina, which he soon labeled the "troublesome state."[3]

The difficulties posed by South Carolina were largely the result of the "bewildered and disorganized" condition of the Republican Party in the state. The party there was "always more clearly the 'Negro Party' " than elsewhere in the South. Yet, the disfranchisement of Negroes, which became nearly total with various constitutional innovations of 1895, precluded the possibility of any numerically

[2] For Roosevelt's successful efforts to become President "in his own right" see John M. Blum, *The Republican Roosevelt* (Cambridge: Harvard, 1954), 63–72.

[3] Charleston (S.C.) *News and Courier,* December 5, 1902.

strong electorate.[4] Some Negroes who escaped disfranchisement sought desperately to retain a semblance of political power by holding on to their positions in the state's Republican organization and by gaining appointments to federal offices; others eschewed politics altogether and concentrated upon achieving economic success as "the only means to the end of correcting existing conditions." [5] Those who still believed political involvement worth the effort and risk suffered from a growing sense of frustration which only aggravated the factionalism within Republican ranks. Fully aware of their deteriorating position, some Negro Republicans, including former Congressman George W. Murray, came to believe that the "only hope of the colored man" in the repressive atmosphere of South Carolina was to attract white men into the "party of Lincoln" who would cooperate with Negroes without attempting to divest them of all power. Murray was willing for whites to occupy the most conspicuous party positions so long as Negroes were allowed to share in the decision-making.[6]

An arrangement of this type had existed throughout most of the 1890's with Thomas E. Miller, Robert Smalls, and other Negroes prominent during Reconstruction sharing the party leadership with such whites as Eugene A. Webtser and the Tolbert family. Late in the 1890's frequent movements for "party reform," a euphemism for the elimination of Negroes from Republican politics, seriously eroded the effectiveness of the Black and Tan organization. A boycott of the state Republican convention in 1900 by the Lily Whites allowed Negroes to capture all party posts. Edmund H. Deas, the so-called Duke of Darlington, a Negro long associated with the Tolberts and with Webster (under whom he served as deputy collector of internal revenue), was elected party chairman. But few Negro Republicans failed to appreciate the hollowness of their victory. It

[4] George B. Tindall, *South Carolina Negroes, 1877–1900* (Columbia: U. of S.C., 1952), 53, 73–91. See also James W. Patton, "The Republican Party in South Carolina, 1876–1895," in Fletcher M. Green (ed.), *Essays in Southern History* (Chapel Hill: U. of N.C., 1949).

[5] S. W. Bennett to Whitefield McKinlay, April 15, 1903, in Carter Woodson Papers, Manuscript Division, Library of Congress.

[6] George W. Murray to McKinlay, July 25, 1902, in Woodson Papers.

was obvious that the Lily White movement, which aimed to eliminate not only Negroes but also such "carpetbaggers" as Webster,
had the backing of the Republican National Committee. Negro Republicans in South Carolina became convinced that the black man
would "soon be as completely shorn of power in Republican politics
as he is now in Democratic politics." [7]

Increasingly, Negroes expressed concern over the so-called pacification policy inaugurated in the South by McKinley and Hanna.
This policy had encouraged the Lily Whites in South Carolina to
boycott the convention of 1900. Negroes interpreted Hanna's lav-
ishing of patronage upon this element as evidence of a basic change
in national party policy.[8] Clearly Hanna was no longer relying on
the recommendations of National Committeeman Webster, whose
position as "boss of South Carolina Republicanism" had previously
entitled him to an influential voice in patronage matters. Even more
disturbing to Negro Republicans were Hanna's overtures to Senator John L. McLaurin of South Carolina. Alienated from the political organization of his sponsor Benjamin R. Tillman, the senator
had espoused what he called "Commercial Democracy," [9] which was
economically akin to McKinley Republicanism. A regular visitor to
the White House by late 1900, McLaurin was soon placed in virtual
control of federal patronage in South Carolina. Although Hanna
considered him the chief agent for the reorganization of Republicanism in the state, it is not altogether clear how or at what point
McLaurin's Commercial Democracy was to be transformed into
McKinley Republicanism. But obviously the assumption that such
a metamorphosis would take place underlay the cooperation between McLaurin and Hanna. With federal patronage and Republican financial assistance at his disposal, McLaurin proposed to build
a new party in South Carolina which would embrace Lily White
Republicans, Gold Democrats hostile to either Bryan Democracy

[7] New York *Times*, October 4, 1900; Charleston *News and Courier*, October
4, November 4, 1900; Murray to McKinlay, July 25, 1902, in Woodson Papers.
[8] Cleveland *Gazette*, May 4, 1901; Bennett to McKinlay, April 15, 1903, in
Woodson Papers.
[9] J. L. McLaurin, "Breaking Up the Solid South," *World's Work*, II (1901),
985–86; David D. Wallace, *South Carolina: A Short History, 1520–1948* (Chapel
Hill: U. of N.C., 1951), 640–42.

or Tillmanism, and others disgruntled with the political status quo. The alliance between Hanna and McLaurin gave credence to the widely circulated rumors that the McKinley administration intended to "rehabilitate the Republican Party by overthrowing Negroes and Carpetbaggers." [10]

Unquestionably McLaurin used his influence to dislodge federal officeholders in South Carolina who were identified with the old line, or Black and Tan, organization. Early in 1901, he secured the appointment of John G. Capers as district attorney of South Carolina, one of the most prestigious patronage posts in the state, which traditionally had been occupied by a candidate recommended by Webster. A Gold Democrat whom Grover Cleveland had appointed to a position in the Justice Department in 1894, Capers was a representative of those "best people" in the state who had recently transferred their allegiance from the Democratic Party to Republicanism. As district attorney, he acted as McLaurin's lieutenant in organizing a new party in South Carolina. Their efforts not only aroused the hostility of Negroes but also prompted Tillman to use his considerable influence to undermine McLaurin's political position in the state. Tillman argued that his former disciple threatened to split the white vote and to bring Negroes "back into politics." [11]

In the midst of this struggle two deaths occurred which profoundly altered McLaurin's plans as well as the course of South Carolina Republicanism. The death of McKinley on September 14, 1901, was followed by that of Webster three days later. While Theodore Roosevelt was establishing himself in the presidency, McLaurin moved immediately to fill the vacancies in the Republican National Committee and the Internal Revenue Service created by the death of Webster. Once Hanna had approved his request that Capers be appointed national committeeman, McLaurin hastened

[10] J. L. McLaurin to William McKinley, April 1, June 1, 1901, McLaurin to Mark A. Hanna, June 17, 1901, in William McKinley Papers, Manuscript Division, Library of Congress.

[11] McLaurin to Hanna, June 17, 1901, McLaurin to McKinley, June 17, 1901, in McKinley Papers; Charleston *News and Courier*, April 20, 1901; B. R. Tillman, *The Struggles of 1876: How South Carolina Was Delivered from Carpet-bag and Negro Rule* (n.p., 1901), 4–6. For a sketch of John G. Capers see John Leonard (ed.), *Men of America* (New York: Hamersly, 1908), 389–90.

to renew his acquaintance with Roosevelt, whom he had known as the presiding officer of the Senate, and to urge him to appoint Loomis Blalock, a textile manufacturer, to succeed Webster as collector of internal revenue.[12] Although McLaurin's frequent visits to the White House seemed to confirm rumors that Roosevelt would adhere to McKinley's pacification policy, McLaurin failed to win presidential support for his proposed party realignment in South Carolina. Not only was he too closely identified with Hanna, whose power Roosevelt wished to curtail, but also his efforts at political reorganization had stirred a violent upheaval within Republican ranks in the state. Led by Deas, Negro Republicans filed with the President their grievances against Capers, whom they described as a "renegade democrat" being used by McLaurin to eliminate the black man from the state's Republican organization. However abrasive Deas may have been, Roosevelt at least was apprised of the Lily White activities of McLaurin and his disciples. Nor was the President unaware of McLaurin's precarious grip on political power as a result of Tillman's systematic campaign against him. By mid-1902 Tillman had sealed his fate by excluding him from the state's Democratic primary. Obviously Roosevelt would not select as his spokesman in South Carolina a lame-duck senator who was in effect a man without a party. Instead he accepted Capers as his patronage referee in the state. Deftly, Capers shifted his allegiance from Hanna to Roosevelt and publicly committed himself to a biracial party in South Carolina.[13]

Roosevelt's gradual abandonment of McLaurin's schemes undoubtedly owed much to the new sources from which he had begun to receive advice on southern affairs. Among these advisers were Booker T. Washington and two Republican politicians experienced in dealing with southern Republicans, Henry C. Payne and James S. Clarkson, whom he appointed postmaster general and surveyor of the New York port, respectively. In October, 1901, Washington

[12] Charleston *News and Courier*, September 19, 21, 26, 1901.

[13] *Ibid.*, October 1, 4, 6, 1901; Washington *Evening Star*, July 27, September 30, October 3, 7, 9, 11, 12, 1901; "The South Carolina Senators Resign," *Outlook*, LXVIII (1901), 231–32; Francis B. Simkins, *Pitchfork Ben Tillman: South Carolinian* (Baton Rouge: La. State, 1944), 385–90.

urged the President to appoint William D. Crum to the revenue post formerly held by Webster. The Negro physician had much to recommend him. Well educated and obviously a man of means, he counted among his friends prominent Negroes such as Washington; P. B. S. Pinchback, formerly lieutenant governor of Louisiana; Whitefield McKinlay, the wealthy realtor in Washington; Harry Smith, editor of the Cleveland *Gazette*; and T. Thomas Fortune, editor of the New York *Age*. Furthermore, the white people of Charleston probably held Crum in higher esteem than they did any other Negro in the city. When the businessmen there decided to sponsor the Charleston and West Indian Exposition in 1901, Crum and Booker T. Washington were selected to direct its Negro department. Crum organized the exhibition, which was generally acclaimed as one of the most notable features of the exposition. But the high esteem in which white Charlestonians held him had little to do with such accomplishments. If they spoke of the Negro doctor, they were likely to recall that when Wilbur Wilberforce's daughter rode in Crum's carriage during a visit to the city, he walked alongside to avoid riding with her.[14] Although Roosevelt recognized Crum's merits, he informed Booker T. Washington that the revenue collectorship had already been promised to Blalock, an indication that McLaurin and Capers had succeeded in winning presidential acceptance of their nominee. But Roosevelt assured Washington that he would consider Crum for any other position in South Carolina which became vacant.[15]

When Blalock went on a drunken spree in Washington in mid-October, 1901, apparently in a premature celebration of his appointment, Roosevelt rejected him as unfit for the revenue collectorship.[16] Notwithstanding his promise regarding Crum, the

---

[14] W. D. Crum to McKinlay, April 21, 1897, in Woodson Papers; Simkins, *Pitchfork Ben Tillman,* 416; Charleston *News and Courier,* September 12, 1901.

[15] Emmett J. Scott to B. T. Washington, October 5, 1901, in Emmett J. Scott and Lyman B. Stowe, *Booker T. Washington: Builder of a Civilization* (Garden City, N.Y.: Doubleday, 1916), 53–54; Washington to Scott, October 4, 1901, in Theodore Roosevelt Papers, Manuscript Division, Library of Congress.

[16] Theodore Roosevelt to Hanna, October 16, 1901, in Roosevelt Papers;

President selected as Blalock's replacement George R. Koester of Columbia, a journalist of ability who was closely identified with McLaurin, Capers, and other "conservative interests." Scarcely had Koester assumed the revenue post early in November, 1901, when a faction of Negro Republicans led by Deas launched an offensive to prevent his confirmation by the Senate. Deas publicly charged him with participating in the lynching of two Negroes in 1893. In his own defense, Koester maintained that he had covered the lynching as a reporter and had persuaded the lynchers to shoot one of the accused rapists rather than burn him alive in resin. The Columbia *State*, an old rival of Koester's own *Evening Record,* joined in the chorus of denunciation. Even more effective was the tactic of Senator Tillman, who, unwilling to weaken his racist image at home, shrewdly damned Koester by praising him as "my kind of man." Throughout the winter of 1901–1902, Deas vigorously pressed the lynching charge and placed in the hands of several Republican senators documentary evidence of Koester's part in the crime.[17] More important was the speaking tour that he made in the North, where his allegations were more likely to provoke a politically significant response among Negroes. As a result of his efforts, Negro societies and organizations in Cleveland, Chicago, Boston, and other cities in which Deas spoke directed resolutions both to the White House and the Senate demanding the withdrawal of "mobocrat" Koester.[18] Roosevelt recognized that his continued support of Koester might well have serious political consequences. Therefore, on June 28, 1902, the President wrote Koester, "All that I regret is that I was not able to get you confirmed. I had high hopes of it at one time." [19]

In Koester's place as revenue collecter Roosevelt appointed

Washington *Evening Star,* October 11, 12, 1901; Loomis Blalock to McKinlay, December 25, 1902, in Woodson Papers.

[17] Charleston *News and Courier,* November 5, 8, 10, December 8, 1901, May 24, June 29, 1902; Atlanta *Constitution,* November 1, 2, 4, 8, 1901; Roosevelt to Washington, November 9, 1901, in Elting Morison (ed.), *The Letters of Theodore Roosevelt* (8 vols.; Cambridge: Harvard, 1951–54), III, 194.

[18] Washington *Colored American,* January 18, February 22, June 7, 1902; Cleveland *Gazette,* February 22, April 12, June 21, June 28, July 5, 1902.

[19] Roosevelt to George R. Koester, June 28, 1902, in Roosevelt Papers.

Micah Jenkins, a Gold Democrat and former Rough Rider. But the appointment of Jenkins, as well as others made in 1901 and 1902, invariably became entangled in the race question. Jenkins created much consternation in Negro Republican circles by dismissing former Congressman George W. Murray from his minor post in the revenue service. Negro Republicans in South Carolina, supported by a sizable segment of the Negro press in the North, threatened "to get even with Roosevelt in the next national convention." Much of their fire was directed at Capers, whose repeated promises to recognize "the best elements of the colored race" did little to allay their fears. Deas in particular waged a persistent campaign against Capers and denounced both Roosevelt and Hanna as traitors to the historic principles of the Republican Party. Deas's varied activities, fully aired in the northern Negro press, tended to transform the struggle in South Carolina from one of politics into one of race, a fact that was not lost upon the President.[20]

Clearly the crisis in Republican affairs in the state troubled Roosevelt. He was not only disturbed by the disruptive activity of the state chairman but also by its political effects beyond the boundaries of South Carolina. In April, 1902, when he visited the Charleston exposition, the President sought additional knowledge of the situation to enable him to steer clear of further complications. On a trip to Fort Sumter aboard the *Algonquin*, he discussed appointments with a group of white conservative South Carolinians. Among those in his party were his old friend Judge William H. Brawley; Mayor Adgar Smyth of Charleston; R. Goodwyn Rhett, a prominent Charlestonian; and James C. Hemphill of the *News and Courier*.[21] The demand among Negroes for some evidence of his commitment to a biracial party prompted Roosevelt to make numerous inquiries regarding Crum. Every response corroborated Booker T. Washington's estimate of him as a man of ability and character. What was actually said aboard the *Algonquin* later became the subject of

[20] Charleston *News and Courier*, June 23, July 3, 4, 6, September 13, 1902; Washington *Colored American*, July 12, 19, September 20, 1902; Cleveland *Gazette*, August 2, 30, 1902.

[21] For the story of Roosevelt's visit to Charleston see the Charleston *News and Courier*, April 8, 9, 10, 15, 1902.

much dispute. But thirty years after the event, Daniel L. Sinkler, a participant, recalled that Hemphill had said to Roosevelt, "Mr. President, I hope you will not appoint any negro to an important office in the South." According to Sinkler, Roosevelt replied, "How could I when my mother was a Southern woman, a Bulloch from Georgia?" Sinkler admitted that the President asked about Dr. Crum and was assured that he was "well liked by the whites." Apparently the confusion lay in the term "important office" and the difference of opinion regarding what constituted such an office.[22] Another version of the conference credited to Micah Jenkins, who was also present, claimed that Roosevelt candidly explained his interest in Crum by saying, "I have to appoint a negro to an office in South Carolina, not that I expect anything from South Carolina, but for the effect it will have in Ohio, Indiana, and the other close states in the north, where there is a large negro vote. I want you to recommend to me an absolutely clean man for the appointment." Crum, according to Jenkins' account, was unanimously recommended by those in the presidential party because at the time no federal office was vacant in Charleston and they assumed that he would be given a minor post elsewhere in the state.[23] That Roosevelt's erstwhile advisers were careful to mention major post offices as unsuitable for Negro appointees may well have been prompted by their fear that Crum would be placed in the Charleston post office to succeed George I. Cunningham, who was slated to become a federal marshal. Instead the President chose another white Republican, Wilmot L. Harris, as postmaster.[24]

Despite the later controversy over what transpired aboard the

22 *Ibid.*, October 22, 1934.

23 *Ibid.*, October 28, 1934.

24 Harris was appointed postmaster of Charleston upon Capers' recommendation. Tillman immediately labeled him a "carpet-bagger" and promised to prevent his confirmation despite assurances from Charleston officials that he was "wholly acceptable." Actually, Harris had been a former per diem pension agent in Charleston who had lived there barely long enough to establish his legal residence when he was appointed postmaster. Tillman later dropped his opposition to Harris in order to concentrate on preventing the confirmation of Crum. See Charleston *News and Courier*, May 29, 31, June 6, 7, July 3, 1902.

Algonquin, Roosevelt was convinced that Crum was fully qualified to serve in a federal position. Developments during the summer and fall of 1902 tended to confirm the President's inclination to appoint him to a post in South Carolina. Northern Negroes became increasingly resentful of what they considered Roosevelt's acquiescence in the machinations of Lily White Republicans, and Deas continued to embarrass the administration by his highly vocal campaign. In September, 1902, Deas filed a complaint with the Civil Service Commission charging Capers and Jenkins with "coercion of subordinates and interference in elections" in direct violation of Roosevelt's executive order of the previous June. As a result of the complaint, Capers' superior, the attorney general, formally reprimanded him for engaging in political activities contrary to civil service regulations.[25]

In view of the circumstances it was not surprising that when Robert M. Wallace, collector of customs in Charleston, died in September, 1902, Roosevelt immediately thought of Crum as his successor. Booker T. Washington again urged his appointment. "I have known him for fifteen years," Washington assured the President, "and he is as far different in my mind from the old irresponsible and purchasable Negro politician as day is from night." [26] Born in 1859, Crum was the youngest of seven children in a family of German-African descent. His grandfather was a German who had emigrated to South Carolina early in the nineteenth century. The name was originally spelled with a *K* until his grandfather anglicized it. Crum's father Darius, listed as a "planter" in the census of 1850, owned considerable land near Orangeburg which required the labor of forty-three Negro slaves. By the end of the Civil War the family fortunes were depleted and Darius Crum was dead. The older sons, who found work in the North, agreed "to help William get an education." With their assistance he graduated from Avery Normal Institute in Charleston, studied briefly at the University of South Carolina, and obtained a medical degree from Howard University

[25] *Twentieth Annual Report of the United States Civil Service Commission, July 1, 1902, to June 30, 1903* (Washington: Government Printing Office, 1903), 129; Atlanta *Constitution*, November 7, 1902.

[26] Washington to Roosevelt, December 1, 1902, in Roosevelt Papers.

in 1881. Two years later, he married Miss Ellen Craft, who, like himself, had been born free and had enjoyed the benefit of a formal education. Shortly after establishing his medical practice in Charleston, Crum became active in Republican politics. He served as party chairman in Charleston County for more than two decades and was a delegate to every Republican national convention from 1884 to 1904.[27] The most active phase of Crum's involvement in politics began early in the 1890's. In 1892 President Harrison appointed him postmaster of Charleston, but the opposition of white Charlestonians was sufficient to force Harrison to withdraw the appointment.[28] Two years later, the selection of Crum as the Republican candidate for the United States Senate represented a victory for the old-liners in their efforts to thwart an incipient Lily White movement. But his candidacy was little more than a symbolic gesture, because he was pitted against Benjamin R. Tillman, the master of South Carolina's Democratic Party.[29] Tillman's victory meant that henceforth Crum would have a powerful antagonist in the Senate to oppose any future federal appointment that he might seek. The enmity between Roosevelt and Tillman which resulted in an open break early in 1902 may have figured in the President's determination to appoint Crum to a post in South Carolina.[30]

[27] *Who's Who in America, 1912–1913* (Chicago: Marquis and Co., 1912), 492; Chicago *Broad Ax*, December 6, 1902; Washington *Colored American*, February 28, 1903; Census of 1850, Orangeburg County, S. C., December 5, 1850 (Microfilm copy in University of Georgia Library, Athens). Crum's wife was the daughter of Ellen and William Craft, whose escape from slavery was widely publicized both in the United States and England. Ellen Craft Crum was born in England and educated in Boston. See "The Flight of Ellen and William Craft, 1849," in Herbert Aptheker (ed.), *A Documentary History of the Negro People in the United States* (2 vols.; New York: Citadel, 1951), 277–78; "An Escape from Slavery in Georgia," *Chamber's Edinburgh Journal*, March 15, 1851, pp. 174–75.

[28] Atlanta *Constitution*, July 2, 18, 1892; *Congressional Record*, 52nd Cong., 1st Sess., 5664, 6164; *Nation*, LV (July 21, 1892), 38.

[29] Simkins, *Pitchfork Ben Tillman*, 272n.

[30] The rupture between Tillman and Roosevelt occurred in February, 1902. The occasion was Roosevelt's withdrawal of an invitation to Tillman to a dinner at the White House in honor of Prince Henry of Prussia, because of a fistfight on the floor of the Senate between Tillman and McLaurin on the day before the dinner. For the story of this altercation see *ibid.*, 8–11.

Roosevelt apparently informed Capers that he favored Crum and left to him the task of securing from the state Republican committee the customary endorsement. Although Negroes dominated the committee, its approval of Crum was by no means a foregone conclusion. In addition to Crum, there were two other aspirants for the collectorship—William H. Johnson, another Negro physician; and Robert R. Tolbert, a veteran white Republican long associated with Deas. Crum had never been close to Deas, whose approach to race relations, compared to his own, was radical. He agreed with Deas regarding the evil of "lynch law, Jim Crow cars, disfranchisement," and other products of "lily-whitism" but disagreed with his tactics. Like others who subscribed to Booker T. Washington's philosophy, Crum believed that the elimination of such discriminatory practices could be more readily accomplished through indirect means. Fully aware of the growing repression of Negro rights, he was careful to avoid any statement which he believed would accelerate the tendency.[31] "Social equality," Crum insisted, "is something that the white man need not fear. All we ask is the God-given right to earn an honest living, and the privilege of enjoying the fruits thereof, unmolested by the lyncher with his shotgun and rope." [32] But it was more than philosophy or rhetoric that separated Crum and Deas.

Anxious for some office himself, Deas apparently was deeply resentful of the fact that his long service to the party had been ignored by both Hanna and Roosevelt, and even more disheartening was the failure of prominent Negroes such as Booker T. Washington to press his claim for office. Whatever places he had achieved in the party or in government service had largely been the result of efforts by Webster and the Tolbert family. Furthermore, Deas never forgave Crum for endorsing the appointment of Capers, even though Crum insisted that he had done so only after assurances from the new Republican "boss" that he would "play fair" with Negroes.[33] Because many Negro Republicans were suspicious of anything that

[31] Crum to McKinlay, October 12, 1902, in Woodson Papers; Charleston *News and Courier*, September 13, 15, 17, 1902.
[32] Quoted in Boston *Guardian*, April 18, 1903.
[33] Crum to McKinlay, September 25, 1902, in Woodson Papers.

smacked of what they called "Caperism," they supported Tolbert for the port collectorship. At least he had proved his friendship for them. For Deas the choice of a port collector involved his own political future. He believed that only with Tolbert's friendship could he retain even nominal control of the party machinery. In explaining his position later, Deas wrote, "I did everything I could to keep my endorsement from Tolbert; did all I could to persuade him out of becoming a candidate but having promised it while I was nearly dead with a fever a day or so after Wallace's death, and when I was in deep distress and trouble as whether I'd have a quorum of members [of the state executive committee] present, by reasons of Capers' and Jenkins' opposition, I had to give it as he was an influential member from the Piedmont, had to give it against my better will and better judgment." [34]

The subcommittee selected by the State Republican Executive Committee to choose a candidate for the collectorship favored Tolbert. Only two members, Capers and Robert Smalls, voted for Crum. Despite Tolbert's showing, it should have been obvious that Roosevelt would find him unacceptable because of his previous involvement in several unsavory episodes in Republican politics.[35] When it appeared that Crum might lose in the race for the post, various forces outside the state, including the considerable influence of James S. Clarkson and of Booker T. Washington's so-called Tuskegee machine, were brought to bear on the situation. One of Washington's allies, Whitefield McKinlay, a native of South Carolina, hastened to the defense of his old friend Crum. For many years McKinlay had acted as a kind of unofficial emissary in the capital city for Negro Republicans from South Carolina. Upon hearing of their support for Tolbert, he severely arraigned them for their behavior as "only in keeping with what is going on in Hayti, proving

[34] E. H. Deas to McKinlay, March 27, 1903, in Woodson Papers.

[35] Robert Smalls to McKinlay, October 22, 1902, Bennett to McKinlay, October 23, 1902, Crum to McKinlay, October 12, 26, 1902, in Woodson Papers. Tolbert himself had been a principal figure in the Phoenix riot of 1898 and his father had been removed as collector of the Port of Charleston for malfeasance in office. See *Appleton's Annual Cyclopaedia and Register of Important Events of the Year, 1898* (New York: Appleton, 1899), 699–700.

conclusively" that Negroes were "incapable of appreciating high ideals." McKinlay clearly intimated that his future activity in Washington in their behalf was contingent upon their support of Crum.[36] Such pressure was sufficient to halt temporarily the factional fighting over the port collectorship and to give Crum's candidacy the appearance of having party as well as racial endorsement. Even Deas assured McKinlay that he would work for Crum at the same time that he continued his fight against "the scoundrel Capers." [37]

Early in November, 1902, Roosevelt publicly announced his intention to place Crum in charge of the Charleston customs house. Much to his surprise, the announcement was greeted by a loud protest in Charleston and throughout the South. When the President reminded white Charlestonians of their glowing accounts of Crum during his visit to the exposition earlier in the year, they in turn reminded him of his promise "to appoint no colored man" to a post of prominence. For several weeks a steady exchange of charges and countercharges regarding the conversation between the President and the white South Carolinians aboard the *Algonquin* dominated the discussion of the appointment. For his part, Roosevelt maintained that his appointment of Crum was in no way inconsistent with any statement made by him during his visit to Charleston. In fact, he recalled that the white Charlestonians had specified only postmasterships as federal jobs in which Negroes were objectionable because of their regular and direct contact with whites.[38]

Whether the collectorship constituted a major or minor office, Roosevelt could argue with considerable justification that it was

[36] Crum to McKinlay, October 31, 1902, McKinlay to Members of the Executive Committee of South Carolina, October 23, 1902, James S. Clarkson to McKinlay, December 13, 1902, T. Thomas Fortune to McKinlay, November 24, 1902, in Woodson Papers.

[37] Deas to McKinlay, March 27, 1903, in Woodson Papers. See also Deas to McKinlay, January 21, March 18, 1903, in Woodson Papers.

[38] Charleston *News and Courier*, November 9, 1902; Thomas R. Waring to R. G. Rhett, November 5, 1902, Rhett to George B. Cortelyou, November 7, 1902, J. Adgar Smyth to Cortelyou, November 10, 1902, J. C. Hemphill to Roosevelt, November 11, 1902, in Roosevelt Papers; Atlanta *Constitution*, November 9, 16, 29, December 6, 13, 1902; Roosevelt to Rhett, November 10, 1902, in Morison (ed.), *Roosevelt Letters*, III, 375–76.

relatively unimportant. Certainly in comparison to the prestige and power enjoyed by the district attorney, internal revenue collector, marshal, and postmasters of the major cities it was insignificant. Whatever the soundness of such an argument, white Charlestonians scarcely considered it a valid reason for appointing a Negro to head the customs house. Nor did they accept Roosevelt's claim that "in making appointments I disregard any question as to how the delegation from that state will be affected as regards myself." [39] In response to communications from Mayor Smyth, Hemphill, Rhett, and other prominent Charlestonians who protested Crum's appointment because of his color, Roosevelt released to the press a letter that he had written to Smyth on November 26, 1902, in which he defended the appointment. Of his many "original appointments" in South Carolina, he pointed out, the Charleston collectorship was the only one which had gone to a Negro. He maintained that "it has been my consistent policy in every state where their numbers warranted it to recognize colored men of good repute and standing in making appointments to office." Unwilling to make an exception in the case of South Carolina, the President assured his Charleston critics that under no circumstances would he subscribe to the "position that the door of hope—the door of opportunity—is to be shut upon all men no matter how worthy, purely on the grounds of color." [40] Obviously what had originated as a politically feasible appointment had been transformed into a matter of support for the rights of Negroes. And Roosevelt lost little time in defending his "good politics" on the grounds of lofty principles.

The President's refusal to acquiesce in the wishes of the spokesmen for white Charlestonians was the signal for highly emotional attacks on his so-called Negro policy. The Crum appointment quickly

[39] This statement was made in a letter to James S. Clarkson, who was experienced in corralling southern delegates. Although Clarkson figured in the appointment of Crum, it is impossible to determine precisely what influence he had. See Roosevelt to Clarkson, September 29, 1902, in Morison (ed.), *Roosevelt Letters*, III, 332–33; Crum to McKinlay, October 12, 1902, in Woodson Papers; E. M. Brayton to Clarkson, December 27, 1902, in James S. Clarkson Papers, Manuscript Division, Library of Congress.

[40] Roosevelt to Smyth, November 26, 1902, in Morison (ed.), *Roosevelt Letters*, III, 383–85.

became the subject of discourses on "race war, Negro domination, Anglo-Saxon superiority, and like rhetorical fustian." [41] The Charleston *News and Courier,* under the editorship of James C. Hemphill, launched an assault upon Roosevelt and Crum which did not cease until both retired from office early in 1909. Convinced that the President did not understand the South, the *News and Courier* insisted that his "reckless and irresponsible course" in the Crum affair would have "the effect of inflaming the mob spirit" in the region.[42] The southern press, making the cause of Charleston its own, denounced Roosevelt for insulting the white South in order "to pander to the negro vote in the Northern states." In fact, a favorite theme was that the President was playing "cheap politics" in an effort to win Negro convention delegates in the South and Negro voters in the North.[43] The New Orleans *States* assured him that southerners would never allow a return to "the dark days of Reconstruction." "His negro appointees will be killed," the *States* boasted, "just as the negro appointees of other Republican presidents have been put out of the way." [44] Such threats merely strengthened Roosevelt's determination to stand by Crum.

But opposition to Roosevelt's appointment of Crum was not limited to southern editors. A sizable segment of the eastern press was only a little less vocal in its hostility to a presidential act which "would serve no good public purpose" and would result in harm to the very people that it was designed to help. The New York *Times* considered Crum's appointment an unnecessary challenge to the "southern solution" to the Negro question, and the New York *Herald* removed the presidential flag from its masthead to show its displeasure.[45] Periodicals of such widely disparate character as *Harper's Weekly* and William Jennings Bryan's *Commoner* were se-

41 Kelly Miller, *Roosevelt and the Negro* (Washington: n.p., 1907), 8.

42 Charleston *News and Courier,* November 28, December 5, 1902, January 6, 1903.

43 See *Literary Digest,* XXIV (1902), 737–38.

44 Quoted *ibid.,* XXVI (1903), 71–72.

45 New York *Times,* November 29, 1902; Charleston *News and Courier,* January 9, 12, 1903.

verely critical of the President's disregard of southern racial mores. Pursuing an argument popular among editors in the South, Bryan suggested that Roosevelt demonstrate his sincerity regarding the "door of hope" by appointing a Negro to an important post in the North. Others maintained that a Negro as postmaster at Oyster Bay would suffice.[46] Roosevelt's appointment of William H. Lewis, a Negro, as district attorney in Massachusetts in 1903, largely removed the utility of such arguments.

Despite the anti-Roosevelt sentiment expressed in the agitation over Crum, the appointment elicited warm approval from quarters which the President considered significant. The New York *Evening Post*, especially its Washington correspondent Francis E. Leupp, enthusiastically supported the appointment and urged Roosevelt to stand up to southern racism.[47] "If the South had a good business head," the Boston *Transcript* declared, "it would see by acquiescing in the appointment to office of colored men of exceptional talent and character that it would strengthen its hold on the colored race. But the South never had a business head and apparently never will acquire it." [48] The *Outlook*, expressing the views of many Republican papers, described Roosevelt's selection of Crum as wholly consistent with the "fundamental principles" of the Republican Party and the American republic.[49]

Grateful as the President may have been for such endorsements, he was undoubtedly even more pleased by the effect of his action among northern Negroes hitherto dissatisfied with his performance. The Washington *Colored American* spoke for much of the Negro community when it exclaimed, "Hip, Hip, Hurrah for President Roosevelt." [50] Even such militant Negro newspapers as Monroe Trotter's Boston *Guardian* and Harry Smith's Cleveland *Gazette*

[46] *Harper's Weekly*, XLVIII (1903), 97, 140; *Commoner*, January 30, 1903, p. 3.

[47] Crum to McKinlay, January 10, 1903, in Woodson Papers; *Literary Digest*, XXVI (1903), 175.

[48] Quoted in *Literary Digest*, XXVI (1903), 175.

[49] *Outlook*, XXXVII (1903), 138–39.

[50] Washington *Colored American*, February 21, 1903.

abandoned their critical attitude toward the President because of his stand in the Crum case.[51] For the moment Negroes looked upon Roosevelt as a worthy "successor to Lincoln" and made the appointment of Crum a test of the Republican Party's loyalty "to the principles of the Great Emancipator." [52]

Shortly after Roosevelt announced his intention to place Crum at the head of the Charleston customs house, opponents began to mobilize their forces with the aim of persuading the President to change his mind. Although they continued to insist that Crum's appointment would disturb the prevailing peace between whites and Negroes, their new emphasis was on issues other than race. Prominent businessmen predicted that placing a Negro in a position of such commercial importance would seriously affect the prosperity of Charleston and go far toward ruining the port facility which they had labored so long to build up.[53]

When such arguments failed to impress Roosevelt, white Charlestonians again shifted their strategy and sought to discover something in Crum's political past which would reflect upon his character. Seizing upon the controversy that had prompted President Harrison to withdraw his appointment as postmaster, Crum's enemies collected evidence purportedly proving that he was a "perennial pie hunter" of the "common variety" who could easily be bought with the promise of political appointment. Essentially the allegations maintained that Crum went to the convention of 1892 pledged to Harrison but once there he announced in favor of James G. Blaine, and only when the Harrison forces promised him the Charleston post office did he return to his original commitment. Crum, therefore, was accused of blatant "political treachery." Crum himself flatly denied the validity of such charges, which he claimed had been based on information acquired from a disreputable Negro politician and "well-known liar" by the name of Brooks Sligh. That his opponents had resorted to "the Sligh game" merely convinced him of their desperation. But Roosevelt was obviously disturbed by this

[51] Boston *Guardian*, January 10, 1903; Cleveland *Gazette*, December 6, 1902, January 3, 31, 1903.
[52] Washington *Colored American*, February 14, 28, March 14, 21, 1903.
[53] Charleston *News and Courier*, January 16, 24, 25, 1903.

development and reportedly declared that he could not be expected to stand by Crum if such charges of political perfidy were true.[54] The Washington correspondent of the *News and Courier* advised Hemphill to avoid "indiscreet arraignments" of Roosevelt "while he is wavering" lest such editorializing force a decision "in Crum's favor." "Teddy is sometimes contrary," he counseled.[55]

Throughout December, 1902, President Roosevelt attempted to determine whether the allegations regarding Crum's fitness for office were valid. He conferred at length with various Republicans present at the convention of 1892 and requested Booker T. Washington to probe every aspect of the case. Judge William H. Brawley, who investigated the matter in South Carolina at the President's request, concluded that Crum was guilty. He assured Roosevelt that Crum had "always been one of the men who had to be placated by promises." The principal source of Brawley's information was Abiel Lathrop, an old-line Republican whom Capers had replaced as district attorney.[56] But other investigations of Crum's role at the convention of 1892 tended to contradict Brawley's findings. Senator Louis E. McComas of Maryland, a Harrison leader in 1892, absolved Crum of any wrongdoing, and Booker T. Washington reported that his inquiries had in no way altered his high opinion of the doctor. Washington described the charges against Crum as "mere rumors" likely to circulate about any Negro Republican in the South who sought to gain public office. James S. Clarkson, who was intimately acquainted with the convention of 1892 and the Crum affair, assured the President that it was "a matter of the past and cannot be a quantity in the present." [57] Convinced of Crum's fitness for office and outraged by the southern reaction, Roosevelt sent his nomina-

[54] *Ibid.*, November 24, 26, 29, 1902; Smyth to E. O. Wollcott, January 9, 1903, in James C. Hemphill Papers, Duke University Library, Durham, N.C.; Crum to McKinlay, January 15, 1903, in Woodson Papers.

[55] R. M. Larner to Hemphill, November 29, 1902, in Hemphill Papers.

[56] W. H. Brawley to Roosevelt, December 9, 12, 1902, Brawley to Cortelyou, December 16, 1902, in Roosevelt Papers; Roosevelt to Brawley, December 3, 1902, in Morison (ed.), *Roosevelt Letters*, III, 387–89.

[57] Washington to Cortelyou, December 16, 1902, February 3, 1903, Washington to Roosevelt, February 5, 1903, in Roosevelt Papers; Clarkson to McKinlay, December 13, 1902, in Woodson Papers.

tion to the Senate on December 31, 1902. "President Roosevelt has done his worst," the *News and Courier* announced.[58]

Neither Crum nor his supporters had any illusions about the difficulties of securing Senate confirmation of his appointment. They not only had to win the support of the Senate Commerce Committee and thwart the strategy of their Charleston opponents, but they also had to make certain that Roosevelt remained firm in his commitment to their cause. The responsibility for pressing Crum's claims devolved upon a group of nationally prominent Negroes including Washington, Pinchback, Fortune, and Kelly Miller, a native of South Carolina and a mathematician at Howard University. Whitefield McKinlay served as a kind of liaison agent for the pro-Crum forces and actually bore the burden of the struggle.[59] In a letter to McKinlay, Crum summarized the position which many Negroes had assumed toward his appointment:

> This question as far as I am concerned is beyond the matter of the collectorship; it is up to the people of this country to say, and at once, whether we are citizens or not. Especially is this a personal matter with every Republican senator in the U. S. Senate. President Roosevelt, be it said to his honor, has been equal to the occasion, and now it remains to be seen whether the Republican Senate will support a Republican President, or allow sectional feeling against a component part of the American body politic to dominate the policy of the Republican administration.[60]

While the Negro press pursued a similar theme and Negro organizations passed resolutions calling upon the Republican Senate to approve the President's appointee, McKinlay was attempting to insure continued support from the White House. In several conferences with the President, he emphasized the "transcendent importance" of the Crum appointment "to the entire race." Shrewdly, McKinlay appealed to the President on both historical and political grounds. "If Southern opponents of the Negro succeed in defeating

[58] Charleston *News and Courier*, January 6, 1903.

[59] Crum to McKinlay, December 24, 1902, January 10, 15, 1903, Smalls to McKinlay, January 26, 1903, in Woodson Papers; Washington *Colored American*, February 23, 28, 1903. See also "Whitefield McKinlay," *Journal of Negro History*, XXVII (1942), 129–30.

[60] Crum to McKinlay, January 10, 1903, in Woodson Papers.

this appointment," he told Roosevelt, "it will establish a precedent which will make it impossible for you or any other president to appoint, for years to come, a colored man to any office in the southern states and greatly endanger the tenure of office of every colored man now in government service in that section." [61]

Although Roosevelt's attitude toward Negroes had much in common with the prevailing racial views of white Americans in general early in the twentieth century, it was reasonable to assume that a man as conscious of history, as outspoken on moral issues, and as politically astute as the President would be impressed by the pleas of Crum's spokesman. Increasingly, Roosevelt came to identify his position in the affair with that of Lincoln. He claimed that the political treatment accorded the Negro by Hanna during McKinley's administration had been devoid of any consideration of "the fundamental ethical elements in the situation." As for himself, he intended "to stand straight for the policies of Abraham Lincoln, not those of Stevens and Garrison." [62] Obviously he convinced himself that the appointment of Crum involved a matter of simple justice to a thoroughly honorable citizen who happened to be black. It scarcely involved what he interpreted as the excesses of abolitionists or Radical Reconstructionists. McKinlay and his cohorts carefully worded their arguments so that their appeal was to the principles of Lincoln rather than those of William Lloyd Garrison and Thaddeus Stevens, whom Roosevelt considered representative of the lunatic fringe.

No less painstaking in their preparations for the battle in the Senate were the white Charlestonians who had high hopes of defeating Crum's appointment. Several business organizations in Charleston called upon commercial bodies in other eastern cities to aid them in opposing an appointment which they claimed would bring economic disaster to the port. In response to such appeals, the

[61] McKinlay to Roosevelt, February 14, 1903, in Woodson Papers. See also Washington to Roosevelt, March 1, 1903, in Roosevelt Papers.

[62] Roosevelt to Lyman Abbott, November 5, 1903, in Morison (ed.), *Roosevelt Letters*, III, 647–48. See also Roosevelt to Silas McBee, January 15, 1903, in Silas McBee Papers, University of North Carolina Library, Chapel Hill, N.C.

boards of trade in several cities expressed sympathy and the New York Cotton Exchange not only lodged a protest against Crum but also promised other "valuable aid." [63] Of more significance, however, were the overtures which the Charleston "aristocrats" made to Senator Tillman. A common hostility to the appointment of a Negro as customs collector ended the long-standing enmity between Tillman and the Charlestonians. At their urging the senator agreed to act as the spokesman of the anti-Crum forces in the Senate. The case allowed Tillman ample opportunity to pursue two of his favorite themes, Roosevelt and the Negro. In recognition of his services the Charleston "aristocrats" feted him at an elaborate banquet early in the spring of 1903. The rapprochement between these historic enemies prompted one up-country editor to observe that if the "low country aristocrats" could so easily reverse themselves on "the likes of Tillman," they might eventually learn to "relish a few Crums." Despite a few such murmurs of dissent, most editorial opponents of Crum's appointment looked upon Tillman as an invaluable ally.[64]

On January 22, 1903, the Senate Committee on Commerce opened its hearing on the appointment. Representing what they described as "the majority of the people of South Carolina," three Charlestonians, Mayor Smyth, Hemphill, and A. C. Tobias, joined Tillman in speaking against Crum. They attacked his character by referring to the "treachery of 1892" and insisted that his presence in the customs house would "ignite the fires of race antagonism." Smyth argued that Crum's color was the sole reason for his appointment, and Hemphill reiterated his charge that his color alone was sufficient to "bar him from public office." "We still have guns and ropes in the South," Tillman reminded the committee, "and if the policy of appointing the Negro to office is insisted upon, we know how to use them." Although Crum's color was obviously the real basis of their objections, the South Carolinians claimed that his

[63] Charleston *News and Courier*, January 22, 1903.

[64] *Ibid.*, January 13, April 4, 1903; Tillman to Hemphill, January 28, February 6, 1903, in Hemphill Papers; W. Ernest Douglas, "Retreat from Conservatism: The Old Lady of Broad Street Embraces Jim Crow," *Proceedings of the South Carolina Historical Association, 1958* (Columbia: South Carolina Historical Association, 1959), 10.

lack of business experience disqualified him as a candidate for the collectorship. Smyth assured the senators that Crum was *persona non grata* with the white businessmen, who were the only people in Charleston in direct contact with the customs house. Following the same line of argument, Tillman produced documents which purported to show that Negroes in Charleston owned little property and constituted an inconsequential segment of the business community. At the conclusion of their appearance before the Commerce Committee Tillman and his colleagues were convinced that the senators had been receptive to their protests.[65]

Following Crum's opponents, Whitefield McKinlay and P. B. S. Pinchback, geared with memorials and resolutions from numerous Negro organizations, spoke in defense of the appointment. They specifically denied the allegations regarding Crum's activity at the convention of 1892 and offered as evidence of his high standing in Charleston the fact that he had been selected by white businessmen to head the Negro department of the exposition. Crum's friends in Charleston had supplied McKinlay with statistics on Negro property-owners which disputed Tillman's figures by demonstrating that "the colored citizens of Charleston own in the aggregate over $1,000,000.00 worth of real and personal property." [66] While the hearings were in progress, Judson Lyons, a Negro from Georgia who was register of the treasury and a member of the Republican National Committee, lent support to the efforts of McKinlay and Pinchback by challenging the claim that a majority of South Carolinians opposed Crum's appointment. "The population of South Carolina," Lyons asserted, "consists of 540,781 white persons and 781,788 colored persons. When it is charged that the people of the State are opposed to . . . Dr. Crum . . . , I am at a loss to understand what people are meant—for certain it is that all the colored people . . . are in favor of his appointment." [67] Crum himself reminded McKinlay of the inconsistency in Hemphill's charge that a

[65] Charleston *News and Courier*, January 22, 23, 24, 1903.

[66] *Ibid.*, January 23, 1903; Washington *Colored American*, February 7, 14, 1903; Crum to McKinlay, January 26, 1903, Bennett to McKinlay, January 27, 1903, in Woodson Papers.

[67] Quoted in *Forum*, XXIV (1903), 495.

lack of business experience made him unfit for the collectorship, since Hemphill's newspaper has endorsed a Lily White Republican physician, Dr. R. L. Frost, for the position. Crum found it strange that "a white Republican physician is so much more qualified from a business standpoint than his fellow in bronze." [68] Stranger still, he might have added, was the fact that his own business enterprises and properties were far more extensive than those of Frost. Although McKinlay and Pinchback challenged various specific charges made by Crum's opponents, the burden of their testimony before the Commerce Committee was an appeal to the "Republican conscience" to stand by the legacy of Lincoln in its consideration of the black man. [69]

After considerable wrangling, the committee finally delivered an adverse report on Crum's appointment. Two Republicans, Senator George C. Perkins of California and Senator John P. Jones of Nevada, joined with the Democratic members of the committee to bring about this initial defeat. Veteran observers claimed, however, that if the nomination had been allowed to reach the floor of the Senate, it would have been approved. White Charlestonians were jubilant over the committee's report and reasoned that Roosevelt would abandon the struggle as he had done in the case of Koester. [70] But they grossly miscalculated; far more was at stake in the Crum affair. As the Springfield *Republican* observed, "the Crum appointment has assumed the importance of a test case." [71] Indeed Negroes had made it a symbol of their crusade to keep ajar the "door of opportunity" in an era of increasing racial repression. That Roosevelt was their hero became evident in the numerous expressions regarding his "manly stand" in the Crum case. Bishop W. B. Derrick of the African Methodist Episcopal Church urged Negroes to demonstrate their appreciation of the President's racial policies by join-

[68] Crum to McKinlay, January 15, 1903, in Woodson Papers.
[69] Charleston *News and Courier*, January 23, 24, 1903; Washington *Colored American*, February 28, 1903.
[70] Charleston *News and Courier*, February 2, 4, 6, 13, 1903; Larner to Hemphill, February 12, 1903, in Hemphill Papers; Francis E. Leupp to Roosevelt, February 5, 1903, in Roosevelt Papers.
[71] Quoted in Chareston *News and Courier*, February 18, 1903.

ing in the formation of a pro-Roosevelt political group to be known as the "Roosevelt Invincibles." [72] Nor was the symbolic nature of the appointment lost upon Crum. "In this present situation," he declared, "I could almost wish that I had not been born free, so that my stand against bondage could have stronger effect." [73] Disappointed by the action of the Senate committee, Crum nonetheless was convinced that the astute way that McKinlay had "bearded the lion and cubs of South Carolina" during the hearing, especially in arousing the "wrath of the rasping, ranting, roaring Tillman," would serve to keep the matter before the public.[74]

By the time the Commerce Committee issued its adverse report, the Crum affair had reached such dimensions that the President was undoubtedly aware that any retreat on his part would run the risk of alienating those who interpreted the Crum appointment as a test case. Although he had some misgivings about the appointment and was disturbed by the hostility of the white South, he recognized that for him to withdraw support from Crum at this juncture would be viewed as a surrender to the blatant racism of his old antagonist Tillman and as the final abandonment of the Negro by the Republican Party. While Roosevelt was agonizing over the matter in mid-January, 1903, the novelist Owen Wister and his wife were guests at the White House for several days. The Wisters, having lived in Charleston during 1902, had become much enamored of the "fine traditions" of the "ancient city." In discussing Crum's appointment at length with the President, Wister frankly expressed his disapproval of selecting a Negro for a public office in Charleston. When Mrs. Wister, the great-granddaughter of William Ellery Channing, also voiced her objections, Roosevelt exclaimed, "Why, Mrs. Wister! Mrs. Wister!" Replying to their objections, he insisted that not only had he taken the "greatest pains" to find a Negro who was eminently fit for office but also that he had specifically chosen the "office of Collector of the Port, because a person holding that posi-

[72] Seth M. Scheiner, "President Theodore Roosevelt and the Negro, 1901–1908," *Journal of Negro History*, XLVII (1962), 176; Charles W. Anderson to McKinlay, February 3, 1903, in Woodson Papers.

[73] Quoted in Jackson (Miss.) *Clarion-Ledger*, March 3, 1903.

[74] Crum to McKinlay, January 26, 1903, in Woodson Papers.

tion would not be brought into contact with many Charleston people in the discharge of his duties." Furthermore, Roosevelt told the Wisters that "he must recognize and support the party of which he was the head" and that he must fulfill his wider obligation to all people. "Why, don't you see—why, you *must* see—that I can't close the door of hope upon a whole race!" he concluded. Voicing a theme espoused by many whites and a few blacks, Wister replied, "You didn't open it when you appointed Dr. Crum. . . . You shut it a little tighter." When the conversation again turned to the Crum appointment during the last day of the Wisters' visit at the White House, the President admitted, "Well, if I had it to do over again, I—don't—*think*—I'd—do it." But having already committed himself and fully aware of the political and moral justification for his action, Roosevelt was determined to stand by Dr. Crum.[75]

Despite a plea from Senator William P. Frye, chairman of the Commerce Committee, to withdraw the nomination, the President again submitted it as soon as the Senate convened in extraordinary session early in March. It was widely rumored that Roosevelt had promised to give Crum an interim appointment unless the Senate performed its duty by acting on his nomination. Noisy threats by Tillman to lead a filibuster, coupled with the desire of some Republican senators to delay any decision until the elections of 1903 had taken place, prompted the Commerce Committee to shelve the appointment.[76] Some Republican newspapers chastised the Senate for evading its responsibility by "hiding behind an inactive committee." All the while, opponents of the appointment returned to the attack, charging Roosevelt with being interested only in delegates

[75] Owen Wister, *Roosevelt: The Story of a Friendship, 1880–1919* (New York: Macmillan, 1930), 116–18. Roosevelt apparently went so far as to suggest to Booker T. Washington that Crum accept another post. He made the suggestion following a conference with Edgar Gardner Murphy, a southern social reformer, sometime in February, 1903. Murphy, like others, thought that the fight over Crum's appointment to the Charleston collectorship would do more harm than good for the uplift of the Negro. See Hugh C. Bailey, *Edgar Gardner Murphy: Gentle Progressive* (Coral Gables, Fla.: U. of Miami, 1968), 115–17.

[76] Charleston *News and Courier*, February 19, March 2, 6, 1903.

and votes rather than the welfare of Negroes. Delighted by the refusal of the committee to act, they claimed that Roosevelt had "been
forced into a hole" and any interim appointment at this stage would
result in Crum's being considered the "personal representative of
the President" rather than as a bona fide official of the federal government. Even at this juncture, the anti-Crum forces seemed to believe that the President could still be induced to abandon the fight.
Their renewed attack on Crum's fitness for office undoubtedly
served little purpose other than to strengthen Roosevelt's determination to make good his threat of an interim appointment.[77] Their
efforts to depict Crum as an impoverished Negro doctor with "barely enough training to practice among his own people" were contradicted by the reports of correspondents of eastern papers, whose
firsthand investigations of Crum's personal life revealed him to be a
man of means and culture. The correspondent of the New York
World, in a widely reprinted article, described his German ancestry,
lucrative medical practice, and extensive contributions to charity.
"He dresses as well as any man in Charleston," he reported, "and
lives in better style than most of them." Describing Crum's appearance as resembling nothing so much as that of a "German burgher,"
the reporter was surprised to discover that he was interested in the
theater, read French literature, and spoke "a smattering of German."[78] That a man who in no way fitted the stereotyped view of
the Negro Republican "pie hunter" should stir such violent animosities was a commentary on the ironies and incongruities spawned
by racial prejudice.

When the Senate recessed without taking any action on the Crum
case, Roosevelt immediately carried through his threat to make a
recess appointment. On March 30, 1903, Crum assumed his duties
as collector of the Port of Charleston.[79] That Roosevelt had dared
to place him in the customs house without Senate approval brought
praise from Negroes and whites who considered it in line with "the

[77] *Ibid.,* February 15, 18, March 20, 21, 1903; Washington *Colored American,* March 14, 21, 1903.
[78] New York *World* quoted in Charleston *News and Courier,* March 5, 1903.
[79] Crum to L. M. Shaw, March 30, 1903, in Papers of the Charleston Customs
House, National Archives, Region 4, East Point, Ga.

policy of Lincoln" and brought denunciation from those opposed to Negro officeholders. The city of Charleston threatened to take the matter to court. Some white citizens in the city wanted to call a mass meeting to protest the President's action; others hinted that they would seek an injunction against Crum. Despite all the noise, nothing happened. While only 1 white employee, Stephen Barnwell, resigned from his position in the customs house rather than serve under a Negro superior, more than 150 white persons applied to Crum for the various jobs at his disposal. Andrew S. Withers, an elderly white man who had long served as deputy collector, was retained by the Negro collector.[80] In fact, the two men made an effective team. "The swarthy collector," Kelly Miller wrote, "now sits calmly at his window overlooking Fort Sumter, straining his eyes for sight of an occasional ship. . . . The citizens are again tracing their favorite phantoms. The good old city has sunken into its traditional ways, reveling in the glory of by-gone days, dreaming of things of yore in the shadow of Calhoun's monument." [81] The Charleston "aristocrats" may well have returned to their traditional ways, if indeed they had ever departed from them, but they rarely missed an opportunity to remind Roosevelt that he and his "personal representative" were *personae non gratae* in their "ancient city." Quick to publicize anything likely to reflect discredit upon Crum, the *News and Courier* gave extensive coverage to disputes involving his selection of Negroes for subordinate positions in the customs house and to the legal difficulties of the Progressive Benefit Association, a small Negro insurance company of which he was president.[82]

During the special session of the Senate which convened shortly after the elections of 1903, Roosevelt again sent in Crum's nomination. Crum's supporters hoped that the changes in the composition of the Commerce Committee as a result of the election would lead to favorable action. But when the special session ended without considering the case, Roosevelt displayed his determination to force action by granting Crum still another recess appointment; the President sent his name to the Senate again early in December, 1903, at

80 Charleston *News and Courier*, March 19, 30, April 1, 1903.
81 Miller, *Roosevelt and the Negro*, 8.
82 Charleston *News and Courier*, June 2, December 5, 8, 1903.

the opening of the regular session of Congress. The appointment of Crum "precisely at . . . noon" on the first Monday in December, 1903, during what Roosevelt interpreted as the "constructive recess" existing at the moment between the end of the special session of the Senate and the beginning of the regular session of Congress provided Tillman with an opportunity to challenge the President on constitutional grounds. The theory of the "constructive recess," in Tillman's view, seriously compromised the constitutional right of the Senate to confirm presidential appointments. He first asked Secretary of the Treasury Leslie M. Shaw to report on the legality of Crum's appointment. Convinced that Shaw's response was evasive, Tillman introduced a resolution directing the Judiciary Committee to define a Senate recess and to advise the senators regarding the constitutionality of "constructive recess appointments." Although Tillman broadened his criticisms of such appointments to include advancements in military rank made by Roosevelt, the Crum appointment remained the critical issue with him. He tried unsuccessfully to forestall any more hearings on Crum's appointment until the Judiciary Committee had reported on his resolution.[83]

In the second round of hearings McKinlay, again representing Crum, presented a series of closely reasoned arguments before the Commerce Committee. Assisting him was C. S. Smith, the cashier of the Charleston customs house, who assured the senators that public sentiment against Crum was "rapidly passing away" and that "only a few Democratic politicians" continued to keep up the fight against him. All the while, the influential Afro-American Council, through its legal and legislative bureau, lent support to Crum's cause by extracting promises from senators to vote for his confirmation. The effectiveness of Crum's opponents during the hearings suffered from a disagreement over strategy between Tillman and the spokesmen from Charleston. On February 18, 1904, the Commerce Committee gave Crum's appointment a favorable report by a strictly partisan vote of eight to five. At this juncture Tillman be-

[83] Cleveland *Gazette*, November 21, 1903; Charleston *News and Courier*, November 11, 12, December 6, 10, 12, 1903, January 23, 26, February 19, 1904; Simkins, *Pitchfork Ben Tillman*, 416–18; *Congressional Record*, 58th Cong., 2nd Sess., 65, 1104–1109, 1356–66, 1549–50, 1603–1609.

came ill and went home to South Carolina. Senatorial courtesy precluded any action on the Crum case in his absence. Crum assured McKinlay that Tillman's extended absence was merely a maneuver to delay his confirmation. Finally, after six weeks, Tillman returned briefly to Washington in mid-April, 1904, but when Crum's appointment was called up for consideration, he claimed that his health made it impossible for him to participate in the debate.[84] Senatorial deference to his request for a delay prompted Roosevelt to write a strong letter to Senator Nelson W. Aldrich urging him to push action on the Crum case immediately. "I feel that Crum is not only entitled to confirmation," the President wrote, "but that politically it would be a bad thing for the Senate to refuse to vote one way or the other upon his nomination. Already we are being taunted with insincerity and timidity in the matter. If Senator Tillman is not well enough to talk, then let him depute someone else the task of objection. His friends are openly boasting that he is merely doing this as a bit of filibustering." [85]

Even a threat by the President to call a special session of the Senate was of no avail in getting action. Tillman returned home, presumably because of illness, and did not again appear in the Senate during the session. When Congress again adjourned without acting on the matter, Roosevelt conferred another interim appointment upon Crum on April 28, 1904.[86] Although the matter would not come before the Senate again until late in that year, the editorial opposition kept it alive by elaborating upon Tillman's constitutional objections to "constructive recess appointments" and by warning against any executive encroachment upon the prerogatives of the Senate. Their efforts to defeat the confirmation of a Negro appointee by resorting to discourses on constitutional principles no more obscured the real basis of their opposition than Roosevelt's

[84] Charleston *News and Courier*, February 19, April 13, 14, 28, 29, 1904; Crum to McKinlay, January 25, April 7, 1904, McKinlay to J. B. Foraker, April 14, 1904, F. L. McGhee to McKinlay, January 12, 1904, in Woodson Papers; Rhett to Hemphill, February 5, 1904, in Hemphill Papers.

[85] Roosevelt to Nelson W. Aldrich, April 16, 1904, in Morison (ed.), *Roosevelt Letters*, IV, 774.

[86] Charleston *News and Courier*, April 29, 1904.

homilies about "the ethical elements in the situation" concealed his game of practical politics.

Throughout the fracas over his appointment, Crum not only remained in constant contact with the nationally prominent Negroes who kept his case a live issue but also performed his duties as collector with discretion and efficiency. Except for one occasion his color seems to have presented no difficulties in dealing with the personnel of foreign ships. The exception occurred in the summer of 1903 when a German vessel, the *Gazelle*, put in port at Charleston. Its captain won the hearts of white Charlestonians by refusing to make the usual courtesy call upon the port collector.[87] Crum ignored the incident, but in view of his German ancestry he could scarcely have failed to note the element of irony in such a slight. In his relations with the local white community he displayed comparable forbearance and was careful to avoid any act which could be used by his detractors. In order to pacify those whites who found his color objectionable, he arranged for them to deal with Deputy Collector Withers.[88]

Crum shunned personal publicity and rarely accepted invitations to make public appearances in northern cities without first consulting McKinlay. An unfortunate experience in the summer of 1903 undoubtedly contributed to his reluctance to accept such invitations thereafter. While in Chicago for a series of speaking engagements before various Negro organizations, Crum had an interview with a reporter from the Chicago *Inter-Ocean* which created a storm of controversy among northern Negroes who had hitherto been his warmest supporters. The *Inter-Ocean* quoted him as saying, "Lynchings savor of the barbarism of the dark ages but we must consider the crimes that provoke them. They are so atrocious that no punishment is too severe." [89] Under such headlines as "Crum Condones

[87] New York *Times*, June 17, 1903; Charleston *News and Courier*, June 29, 1903.

[88] Crum's correspondence in the Woodson Collection and in the papers relating to the Charleston Customs House reveals his reliance upon Withers. There appears to have been a division of labor between the two men. But there is no evidence to suggest that Crum surrendered direction of the customs house to Withers.

[89] Quoted in Boston *Guardian*, July 11, 1903.

Lynching," Negro newspapers denounced him for accepting as valid the southern argument that attacks upon white women by Negro rapists caused all lynchings. The Cleveland *Gazette* spoke for much of the Negro press when it questioned Crum's fitness for public office as a result of this flagrant effort on his part to "win favor in the eyes of that South that has so bitterly opposed his confirmation." [90] Repeatedly, Crum denied making any statement which could possibly be interpreted as an endorsement of lynching under any circumstances. He was hopeful that the *Inter-Ocean* report, "like other lies," would "die of its own weight." But his chief concern was not that the incident would damage him personally but that it would be harmful to the cause of which he was the symbol. Immediately, McKinlay, Pinchback, Washington, and their allies exerted their influence to minimize any divisiveness that the ill-fated interview had caused among Negroes. Crum assured McKinlay that newspaper reporters would "have a hot time chasing me for another interview." [91]

Early in his tenure as collector, Crum adopted the position of "saying nothing and attending strictly to his duties" while his enemies in Charleston ranted "to their hearts' content." [92] In his personal correspondence with McKinlay, however, he revealed his sensitivity to the abuse heaped upon him and his tendency to suspect that virtually everyone, save Roosevelt and McKinlay, had "played him false." He was first suspicious of Deas and Smalls, but later came to believe that Capers had done "more dirt than all the rest." On more than one occasion he despaired of "the whole business." For example, when the Republican Senate postponed consideration of his appointment out of deference to "the ranting Tillman," he was so "disheartened" and "sick" that he threatened to resign the collectorship rather than suffer "further humiliation from my [Republican] friends." [93]

Equally disturbing was a ruling by the Treasury Department early in May, 1903, that no salary or fees could be paid to him until

[90] Cleveland *Gazette*, July 4, 1903.
[91] Crum to McKinlay, July 15, 1903, in Woodson Papers.
[92] A. T. Jennings to McKinlay, December 3, 1903, in Woodson Papers.
[93] Crum to McKinlay, October 22, 1902, April 7, 1904, in Woodson Papers.

the Senate had confirmed his appointment. The treasury officials ruled that the law prohibited payment of salaries to persons "appointed to a vacancy if that vacancy existed while the Senate was in session." Like many of his supporters, Crum considered this decision merely another obstacle thrown in his path by those hostile to Negro officeholders. "I have been unable to discover why I should be particularly picked out for this test," Crum wrote McKinlay, "unless there are influences at work either to create more political capital or trying to encompass our defeat in a more astute way." [94] Whatever the reason for withholding Crum's salary, the fact that it was done was useful to Roosevelt in defending his administration against Tillman's charges about the legality of recess appointments. Although all fees and salaries would be paid once Crum was confirmed by the Senate, there was a strong possibility that such approval might never be achieved. Crum's determination to hold on to the collectorship under such circumstances suggested that his interest in the office involved more than a desire to share in the "federal pie."

While the controversy over Crum raged in the Senate and in the press, the squabbles among South Carolina Republicans began to abate. If the achievement of a harmonious pro-Roosevelt delegation to the national convention of 1904 was a motive in the President's selection of Crum, such a goal seemed near realization by the beginning of that year. And the evidence suggests that whatever other considerations came to be involved in the appointment, Roosevelt never lost sight of its original political import. When Crum first took office in March, 1903, the President advised him "to keep in touch with Mr. Capers and those acting with him." Although Crum privately expressed suspicions about Capers, he was apparently willing to make his peace with the white Republican "boss" in order to avoid jeopardizing the cause which his appointment symbolized.[95] For wholly different reasons, Deas too became less vocal in his attacks on Capers and Roosevelt. His last major struggle against "Caperism" before the election of 1904 was a protest filed with the

[94] Crum to McKinlay, May 12, 1903, in Woodson Papers.
[95] Roosevelt to Crum, March 26, 1903, in Morison (ed.), *Roosevelt Letters*, III, 459; Crum to McKinlay, March 4, 1903, in Woodson Papers.

Republican National Committee in November, 1903, challenging Hanna's appointment of Capers to that body. But the committee, including its only Negro member, Judson Lyons of Georgia, upheld the appointment. Clearly the struggle over Crum, who was supported at least publicly by Capers, dissipated the force of Deas's free-wheeling crusade which alternately attacked Capers, Roosevelt, and Hanna. Although it appears that Hanna made a last-minute attempt to patch up his relations with Deas, there is nothing to suggest that such efforts were successful.[96] Deas's threat to lead an anti-Roosevelt movement in South Carolina scarcely meant that he would cast his lot with Hanna, who, after all, had denied him a place on the national committee. In fact, Deas gave every appearance of a man suffering from acute political frustration. By the beginning of 1904, he, like other Negroes originally hostile to Capers, was willing to make his peace with those he called the "powers that be." While Deas well may not have relished the prospect, he could at least claim much credit for preventing a wholesale capitulation to Lily Whiteism and for initiating the chain of events which prompted Roosevelt to consider the appointment of Crum politically feasible.

The meeting of the state Republican committee on January 20, 1904, indicated that "the Duke of Darlington" had for the moment acquiesced in Capers' leadership and that a pro-Roosevelt sentiment prevailed in the state organization. Chaired by Deas, the committee passed resolutions which called for the early confirmation of Crum and which commended Roosevelt for defending the civil rights of Afro-Americans. The New York *Age* described the meeting as "a veritable political love feast," at which Deas and Capers "buried the hatchet and smoked the cheroot of peace." In explaining the new harmony within Republican ranks, Deas commented that politics "is a funny thing" and that politically "most folks do not know where they will go to sleep." [97]

By the time of Hanna's death on February 15, 1904, the Republican Party in South Carolina had been transformed into the Roose-

[96] Charleston *News and Courier*, June 29, December 13, 1903.
[97] *Ibid.*, January 21, 1904; Washington *Colored American*, February 4, 1904.

velt party. At the state Republican convention ten days later, Capers and Deas secured the election of a solidly pro-Roosevelt delegation to the national convention. The delegation consisted of eighteen members: four delegates at large and two from each of the seven congressional districts. The first ballot for delegates-at-large resulted in the election of Capers, Deas, and Loomis Blalock, who had remained a Roosevelt partisan in spite of his failure to get the revenue collectorship two years earlier. Contenders for the fourth position, led by George W. Murray, withdrew in favor of Crum, whose membership in the delegation was considered necessary in order to dramatize the party's endorsement of his struggle to keep open the "door of opportunity." Late in April, 1904, Postmaster General Henry C. Payne visited Charleston and was delighted to learn of the harmony existing within the Republican Party in South Carolina. Shortly afterward, when he and the President made final plans for the national convention, they considered having Crum deliver one of the speeches seconding Roosevelt's nomination. But the honor finally went to Harry S. Cummings, the first Negro to hold elective office in Maryland. At the Republican National Convention in June, 1904, the eighteen members of the South Carolina delegation, a third of whom were Negroes, enthusiastically joined in the unanimous nomination of Roosevelt.[98]

The presidential campaign served to revive interest in the Crum appointment. The Democrats used it as an example of the excesses of Roosevelt's "Negro policy" and as evidence of his penchant for unconstitutional action. The whole question of the legal ramifications of the "recess appointments" received a thorough airing. Following Roosevelt's triumph at the polls in November, 1904, there was some speculation whether he would continue to stand by Crum. But those who expected him to "name a new man" for the port position as soon as Congress reconvened were in for a disappointment.[99] On December 6, 1904, the President again nominated Crum

[98] Charleston *News and Courier*, February 25, April 27, 1904; Murray to McKinlay, March 25, 1905, Crum to McKinlay, June 8, 1904, in Woodson Papers; Roosevelt to H. C. Payne, May 10, 1904, in Morison (ed.), *Roosevelt Letters*, IV, 794; *Official Proceedings of the Thirteenth Republican National Convention, 1904*, pp. 102, 165.

[99] See Charleston *News and Courier*, November 4, 16, 1904.

for the post and informed the Senate through Senator Jacob H. Gallinger that further delay on the appointment would be inexcusable. Even Tillman was ready to give up the fight, because he believed that the new composition of the Senate as a result of the elections left little hope of defeating Crum. "I do not see the use of butting my head against a stone wall," he declared. But as a last gesture of defiance, he served notice that he would oppose any consideration of the Crum case until the Judiciary Committee responded to his inquiry regarding Roosevelt's theory of the "constructive recess appointments." Less willing to accept Crum's confirmation as inevitable, the *News and Courier* continued its opposition and denied that the Negro collector was in any way responsible for the "highly creditable" conduct of the customs house. It argued that Deputy Collector Withers, "a native white South Carolinian," had "done all the business of the office," which would have "been managed equally well if Dr. Crum had been sunk into the depths of the ocean." [100] Despite such allegations, the Senate in its executive session on January 6, 1905, finally confirmed Crum as collector of the Charleston port. Shortly after, the Judiciary Committee compensated in part for whatever pangs of defeat Tillman may have suffered by reporting that Roosevelt had been in error in his application of the "constructive recess" theory in the Crum case.[101] If, as the Cleveland *Gazette* maintained, Crum owed his confirmation to the fact that Negroes had voted overwhelmingly for Roosevelt in the election of 1904, Crum's struggle was at least partially responsible for creating that "overwhelming Roosevelt vote" among Negroes.[102]

Although the Senate had finally approved Crum, Roosevelt was scarcely allowed to forget the struggle which the appointment had occasioned. Thereafter almost any controversy which involved his action toward Negroes was likely to prompt references to the Crum incident. When he dismissed three companies of Negro troops as a

---

[100] Roosevelt to Jacob H. Gallinger, December 31, 1904, in Morison (ed.), *Roosevelt Letters*, IV, 1084; Charleston *News and Courier*, December 7, 9, 10, 17, 1904; Cleveland *Gazette*, December 10, 1904.

[101] Charleston *News and Courier*, January 7, 1905; "Square Deal for Dr. Crum," *Current Literature*, XXXVIII (1905), 201.

[102] Cleveland *Gazette*, January 14, 1905.

result of the so-called Brownsville affray in 1906, many of those who had hailed his treatment of Crum as evidence of his loyalty to Republican principles turned violently against him and accused him of blatant racism.[103] Speaking before the Massachusetts Club in Boston early in January, 1907, former Secretary of the Navy John D. Long discussed the relationship between Roosevelt's actions in the Brownsville affray and his appointment of Crum. He declared that both had resulted from the President's impulsiveness. Then, without any particular regard for consistency, Long concluded that Roosevelt's dismissal of the Negro troops was motivated by his desire to "make up" for the "outrage committed by him in the Crum case." [104] To be sure, Roosevelt's tactics often resembled what later became known as consensus politics. Given the sustained action over the Crum incident, Long's interpretation appears more valid than a later suggestion that Roosevelt's handling of the Brownsville episode was designed to counteract or balance the effect of his dinner with Booker T. Washington.[105]

Roosevelt's most comprehensive statement regarding the Crum incident was contained in a fifteen-page letter which he wrote in the spring of 1906 to his friend Owen Wister. The occasion for this review of the case was his reading of Wister's new novel *Lady Baltimore*, one of the first copies of which had been dispatched to the White House. In discussing the book later, Wister wrote, "So I wrote *Lady Baltimore*, not as a tragedy but as a comedy; calling Charleston Kings Port. . . . Into the action of the comedy, I wove the incident of Dr. Crum's appointment as Collector of the Port." [106] Indeed, much of the novel was devoted to the Negro question as viewed through the eyes of "the survivors of Charleston's great civilization," whose "lavender and pressed-rose memories" had captivated Wister. A principal figure in the novel was John Mayrant, the

---

[103] See Emma Lou Thornbrough, "The Brownsville Episode and the Negro Vote," *Mississippi Valley Historical Review*, XLIV (1957), 469–93; James A. Tinsley, "Roosevelt, Foraker and the Brownsville Affray," *Journal of Negro History*, XLI (1956), 43–65.
[104] Charleston *News and Courier*, January 22, 1907.
[105] See Tinsley, "Roosevelt, Foraker and the Brownsville Affray," 64.
[106] Wister, *Roosevelt*, 247.

impoverished scion of an aristocratic family who held a minor job in the customs house. That Mayrant had to occupy such a lowly position under any circumstances was embarrassing enough, but the appointment of a Negro as head of the customs house was more than his pride would tolerate.[107]

Wister's fictional account of the Crum affair elicited a strong reaction from President Roosevelt, who described *Lady Baltimore* as "a tract of the times" which would "fail to do good." He wrote Wister, "Your particular heroes, the Charleston aristocrats, offer as melancholy an example as I know of a people whose whole life has been warped by their own wilful perversity." The President reviewed the circumstances which he claimed had led to Crum's appointment and emphasized that the Charleston aristocrats with whom he had conferred during a visit to the exposition in 1902 had raised no objection to his appointment of Negroes to any office other than that of postmaster. He recalled how they had "specially mentioned the then colored collector of customs in Savannah as a case in point." The well-publicized fact of Crum's mixed ancestry may well have prompted Roosevelt's remarks to Wister regarding the hypocrisy of his beloved Charlestonians. "They shriek in public about miscegenation," he wrote, "but they leer as they talk to me privately of the colored mistresses and colored children of the white men whom they know." The President denied that the aim of his policy toward Negroes was to bring about "Negro domination" or even to encourage a majority of Negroes to vote. "Absolutely all I have been doing," he declared, "is to ask . . . that these occasionally good, well educated, intelligent and honest colored men . . . be given the pitiful chance to a little reward, . . . a little respect if they can by earnest useful work succeed in it." But Roosevelt admitted that he may have erred in appointing Crum. "I am not satisfied," he wrote, "that I acted wisely in either the Booker Washington dinner or the Crum appointment, though each was absolutely justified from every proper standpoint save that of expediency." [108]

While Roosevelt pondered whether he had acted wisely, Crum

---

[107] See Owen Wister, *Lady Baltimore* (New York: Macmillan, 1906).
[108] Roosevelt to Owen Wister, April 27, 1906, in Wister, *Roosevelt*, 248–56.

was busy improving the port's physical facilities and increasing the efficiency of the customs house. The annual customs receipts more than doubled during his tenure, a fact which belied the dire predictions of his detractors in 1903. Largely as a result of his persistence the customs house obtained a longer pier, a deeper channel to its wharf, and a gasoline launch for boarding vessels. Virtually all inspectors from the customs service were impressed by the immaculate appearance of the customs house during his term of office. One inspector reported that "the word neatness is one of the strongest in the Collector's vocabulary." Crum's interest in the appearance of the building was undoubtedly a major factor in persuading the Treasury Department to approve his proposal for a major renovation project. Even the *News and Courier* and members of the white business community who had railed against his fitness for office were impressed by his efficiency and grudgingly praised some of his accomplishments.[109]

Although Crum continued to participate in the affairs of the Republican Party, he was careful to avoid any activity which would compromise his image as a dedicated federal official. He remained aloof from various maneuvers which resulted in the failure of Capers to secure reappointment in 1906 as district attorney. Those who engineered his defeat were thwarted in their effort to remove him as a factor in South Carolina politics, because Roosevelt kept him as his "patronage referee" and in 1907 appointed him federal commissioner of revenue. Thereafter, Capers directed the Republican affairs of South Carolina from his office in Washington. That he was still the Republican "boss" in the state became evident during the preconvention campaign of 1908. Deas and other Negro Republicans who had never been wholly reconciled to Capers' leadership failed in their efforts to prevent his selection as a national convention delegate. Capers' endorsement of Secretary of War William

[109] Charleston *News and Courier*, December 25, 27, 1907, March 27, April 4, June 30, 1908. Among the numerous bound volumes of Crum's correspondence relating to the customs house see Crum to Shaw, November 21, 1904, Crum to J. B. Reynolds, November 21, 1907, Crum to Cortelyou, January 3, 1908, Crum to James K. Taylor, February 26, 1908, in Papers of the Charleston Customs House.

Howard Taft, Roosevelt's choice as his successor in the White House, may have been partially responsible for the various anti-Taft movements among Negro Republicans in South Carolina. Another factor which undoubtedly figured in this opposition to Taft was his part as secretary of war in the controversy over the Brownsville affair. Throughout these intraparty struggles, Crum remained in the background and shied away from any situation which would force him to choose between the factions of Capers and Deas.[110]

Early in May, 1908, Taft arrived in Charleston en route to the Panama Canal. Crum joined other local dignitaries who greeted him at the railway station. Following a lunch with Mayor R. Goodwyn Rhett and his family, Taft was entertained by Crum at a reception in the customs house, where Negro Republicans and Charleston "aristocrats" mingled freely. During the reception Taft repeatedly expressed his high regard for Crum and his administration of the port. Rather than being repelled by such praise, James C. Hemphill joined Crum in escorting Taft aboard the cruiser that took him to Panama.[111] The free and easy manner with which the Charleston "aristocrats" associated with Crum and his "bronze friends" during Taft's visit suggested that perhaps Charleston had indeed come "to accept a few Crums."

Within a few weeks, however, their behavior became the chief topic of debate in the South Carolina senatorial campaign of 1908. In his bid for the Senate, Mayor Rhett of Charleston encountered strong opposition from several other Democrats, especially John P. Grace and O. B. Martin, who were quick to make political capital out of his willingness to associate with the Negro port collector. Actually, Rhett's opposition to Crum was only a little less virulent than that of his predecessor, Smyth. But unfortunately for him, he was credited with reestablishing "diplomatic relations between Charleston and the White House" in October, 1905, when he visited Roosevelt in an effort to persuade him to include the city on his tour of the South later in the year. Ironically, Martin and Grace

---

[110] Charleston *News and Courier*, January 20, 23, 30, 1906, June 5, November 11, 14, 29, December 7, 23, 1907, January 3, 24, 28, 1908.
[111] *Ibid.*, May 2, 1908.

accused Rhett of being a "Republican in disguise" who had con-nived with Roosevelt to secure the appointment of Crum. Repeat-edly, Rhett was forced to defend his loyalty to the Democratic Party and his record of white supremacy by calling upon various individ-uals to attest to his opposition to Crum. Although neither Grace nor Martin won the Senate seat, their distortions of Rhett's relationship to Roosevelt and the Crum appointment helped to defeat a Charles-ton "aristocrat" who had been one of the original opponents of the Negro collector.[112]

The prominence of Crum's name in the Democratic senatorial campaign only served to rekindle public hostility toward his pres-ence in the customs house. That the attitude of white Charleston-ians had undergone no basic change became evident by late 1908, when Roosevelt announced his decision to appoint him to another term. The *News and Courier* returned to its campaign of vitupera-tion and its editor, Hemphill, reviewed the whole episode in a lengthy piece in *Harper's Weekly*. Tillman again promised to lead the fight in the Senate against his confirmation.[113] Whitefield Mc-Kinlay, who resumed his role as Crum's chief advocate, was de-spondent about the outcome. After consulting Senator Albert J. Beveridge, McKinlay lamented, "I am afraid the jig is up, and it has depressed me very much as it is a fight we cannot afford to lose." [114] Crum himself was worried because the election of Taft as President in 1908 raised serious questions as to whether he would continue to receive strong support from the White House after March, 1909. Taft's overtures to white southerners during and after the campaign, as well as the warm friendship which had developed between him and Hemphill, made Crum anxious. For wholly dif-ferent reasons, southern Democratic politicians were concerned about Taft; they feared his efforts to "break the solid south." Some charged that Tillman and his southern colleagues in the Senate welcomed Crum's reappointment as an opportunity to embarrass

---

112 *Ibid.*, July 15, 16, 20, 23, 24, 29, 30, August 1, 3, 8, 20, 23, 1908.
113 James C. Hemphill, "The President, the South, and the Negro," *Harper's Weekly*, LIII (January 9, 1909), 10, 31; Atlanta *Constitution*, February 4, 1909.
114 McKinlay to Washington, February 7, 1909, in Booker T. Washington Papers, Manuscript Division, Library of Congress.

the new President by forcing him to take a stand on the Negro question.[115]

Whatever the validity of such claims, Roosevelt and Taft concluded that Crum's appointment should not be allowed to become the subject of further controversy. When Tillman threatened a filibuster in opposition to the reappointment, they enlisted the assistance of Booker T. Washington, who prevailed upon Crum to relinquish the collectorship at the expiration of his commission early in 1909. In a confidential letter to McKinlay, Washington described Taft's position as based on the conviction that if Crum "could not be confirmed by the Senate at one time," he "could not be confirmed at another time." But Washington placed part of the responsibility upon Crum himself, who, unlike other Negro officeholders in the South, seemed unable to win support from influential white southerners. When his nomination was duly withdrawn from the Senate, Crum publicly stated that he desired to retire from office with Roosevelt, "his chief and friend." Gracious to his detractors in Charleston, he declared that "all these years I have been treated with kindness and courtesy by those who have had official business with this office and have not had unpleasant contacts with anyone in the city." Shortly afterward, Taft appointed William C. Durant, a white Democrat who had recently shifted his allegiance to the Republican Party, to succeed him as collector of the port.[116]

Crum's retirement prompted a mixed reaction among Negroes. Those who believed that his presence in the customs house had been harmful to the race in general were relieved that the prolonged agitation had finally ended; others denounced Taft's unwillingness to sustain him in office as a surrender to Lily Whiteism, and Crum's reluctance to continue the fight as mere cowardice. Few Negroes found much occasion for rejoicing when in 1910 Taft appointed Crum as minister to Liberia, a post usually reserved for Negro

[115] Crum to McKinlay, January 16, 1909, in Woodson Papers; Atlanta *Constitution*, February 5, 6, 1909.
[116] Washington to McKinlay, February 9, 1909, in Washington Papers; Charleston *News and Courier*, February 3, 5, 6, 10, March 5, 1909; Roosevelt to William H. Taft, February 26, 1909, in Morison (ed.), *Roosevelt Letters*, VI, 1538; "Dr. Crum's Retirement," *Outlook*, XCI (1909), 570.

Americans.[117] Crum's death two years later from an African fever prompted the Cleveland *Gazette* to observe, "Thus is written the closing chapter in the Taft administration's sacrifice of one of the race's leading and best men upon the altar of that baneful Southern prejudice." [118]

Obviously political considerations had weighed heavily in Roosevelt's original decision to appoint a Negro to head the Charleston customs house. From the standpoint of practical politics, the appointment could scarcely have been more successful. It not only helped to unify the Republican Party in South Carolina and to insure a pro-Roosevelt delegation to the national convention of 1904; it also won for the President substantial support among northern Negroes who previously had doubted his good faith. Few controversies of his administration provided him with a better opportunity to combine his talents as "the great politician" and "the preacher militant." In both capacities he performed superbly. Nothing was more characteristic of the Rooseveltian style than his use of a politically inspired appointment to instruct his countrymen in questions of justice, morality, and honest, efficient public service. In time the struggle over Crum's appointment became a contest between the President and his old enemy Tillman. It is difficult to ascertain whether Roosevelt persisted in his loyalty to Crum after the election of 1904 because of his determination to extend a Square Deal to an honorable black man or because of his desire to triumph over a senator whom he found contemptible.

The prolonged agitation over the Crum affair offered abundant evidence of the rising tide of racism which threatened to obliterate completely the civil rights of Negro Americans. In an effort to thwart this trend, Negroes made Crum's appointment the focus of a crusade to dramatize the sorry political plight of their race and to test the loyalty of the Republican Party to its historic principles. Although Roosevelt appointed Crum and stood by him in the face

---

[117] Cleveland *Gazette*, June 18, 1910; Washington to Taft, May 25, 1910, Washington to Charles W. Anderson, June 14, 1910, in Washington Papers; Atlanta *Independent*, February 13, March 13, 1909; Washington *Bee*, March 6, 1909.
[118] Cleveland *Gazette*, December 14, 1912.

of strong opposition, it would be erroneous to interpret his action as evidence that his administration pursued a well-defined policy aimed at advancing the cause of civil rights for Negroes. No such policy existed. Roosevelt himself subscribed to the idea that Negroes as a race were inferior. But he believed that there were individual Negroes of ability who were entitled to recognition and reward. Though sympathetic with the plight of the Negro masses, he did not seriously concern himself with it. In fact, he appeared to be content to admit that the Negro problem baffled him. In the race issue, as in other matters, there were discrepancies between Roosevelt's rhetoric and his action. Part of the explanation lay in the character and personality of the man. Roosevelt's deep social consciousness and commitment to the Square Deal seemed to be at war with his strong convictions about racial differences. Political expedience often dictated the swing of the pendulum. The result was a series of ambivalent acts which "alternately pleased and angered Negroes." [119]

[119] August Meier, *Negro Thought in America, 1880–1915: Racial Ideologies in the Age of Booker T. Washington* (Ann Arbor: U. of Mich., 1963), 164.

V

The Miller Incident

While there is no objection to the employees of the Printing Office forming a union or belonging to a union, yet ... I will not tolerate discrimination against a man because he does not belong to the union any more than against him because he does belong to it.

THEODORE ROOSEVELT

During the summer of 1903 the relative calm of President Theodore Roosevelt's vacation at Oyster Bay was interrupted by the controversy over the so-called Miller incident. The case involved William A. Miller, an assistant foreman in the Government Printing Office, who presumably had been dismissed because he was a non-union man.[1] Although the President turned the incident to his own political advantage, its significance extended far beyond the realm of good politics. It dramatized the prevailing controversy over the issue of the closed shop, raised questions about the relationship of labor unions to government employees, and brought to a climax the long-standing agitation regarding the administration and economy of the Government Printing Office. The probe of the GPO

[1] The most complete assessment of Roosevelt's policies toward organized labor is Irving Greenberg, "Theodore Roosevelt and Labor, 1900–1918" (Ph.D. dissertation, Harvard University, 1959). For a briefer but perceptive analysis see Stephen Scheinberg, "Theodore Roosevelt and the American Labor Movement, 1901–1909" (M.S. thesis, University of Wisconsin, 1959).

prompted by the Miller affair opened a Pandora's box that resulted in a more comprehensive investigation of other executive depart-ments. Throughout the prolonged controversy over Miller, the President not only functioned as a skillful politician but also as an ardent champion of efficiency. His action in the case gave a new dimension to the meaning of the Square Deal and dramatized his search for an equilibrium between the contending forces of labor and capital.

When Roosevelt became President in 1901, the United States was already in the throes of what has been termed an "organizational revolution." The proliferation of organizations representing widely diverse interests indicated that groups other than big business were discovering the powers of combination. The competition among these interest groups became especially acute in the struggles be-tween labor and management. Clearly, both labor and capital un-derwent significant organizational changes in the early years of the twentieth century. In the period from 1897 to 1904 organized labor not only assumed a new role of militancy but also witnessed a rapid expansion in membership. Under the conservative leadership of Samuel Gompers, the American Federation of Labor waged a vigor-ous campaign to improve the economic lot of the worker by cham-pioning collective bargaining and by opposing the open shop. That the membership of the AFL increased from 548,000 in 1900 to 1,676,000 in 1904 was generally interpreted as evidence of the "mass advance" of the union movement. Although Eugene Debs's Social-ist Party enjoyed remarkable growth in the same period, it never achieved a numerical strength of great consequence, and the pro-gram advocated by Debs was anathema to those unionists who sub-scribed to the approach of Gompers. Neither the AFL nor the Socialists, for all their achievements, were successful in organizing such basic industries as steel, iron, and textiles. Even a compara-tively well-organized trade, printing, enrolled only about one-third of the workers as union members.[2]

[2] Philip Taft, *Organized Labor in American History* (Evanston: Harper, 1964), 159–65; Albert K. Steigerwalt, *The National Association of Manufac-turers, 1895–1914: A Study in Business Leadership* (Ann Arbor: U. of Mich., 1964), 108–22; Selig Perlman and Philip Taft, *History of Labor in the United States, 1896–1932* (New York: Macmillan, 1935), 129.

Despite the obvious limitations of the union movement, its advance was sufficient to provoke a vigorous response from industrial management. Small manufacturers and independent businessmen led the countermobilization by establishing various trade and employers' associations. Ultimately the National Association of Manufacturers assumed leadership of the movement and exerted its considerable influence to thwart the goals of organized labor. The belligerently antilabor position of the NAM was typified by its president, David M. Parry, who carried on a relentless campaign against unions as instruments of socialism, violence, and un-Americanism. The mobilization of labor and the countermobilization of industry profoundly disturbed the industrial peace and left in its wake numerous labor disorders. According to one authority, there were 3,494 strikes in the year 1903 alone. Those representatives of management and labor, including Senator Mark Hanna and Samuel Gompers, who were interested in the maintenance of industrial harmony sought to preclude such disorders by establishing the National Civic Federation in 1901.[3]

Theodore Roosevelt's views regarding the relationship of capital and labor had much in common with the philosophy espoused by the federation. His actions as President were prompted in large part by the same motives which brought the federation into existence and induced its leaders to arrange a settlement in 1901 of a labor dispute involving the steel industry. Roosevelt feared the class violence and social disorder which he associated with the Haymarket riot and the Pullman strike. But he had come to believe that the continuation of a shortsighted policy of repression by organized capital against organized labor would aggravate class tensions and drive the workingman into the arms of radicals such as Debs. In his view the maintenance of orderly industrial progress necessitated a more positive role by the federal government. If his attitude toward labor unions was colored by his fears of socialism, disorder, and class antagonism, it was also influenced by his appreciation of the basic rights belonging to the competing interest groups. As President he assumed that it was his responsibility to protect these rights

[3] Steigerwalt, *The National Association of Manufacturers*, 117–22; Marguerite Green, *The National Civic Federation and the American Labor Movement* (Washington: Catholic U., 1956), 1–89.

by preventing both capitalists and labor leaders from misusing their power. His was the role of an arbiter whose chief concern was "the public interest." But what constituted the public interest was often equated with what constituted his own political interest.[4]

Although Roosevelt proclaimed his sympathy for labor and actually accepted membership in a railroad brotherhood, it would scarcely be accurate to depict him as a champion of the trade union movement. Quick to oppose labor's use of the boycott and union intervention in politics, he agreed with those capitalists who saw the collective force of labor as potentially dangerous. His "fundamental bias," as Professor George Mowry has asserted, lay with the capitalist.[5] But his official acts were those of an enlightened Chief Executive who feared that the excesses of management would force organized labor to the left and thereby disrupt industrial progress. As in other matters, Roosevelt manifested his disdain for extremes in either labor or capital. He was equally critical of David Parry and of Sam Parks, the militant labor leader. That he early became identified as a special friend of labor owed much to the fact that he departed from the overtly antilabor policies of his predecessors by assuming that labor as well as capital had rights which must be protected. By comparison with the policies of his predecessors those of his administration appeared to be more prolabor than they actually were.

As President, Roosevelt first became involved in a major labor-management dispute during the anthracite coal strike of 1902–1903. Despite the "record of confusion" concerning this disturbance, his role in it was generally interpreted as highly favorable to the cause of the miners represented by John Mitchell and the United Mine Workers.[6] Such an interpretation of his efforts was not surprising since at the time "the sharpest memory of Presidential intervention in a labor conflict was that of Grover Cleveland's per-

[4] George E. Mowry, *The Era of Theodore Roosevelt and the Birth of Modern America, 1900–1912* (New York: Harper, 1958), 141–42; Richard Lowitt, "Theodore Roosevelt," in Morton Borden (ed.), *America's Ten Greatest Presidents* (Chicago: Rand McNally, 1961), 198–99.

[5] Mowry, *Era of Roosevelt*, 141.

[6] Robert H. Wiebe, "The Anthracite Coal Strike of 1902: A Record of Confusion," *Mississippi Valley Historical Review*, XLVIII (1961), 229–51.

emptory military and legal aid to management during the Pullman strike of 1894." [7] Although other individuals, including Hanna, shared in the responsibility for settling the strike, Americans were inclined to give Roosevelt the credit. Later in his administration he was to find the principles established by the arbitral commission useful in defining his role as the reconciler of the conflicting interests of labor and capital. Of particular value was the statement that "no person shall be refused employment or in any other way discriminated against on account of membership or non-membership in any labor organization." [8] Such a statement provided a rationale for his Square Deal for labor.

By the spring of 1903, less than two years after Roosevelt assumed office, much of the business community was of the opinion that his administration had adopted an antibusiness, prolabor position. The announcement of the decision of the Anthracite Coal Strike Commission in March, 1903, coupled with the initiation of antitrust suits against several large corporations and the creation of a Bureau of Corporations for the purpose of investigating the conduct of interstate companies, seemed to corroborate charges of his antibusiness bias. Rumors to the effect that Wall Street would defeat his bid for the Republican nomination in 1904 made him uneasy. Although Roosevelt talked menacingly about "the Wall Street crowd" and identified his political rival Hanna with it, he attempted at the same time to mollify the apparent hostility of the business community by avoiding actions after mid-1903 which would be viewed as inimical to its interests.[9] The labor union issue in the Government Printing Office prompted by the Miller incident provided the President additional opportunity to regain some of the confidence of the business community which his role in the anthracite coal strike had cost him.

In 1903 few agencies of the federal government were more vul-

[7] John M. Blum, *The Republican Roosevelt* (Cambridge: Harvard, 1954), 58–59.

[8] Anthracite Coal Strike Commission, *Report to the President* (Bureau of Labor Bulletin No. 46, 1903), 64.

[9] Blum, *The Republican Roosevelt*, 59–60; Robert H. Wiebe, *Businessmen and Reform: A Study of the Progressive Movement* (Cambridge: Harvard, 1962), 172.

nerable to close scrutiny than the Government Printing Office. Its new building occupied in that year and hailed as a model business structure did not obscure the fact that the "greatest print shop in the world" was in serious trouble. Some critics considered the deficiencies of the GPO so serious that they urged the government to get out of the publishing business altogether and return to a system of letting contracts to private printers. It was generally agreed that one source of difficulty was the ambivalent position which the GPO occupied within the federal structure. The director of the printing office, known after 1874 as the public printer, was appointed by the President with the consent of the Senate and presumably was responsible only to the President. But the Joint Committee on Printing, long headed by Senator Thomas C. Platt of New York, had absolute power over all contracts for advertising and for the purchase of paper. The committee showed its greatest activity during the letting of contracts for paper. The choice of contractors occasionally prompted charges that political favoritism rather than economy was the primary factor in such decisions.[10] Another source of criticism concerned the use of positions in the Government Printing Office by congressmen as patronage rewards for their friends. When 2,709 additional employees of the GPO were placed on the classified list of the civil service in 1895 by President Grover Cleveland, one civil service reformer wondered "where Senator [Arthur P.] Gorman would quarter his men in the future." But even after 1895 the printing office remained a rich source of patronage because of the methods by which the civil service regulations were applied. Whenever the GPO needed an additional employee, the Civil Service Commission furnished the public printer with the names of the three highest eligibles on its classified list. If one of these persons was favored by a powerful congressman, he almost invariably received the appointment. Congressional influence also figured significantly in promotions and reinstatements. Although Congress maintained a constant interest in such matters as personnel and paper contracts,

[10] J. D. Whelpley, "The Nation's Print Shop and Its Methods," *Review of Reviews*, XXVIII (1903), 556–60; Lloyd M. Short, *The Development of National Administrative Organization in the United States* (Baltimore: Johns Hopkins, 1923), 199–201.

it manifested little concern for the efficiency and economy of the GPO.[11] In 1901, Francis E. Leupp observed that only the exposure of some abuse prompted Congress to inquire into the actual operation of the bureau. Even then, according to Leupp, Congress merely "goes through the forms of a solemn inquiry, expresses its surprise at the facts discovered, applies perhaps some temporary palliative, and then promptly forgets all about the subject until the next shock comes." [12] But if Congress gave little attention to the performance in the GPO, Presidents scarcely compensated for its neglect. Not until the administration of Theodore Roosevelt was a determined effort made to initiate broad reforms in the printing office.

By the time Roosevelt assumed office the GPO had become a large, unwieldy bureau which for all intents and purposes enjoyed virtually complete administrative independence. In the absence of direction from either Congress or the President, the public printer had assumed "almost unlimited authority" in the management of the printery. The principal officials of the GPO were men of long tenure who had the confidence and support of the dominant political figures in Congress. The public printer, Frank W. Palmer, was a seventy-six-year-old veteran of Republican politics and journalism who had been closely associated with James S. Clarkson and other political warhorses during the administration of President Benjamin Harrison. First appointed by Harrison in 1889, Palmer remained in office until 1894, when Cleveland replaced him with a Democrat. Reappointed by President William McKinley in 1897, he concentrated upon acquiring a new building for the printery and upon securing sinecures within the GPO for loyal Republicans. Although an investigation by the Civil Service Commission in 1897 largely terminated his overt defiance of its regulations, his almost absolute control over promotions and reinstatements allowed him ample opportunity to advance the interests of deserving Republicans. Under his direction the GPO attempted few of the reforms

11 A. Bower Sageser, *The First Two Decades of the Pendleton Act: A Study in Civil Service Reform* (Lincoln: University of Nebraska, 1935), 214; Whelpley, "The Nation's Print Shop and Its Methods," 562.

12 Francis E. Leupp, "The Government Printing Office," *Harper's Weekly*, XLV (1901), 139.

necessary to keep abreast with the increasing demands placed upon it. Critics complained of the extravagance and costliness of government printing, the lack of labor-saving devices, and the public printer's resistance to innovation. Despite obvious pressures for rapid production and the spectacular performances of the GPO on occasion, critics were by no means convinced that even the peculiar conditions under which the government printery operated necessitated a work force of 4,000 employees and an annual appropriation of $5,000,000.[13] An analysis of the Government Printing Office in 1903 by a knowledgeable writer concluded that its shortcomings resulted largely from its exposure to "direct Congressional influence carrying a large quota of patronage," its lack of "close supervision by a high administrative authority," and "the cumulative and progressive abuses of a century." [14] Even President Roosevelt was concerned about the quantity and cost of public printing. "The excessive cost of government printing," he stated in his annual message of 1902, "is a strong argument in support of the position of those who are inclined on abstract grounds to advocate the government's not doing any work which can with propriety be left in private hands." [15]

The agitation of the so-called labor question after 1897 increasingly focused attention on another aspect of conditions in the GPO which some critics interpreted as the primary source of its difficulties. It concerned the role played by labor unions. Actually, the GPO had been a closed shop since its establishment. In 1860 when the government purchased the printing plant of Cornelius Wendall and J. C. McGuire, it inherited a closed shop. That the printery remained a *de facto* closed shop even under government control did not become an issue until almost four decades later. Those in charge of government printing recognized that they must look to the unions for their labor supply because the printing trades were among the best-organized crafts. Public printers therefore attempted to remain

[13] Whelpley, "The Nation's Print Shop and Its Methods," 560; "Francis Wayland Palmer," in John W. Leonard (ed.), *Men of America* (New York: Hamersly, 1908), 175; Sageser, *The First Two Decades of the Pendleton Act*, 214.

[14] Whelpley, "The Nation's Print Shop and Its Methods," 563.

[15] Hermann Hagedorn (ed.), *The Works of Theodore Roosevelt* (24 vols.; New York: Scribner, 1924–26), XVII, 193–94.

on friendly terms with the printing unions and acquiesced in their demands that all employees of the GPO should be union members. Although the GPO employed non-union personnel, few individuals survived the six-month probationary period unless they were "gathered into the union fold" and complied with the rules established by the appropriate union for employees in various divisions of the GPO.[16]

Public attention was first called to the existence of the closed shop in the GPO in 1897, when a group of electrotypers refused to pay their dues to the typographical union. Because such an act was tantamount to withdrawal from the union, it risked a showdown on the question of whether non-union employees could retain their jobs in the GPO. Fearful of forcing the issue, Public Printer Palmer prevailed upon the recalcitrant electrotypers to pay their dues and "avoid trouble."[17] Three years later, Edward Zimmermann, a new employee in the bindery division of the GPO, created a minor stir by refusing to join the International Brotherhood of Bookbinders. In response to his protest against making union membership a prerequisite for permanent employment in the GPO, the public printer stated that "in order . . . to hold a position in the Government Bindery it is necessary to become a member of the International Brotherhood of Bookbinders." Zimmermann acquiesced in this official ruling and spared the public printer an embarrassing situation.[18] But in 1903, when the Miller case raised a similar issue, Palmer tried without success to avert a crisis which he believed would raise serious difficulties with the labor unions. Obviously, he preferred to avoid anything that would point up the apparent contradiction between the existing employment practices in the GPO and the regulations of the Civil Service Commission.

[16] Sterling D. Spero, *Government as Employer* (New York: Remsen Press, 1948), 378–83; *100 GPO Years, 1861–1961: A History of United States Public Printing* (Washington: Government Printing Office, 1961), 35 ff.; R. W. Kerr, *History of the Government Printing Office with a Brief Record of the Public Printing for a Century* (Lancaster, Pa.: Inquirer Printing and Publishing Co., 1881); Lawrence F. Schmeckesier, *The Government Printing Office, Its History, Activities and Organization* (Baltimore: Johns Hopkins, 1925), 1–17.

[17] Spero, *Government as Employer*, 379–80.

[18] *International Bookbinder*, II (September, 1901), 8–9.

William A. Miller of Minneapolis, a veteran of the printing and binding trades, secured employment in July, 1900, as an assistant foreman in the bindery division of the GPO and was placed in charge of the blank-book section. Apparently, Congressman Joel P. Heatwole of Minnesota was influential in arranging his appointment. Although Miller was a man of "rough speech" who antagonized subordinates as well as superiors, the latter never questioned his efficiency as an assistant foreman. Miller himself claimed that his efforts to achieve greater production and to streamline the business procedures in the government bindery constituted the real basis for the opposition to him. Never inclined toward modesty, he boasted of being responsible for changes which effected substantial financial savings for the government. Among these were the introduction of new types of machines, the establishment of a uniform system of recording work, and the development of cheaper bindings and an inexpensive "route book" for the Post Office Department.[19]

In an interview with a reporter of the Minneapolis *Journal* in 1902 Miller denounced labor unions in government service, especially the International Brotherhood of Bookbinders, which he had joined after being employed in the GPO. He accused the bookbinders' union of forcing upon employees in the GPO rules and regulations which prevented the implementation of reforms designed to increase production and reduce costs. The publication of his interview brought to a climax the growing antagonism between Miller and the International Brotherhood of Bookbinders. Stung by his criticism of the union and resentful of his high-handed, dictatorial behavior as an assistant foreman, the bookbinders' union brought him to trial in September, 1902, for violating that "part of the obligation which forbids a member, by word or deed, endeavoring to injure the interests of any member of the society [International Brotherhood of Bookbinders]." The union specifically charged him with forcing members "to do fourteen books a day"

[19] F. W. Palmer to J. P. Heatwole, November 21, 1902, W. A. Miller to Philander C. Knox, June 13, 1903, in James R. Garfield Papers, Manuscript Division, Library of Congress; *Twentieth Annual Report of the United States Civil Service Commission, July 1, 1902, to June 30, 1903* (Washington: Government Printing Office, 1903), 147; New York *Times*, July 26, 1903.

in violation of the union's limit of ten books per day. Convicted of the charge, Miller was promptly suspended from the union for fifteen days.[20]

When he appealed to Public Printer Palmer, he was assured that "if these binders undertake to fight the government, they will find that they are going up against a hard proposition." But Palmer realized that if Miller were allowed to remain on the job during his suspension, it might well mean trouble, because members of the International Brotherhood were under obligation to refuse to work with anyone not in good standing with the union. Despite indications that the GPO would not bow to the wishes of the bookbinders' union, Palmer persuaded Miller to take a fifteen-day leave with pay, and at the end of that period assigned him to another building. But all such efforts failed to improve relations between Miller and the unionists. Miller continued what the union described as his "scurrilous and obscene" harassment of its members, and he accused officials of Local No. 4 of the bookbinders' union of "laying" for him. Finally, on April 6, 1903, the union prepared new charges against him and summoned him to stand trial a second time. It not only charged Miller with giving to Congressman Heatwole a copy of the testimony on which he had been suspended earlier and which he had secured clandestinely but also claimed that he had furnished Congressman F. H. Gillett of the House Appropriations Committee with a scale of prices and other information purporting to prove that the cost of binding in the GPO was far in excess of that in privately owned binderies. On May 12, 1903, the union voted to expel him from membership. Rather than risk a confrontation with the bookbinders over the closed-shop issue, Palmer suspended him on the following day. Miller had ignored all summonses to testify in his own behalf before the union because he insisted that its officers, President Robert D. Barrett and Secretary James A. Stockman, had "rigged" the trial. Palmer, in the meantime, had become annoyed with Miller and his cavalier attitude toward both union and government officials. He concluded that he must fire Miller or face a general strike in the GPO. Palmer chose the former course and dis-

[20] "The Bookbinders' Trouble in the Government Bindery," *International Bookbinder*, V (August, 1903), 155–57.

missed him from the printing office five days after his expulsion from the bookbinders' union. Miller alleged that the public printer had merely carried out the instructions of the union officers and suggested that he would not have acted so hastily in dismissing him if Congress had been in session. He intimated that the public printer was not the only one in the GPO who had important friends in Congress.[21]

Clearly, Miller had no intention of accepting his dismissal without protest. His first move was an appeal to Attorney General Philander C. Knox. After explaining to Knox that his attempts at reform in the GPO had made him an object of persecution by the union, Miller concluded, "These conditions, of restricting work, of interfering with the cheapening of work, insulting and disrespecting the orders of foremen, *is not known* among the printers and pressmen employed in the Government Office. . . . There is no place in the country where such conditions would be tolerated, as are inflicted by the local bookbinders employed in the Government Printing Office." [22] The attorney general thought Miller's letter of sufficient import to send it to Oyster Bay, where the President was vacationing. George B. Cortelyou, who had been appointed secretary of the new Department of Commerce and Labor in February, 1903, was also informed of Miller's charges. He was deeply concerned because the case was the first labor controversy of significance which had erupted during his tenure of office. A former secretary to three Presidents and a confidant of Roosevelt, Cortelyou assumed a principal role in the Miller affair from the beginning and was in large part responsible for the action taken by the Roosevelt administration. He was the first official to apprise the President of the implications of the affair. Relying heavily upon his advice, Roosevelt directed him to confer with Palmer and to stress the seriousness of Miller's charges.[23] The President was anxious for the public printer

21 *Ibid.*, 156–57; Miller to Knox, June 13, 1903, Palmer to Theodore Roosevelt, July 7, 1903, in Garfield Papers.

22 Miller to Knox, June 13, 1903, in Garfield Papers.

23 William Loeb to George B. Cortelyou, July 2, 1903, Palmer to Cortelyou, July 7, 1903, Cortelyou to Roosevelt, July 11, 1903, in Theodore Roosevelt Papers, Manuscript Division, Library of Congress.

to understand that "the Government in all its branches [must] be carried on on the principle of absolute justice to every man, capitalist or laborer, whether in or out of any organization." To insure that Palmer would not treat the matter lightly, Roosevelt called his attention to the possibility that he may have been party to "what may turn out to be a criminal conspiracy." [24]

While the President and his advisers sought further light on the situation in the GPO, Miller filed an official complaint with the Civil Service Commission charging that his removal from office was a violation of civil service regulations. Upon investigating the matter, the commission concluded that Miller had been dismissed "not because of any delinquency or misconduct in any way connected with his employment or duties in the Government Printing Office, but because he had been charged by an organization entirely independent of the public service with having violated its constitution." In the opinion of the commission, Palmer had violated Civil Service Rule XII, which provided that "no person shall be removed from a competitive position except for such cause as will promote the efficiency of the public service." On July 6, 1903, the Civil Service Commission directed him to reinstate Miller, despite Palmer's contention that the removal had been prompted by a desire to "promote efficiency in the public service by averting a threatened calamity." [25] Convinced that the Brotherhood of Bookbinders as well as other unions in the GPO would strike if Miller were reinstated, Palmer hesitated to carry out the directive from the Civil Service Commission. He apparently hoped that the President would intervene in some way to avert the "threatened calamity" which he anticipated.[26]

But a preliminary inquiry by Roosevelt and his advisers led to a conclusion similar to that of the commission. "I am satisfied," Acting Attorney General William A. Day informed Cortelyou on July 10, 1903, "that the only reason for Miller's removal was the verdict of the union." Day was convinced that if Palmer had challenged the

[24] Loeb to Cortelyou, July 2, 1903, in Garfield Papers.
[25] Palmer to John R. Proctor, July 10, 1903, in Garfield Papers; *Twentieth Annual Report of the United States Civil Service Commission*, 147–50.
[26] Palmer to Roosevelt, July 7, 1903, in Garfield Papers.

union "at the time, he probably would have had no serious trouble." But he recognized that the reinstatement of Miller was "a different matter." Both Roosevelt and Cortelyou shared Day's opinion that the incident was complicated "because of the labor union feature." [27] On July 9, 1903, the President instructed Cortelyou to make "an immediate and thorough investigation" of the incident in view of the serious charges made by Miller. Both Miller and Palmer were to be allowed ample opportunities to make full statements to Cortelyou.[28]

In a critique entitled "The Government Printing Office," Miller specified what he considered its principal weaknesses and abuses. First, he contended that the printery, though "one of the most expensive investments of the U. S. taxpayer," was a "floating mass" without direct affiliation with any department and without any clear line of administrative responsibility. The only time the GPO received any attention whatsoever, he maintained, was at the hearings of the Appropriations Committee. His second criticism concerned the ineptness of Palmer as an administrator. Not even his advanced age nor his small salary of $4,500 a year could excuse his mismanagement of GPO affairs. According to Miller, Palmer's annual reports were little more than a potpourri of "blatant discrepancies," and there was "no telling what an investigation would uncover." But Miller's severest criticism was reserved for the labor unions, which, he claimed, actually forced upon the government printery policies in clear defiance of the printing statutes and civil service regulations. He described in detail two examples of union abuses. One was the manner in which the bookbinders' union, "with the acquiescence of the Printer," defied the law establishing the eight-hour day and the hourly wage of fifty cents. The bookbinders, he alleged, charged four dollars a day whether or not they worked eight hours and limited the number of books they bound per day to ten. The other abuse which he cited concerned the regular theft of excess or waste gold leaf. Because the union instructed finishers to requisition an excessive amount of gold leaf for a job, and then to

[27] William A. Day to Cortelyou, July 10, 1903, in Roosevelt Papers.
[28] Loeb to Cortelyou, July 9, 1903, in Garfield Papers.

sell whatever was not used or absorbed as gold leaf dust in rubber cushions, Miller maintained that the Government Printing Office used "ten times more gold leaf than it should." [29]

If the President expected the public printer to present conclusive evidence to refute such charges, he was sorely disappointed. Palmer, in fact, consistently damned himself in Roosevelt's eyes by maintaining that Miller's dismissal was prompted by his desire to avert a general strike in the government printery. He refused to give Miller credit for any significant improvements in the bindery and characterized him as a ruthlessly ambitious man who had been "angling for the foremanship though the incumbent was a faithful employee of more than thirty years." As far as Palmer was concerned, Miller's dismissal was the result of "his own acts and unwise, untruthful criticisms." [30] Roosevelt considered Palmer's explanation incredible. "He admits in effect," the President wrote, "that he has turned over the discipline of his office to an outside labor organization." [31] No less impressed by Palmer's "poor showing," Cortelyou discussed the situation with Secretary of the Navy William Moody, who had had "much to do with this kind of thing" and suggested as a result of his conversations that a general investigation of the GPO was absolutely necessary. Of immediate concern to him was the possibility of a strike if Palmer reinstated Miller solely at the direction of the Civil Service Commission. But, as Cortelyou told Roosevelt, the unions would "think twice before ordering a strike if that direction were supplemented by positive instructions from yourself, for your action . . . would carry great weight with the country at large and will probably be regarded as final." [32]

Roosevelt agreed to Cortelyou's suggestions regarding both a general investigation and a presidential directive on the reinstatement of Miller, even though he did not wish to "get into a needless conflict with a labor union, especially in the year before a presidential

[29] W. A. Miller, "The Government Printing Office," July, 1903, in Garfield Papers.

[30] Palmer to Roosevelt, July 7, 1903, in Garfield Papers.

[31] Roosevelt to Cortelyou, July 13, 1903, in Elting Morison (ed.), *The Letters of Theodore Roosevelt* (8 vols.; Cambridge: Harvard, 1951–54), III, 514–15.

[32] Cortelyou to Roosevelt, July 11, 1903, in Roosevelt Papers.

election." [33] Whatever the political feasibility of avoiding such a conflict, he did not believe he could "afford to evade so important an issue." Failure on his part to prevent the bookbinders from usurping what he considered governmental functions might ultimately result in union domination of the government itself. "The labor unions were very arrogant and domineering because they did not believe I would face the music," Roosevelt later wrote a friend, "and it was necessary to give them a good jolt to make them understand at the outset that I would not tolerate anything in the nature of tyranny on their part." [34] Thus, he viewed the Miller case as more than an occasion for seeing justice done an individual; it provided an opportunity for him to limit the power of unions in government and to investigate the operations of the GPO. He placed Cortelyou in charge of the GPO investigation, which was directed first to look into the cost of public printing. Convinced that Palmer had "no real control over his establishment," Roosevelt suspected that there had been "the wildest extravagance in expenditures under him." But he advised Cortelyou that he wanted nothing "done publicly until I know just how far it is advisable to go." [35]

At the same time that Cortelyou launched his investigation, the President released for publication two letters regarding the Miller case designed to clarify not only his position in that particular case but also his policy toward labor unions in government. The first letter, dated July 13, 1903, which instructed Palmer to reinstate Miller in accordance with the wishes of the Civil Service Commission, stated that his "final decision" on the fate of Miller must await the outcome of a thorough investigation by Secretary Cortelyou. "There is no objection," the President declared, "to the employees of the Government Printing Office constituting themselves into a union if they so desire; but no rules or resolutions of that union can be permitted to overrule the laws of the United States, which it is

[33] Roosevelt to Cortelyou, July 13, 1903, in Morison (ed.), *Roosevelt Letters*, III, 514–15.

[34] Roosevelt to Albert Shaw, August 1, 1903, in Morison (ed.), *Roosevelt Letters*, III, 537.

[35] Roosevelt to Cortelyou, July 13, 1903, in Morison (ed.), *Roosevelt Letters*, III, 516; Scheinberg, "Roosevelt and the American Labor Movement," 79–80.

my duty to enforce." In the second letter, on July 14, 1903, Roosevelt justified his action in the Miller case by citing a passage in the report of the Anthracite Coal Strike Commission which stated that workingmen ought not to be discriminated against "on account of membership or non-membership in any labor organization." [36]

These two letters, in effect, placed the President on record in favor of the open shop, especially in government service. A month later Roosevelt extended the principle of the open shop to all executive departments by presidential order. This ruling affected several thousand union members other than the five hundred local bookbinders. Although his statements in the Miller case were worded in such a way that they might easily be construed as favoring the open shop generally, the real import was that they established a precedent on the question of labor unions and government employment. Cortelyou assured Roosevelt that the Miller incident had come "at a very opportune time, for several of the departments are embarrassed by the question [of labor unions] in one form or another." In accordance with the President's instructions, Palmer, on July 6, 1903, informed Miller of his reinstatement. Roosevelt also made it eminently clear that any person who participated in a strike because of the reinstatement would never regain employment in government so long as he was President. Unwilling to test the President's threat at this juncture, the members of the bookbinders' union agreed, "under protest," to work with Miller, pending the outcome of Cortelyou's investigation of charges made regarding affairs within the GPO.[37]

Roosevelt's announcements concerning the relationship of unions and government employees, made in the midst of the agitation over the labor question generally, quickly became the focus of national attention. The daily and periodical press, which spoke for middle-

[36] Roosevelt to Cortelyou, July 13, 14, 1903, in Morison (ed.), *Roosevelt Letters*, III, 516. See also New York *Tribune*, July 15, 1903.

[37] Cortelyou to Roosevelt, July 17, 20, 1903, in Roosevelt Papers; Roosevelt to Henry Cabot Lodge, September 3, 1903, in Henry Cabot Lodge (ed.), *Selections from the Correspondence of Theodore Roosevelt and Henry Cabot Lodge, 1884–1918* (2 vols.; New York: Scribner, 1925), II, 51. See also Paul P. Van Riper, *History of the United States Civil Service* (Evanston: Row, Peterson, 1958), 188; Washington *Evening Star*, August 20, 21, 1903.

class Americans, was enthusiastic about his decision in the Miller case. The New York *Tribune* lauded Roosevelt for "this strike against the tyranny of labor unions" which presumed to place their own constitutions above the Constitution of the United States. Like other editorial allies of the President, the *Tribune* depicted his action as a characteristic defense of justice, law, order, economy, efficiency, and a host of other virtues. The New York *Times* spoke of "the monumental impudence" of the bookbinders' union in attempting to impose its will upon a federal agency.[38] Conceding that Miller's charges about misconduct in the GPO might well contain exaggerations, the Chicago *Tribune* was convinced that he was correct regarding the extravagances in printing costs.[39] The *Outlook*, a pro-Roosevelt weekly, warned organized labor that the people of the United States were not "ready to resign their sovereignty into the hands of a private organization" and emphasized that "the right of man to work" was not determined by his membership in a union.[40] "It is high time," *Harper's Weekly* declared, "that labor unionists who were unduly elated by Mr. Roosevelt's intervention in the anthracite coal strike should be made to understand that there are limits beyond which a President cannot and dare not go." [41] Other journals which emphasized the detrimental effect of unions upon the efficient and economical operation of the government printery generally agreed with the analysis of the Chicago *Tribune*: "It costs far too much to run the printing office and the principal reason is that its control passed out of the hands of government officers into the hands of the unions." [42] For wholly different reasons, a sizable segment of the Negro press praised Roosevelt for forcing Miller's reinstatement. The *Colored American* claimed

[38] New York *Tribune*, July 21, 22, 23, 24, 26, 28, 29, 31, August 2, 21, 28, September 19, 22, October 1, 1903.

[39] Chicago *Daily Tribune*, July 28, 1903. See also "U.S. and Union Constitutions," *Public Opinion*, XXXV (1903), 134; "The President and the Labor Union," *Literary Digest*, XXVI (1903), 126.

[40] *Outlook*, LXXIV (1903), 772. See also *Independent*, LV (1903), 1817–19, 1886; *Nation*, LXXVII (July 23, 1903), 61; *ibid.*, LXXVII (July 30, 1903), 83; *ibid.*, LXXVII (September 10, 1903), 197; *Literary Digest*, XXVII (1903), 278–79.

[41] *Harper's Weekly*, LXVII (1903), 1284. See also *ibid.*, 1429, 1465.

[42] Chicago *Daily Tribune*, July 28, 1903.

that the policies of racial discrimination practiced by the various printers' unions had virtually eliminated Negroes from the GPO. The editor hoped that Roosevelt's action in the Miller case would help to remove some of the barriers to the employment of Negroes in government agencies.[43]

Few papers editorialized at such length about the Miller affair as the *Wall Street Journal*. Consistently laudatory of Roosevelt's handling of the matter, the *Journal* discoursed about "how hard is the lot of a President . . . who is determined to be just." It reminded those representatives of corporate wealth who had criticized Roosevelt's role in the anthracite coal strike as an effort to win favor with organized labor to ask themselves "what his political motive must be in antagonizing the most powerful labor organization in the country" by his stand in the Miller affair. The *Journal*, of course, maintained that no such motive existed in either instance and that Roosevelt acted on the assumption that the Miller case involved "a question of simple morality." According to its assessment of the situation, which was equated with that of Roosevelt, the closed shop, especially in government agencies, was immoral and, even worse, un-American. Labor unions, not Miller, were on trial, and the manner in which they reacted to the President's decision would largely determine "the future of trade unionism in this country." The implication was that any effort to oppose the President in the matter would virtually destroy the union movement.[44]

Although organized labor did not consider its response to the President's reinstatement of Miller as crucial as the *Wall Street Journal* suggested, it did recognize that the case was considerably more than a routine affair. For unionists, its importance lay in the fact that it involved the closed-shop issue and a precedent regarding government employees and labor organizations. Many labor spokesmen viewed the closed shop as an indispensable asset in their organizing campaigns and saw the open shop as a potent weapon by which anti-union capitalists could thwart their efforts.[45] In the hands of

[43] Washington *Colored American*, August 1, October 10, 1903.
[44] *Wall Street Journal*, July 24, 25, 27, 31, August 22, 25, 28, September 22, 29, October 1, 3, 1903.
[45] Greenberg, "Theodore Roosevelt and Labor," 193–95.

such anti-unionists as David Parry, the closed shop became a powerful propaganda instrument useful in convincing middle-class Americans that unions threatened individual rights and constituted a new type of trust. Union leaders were not surprised that Parry, so critical of the anthracite coal strike decision, heaped praise upon Roosevelt for his handling of the Miller affair and attempted to infer from the latter that the President favored the open shop in industry no less than in government.[46] Though highly critical of what they considered Parry's perversion of the facts, union leaders nonetheless fully appreciated the predicament in which Roosevelt's action had placed them. At best the closed shop in government service was not easily defended; in the case of Miller justification was all the more difficult because enforcement of the closed shop appeared to conflict with public policy and civil service regulations. For organized labor to oppose Roosevelt's decision in the case would almost certainly be used by Parry and others to support their charge of lawlessness against unions. On the other hand, to accept the decision without some form of rebuttal or defense was likely to give the impression that Miller's charges against unions were valid, which in turn would also provide additional ammunition for the anti-union propagandists.

Such a dilemma would have posed difficulties even for a highly unified and militant labor movement. Labor's response in 1903 merely exposed the divisiveness and cautiousness that characterized unions early in the twentieth century. Samuel Gompers, John Mitchell, and other leaders of the American Federation of Labor restrained hasty action on the part of constituent unions and attempted to work out some settlement which would save face for organized labor without appearing as a defiance of either the civil service regulations or the President's order. The Knights of Labor denounced unionist critics of the President, who was described as

[46] James S. Clarkson to Roosevelt, July 29, 1903, in Roosevelt Papers; *American Federationist*, X (1903), 1163. For examples of laudatory letters regarding the President's decision in the Miller case from members of the National Association of Manufacturers, see N. B. Numermacher to Roosevelt, July 22, 1903, Franklin Nourse to Roosevelt, July 23, 1903, Charles Nelles to Roosevelt, July 24, 1903, in Roosevelt Papers.

"one of the best friends of organized labor," and suggested Senator Hanna serve as a referee in the dispute between the President and the bookbinders.[47]

From the outset, however, the Socialists insisted that Roosevelt's stand in the Miller case revealed his basic prejudice against workingmen, a bias temporarily obscured by his pretentious and noisy assertions during and immediately after the anthracite coal strike. One Socialist leader, Victor Berger, characterized his action in the Miller case as an open invitation for the employment of "scabs" everywhere.[48] Eugene Debs claimed that "the president has slipped a long keen blade into the vitals of organized labor." Such an act, he maintained, should demonstrate to American workers "that socialism is what they want as that is the only thing that will enable them to meet President Roosevelt on his own ground and make him and the capitalist exploiters he represents take to the timber before a triumphant working class." [49] The Socialist press denounced the timidity displayed by labor unions in the face of the Rooseveltian challenge and suggested that the real reason they hesitated to oppose it was his threat "to put typesetting machines in the government office, thus dispensing with the labor of a good many men." The *Social Democratic Herald* called upon all loyal workingmen to oppose Roosevelt in the election of 1904.[50]

Throughout the summer and fall of 1903 the political implication of the Miller incident was a persistent source of concern for the President and his advisers. Early in September, 1903, the Central Labor Union of Washington, D.C., representing seventy-two affiliated labor organizations, openly condemned the President's reinstatement of Miller and asserted that it "could not be regarded in any but an unfriendly light." Similar expressions were forwarded to Roosevelt from unions in Chicago; Milwaukee; Minneapolis; Lynn, Massachusetts; and various other industrial cities. The International Association of Structural Iron and Bridge Workers, meeting in Kansas City late in September, also censured the President be-

[47] New York *Times,* September 25, 1903.
[48] Milwaukee *Social Democratic Herald*, November 14, 1903.
[49] Chicago *Socialist*, October 31, 1903.
[50] Milwaukee *Social Democratic Herald*, August 15, September 5, 1903.

cause of the Miller affair. Critics of Roosevelt's position, led by the International Brotherhood of Bookbinders, apparently hoped to secure passage of a similar resolution at the AFL convention in November.[51] Even more ominous for Roosevelt's political future were suggestions by various union spokesmen that workingmen should join in a movement to defeat his election in 1904. Neil C. McCallum of Chicago, a prominent union official and an advocate of such a movement, predicted that Roosevelt's decision in the Miller case would cost him labor's vote and probably cause his "political downfall." [52] Veteran political observers generally agreed that the Miller incident would figure prominently in the forthcoming presidential campaign. A few intimated that the President might well "lose the labor vote" since his reinstatement of Miller tended "to undo anything that his coal strike commission did, so far as the labor vote is concerned." One widely circulated rumor credited "certain elements of Wall Street" with using the Miller affair to "stir up labor unions against the President." Other rumors claimed that the President's alienation of labor had substantially increased Hanna's prospects for winning the Republican presidential nomination. Of more immediate concern to Roosevelt and his campaign strategists were the efforts by Democrats to capitalize on the Miller affair. The newspaper publisher William Randolph Hearst, an aspirant for the Democratic presidential nomination, made much of Roosevelt's stand in the case and used it in a way designed to enhance his own image as a friend of organized labor. As a result of Hearst's appeal, various labor organizations, including the letter carriers' association, endorsed his candidacy.[53]

[51] "Labor Opposition to the President," *Literary Digest*, XXVII (1903), 413–14; Lynn, Mass., Central Labor Union to Roosevelt, September 22, 1903, Local Union No. 559, Team Drivers' International Union, Augusta, Maine, to Roosevelt, September 18, 1903, Roosevelt to Cortelyou, September 23, 1903, in Roosevelt Papers; Washington *Post*, September 6, 1903; New York *Times*, September 7, 1903; Washington *Evening Star*, September 16, 1903; New York *Tribune*, September 22, 1903; Atlanta *Constitution*, September 30, 1903.
[52] "The Administration and Union Labor," *Literary Digest*, XXVII (1903), 279.
[53] "American Politics," *Forum*, XXXV (1903), 174–75; New Orleans *Picayune*, September 17, October 14, 1903; *Commoner*, III (September 25, 1903), 4; *ibid.*, III (October 2, 1903), 4; Washington *Evening Star*, September 16, 1903; Jackson (Miss.) *Evening News*, August 4, 1903.

None of the President's political advisers appeared more agitated by the implications of the Miller incident than James S. Clarkson, the veteran Republican politician whom Roosevelt had appointed surveyor of the New York port. Clarkson conferred with David Parry as well as with various representatives of labor unions and was alarmed by the impact of the President's handling of the affair. He assured Roosevelt that "the Socialist vote will play a great part in the election next year" and cautioned him against any further action in the Miller case that might force organized labor into the Socialist camp. Clarkson also urged that the President have his own representatives present at the forthcoming conventions of various unions in order to counteract the influence of Hearst's forces.[54] Conferences with union officials convinced Mark Hanna that Clarkson was unduly alarmed. The senator suggested to Roosevelt that the nomination of Hearst by the Democrats would be to "the Republicans' advantage." Hanna agreed that the presence of a few carefully chosen party representatives at the labor conventions might be helpful, but he emphasized that any attempt to have the conventions endorse specific Republican candidates would be "hurtful." [55] Albert Shaw, editor of the *Review of Reviews* and one of Roosevelt's close friends, regretted that the Miller case had not been handled in "a somewhat more routine and roundabout way" and advised the President to get in contact with the leaders of the printers' unions in order to erase any "wrong impression" which his decision had created. News reached the White House in the meantime that virtually all officials and "about 60% of the members" of all unions represented in the Government Printing Office were Democrats.[56]

Neither Roosevelt nor Cortelyou was as alarmed over the political repercussions as Clarkson. But both were anxious to preserve the image of the Roosevelt administration as favoring the open shop without being accused of an antilabor bias. Cortelyou not only retained friendly relations with officials of Local Union No. 4 of the

---

[54] Clarkson to Benjamin Barnes, July 15, 1903, Clarkson to Roosevelt, July 29, 1903, in Roosevelt Papers.

[55] Mark Hanna to Roosevelt, August 4, 1903, in Roosevelt Papers.

[56] Roosevelt to Shaw, August 1, 1903, in Morison (ed.), *Roosevelt Letters*, III, 537; James R. Garfield Diaries (Garfield Papers), July 29, 1903, p. 210.

International Brotherhood of Bookbinders, which was still pressing charges against Miller, but also met informally with the leaders of other labor organizations, especially the powerful typographical union, to explain "the meaning" of Roosevelt's action in the Miller case. Whether because of these explanations or for some other reason, the typographical union refused to ally itself with the cause of the bookbinders.[57] In fact, W. P. Prescott, a prominent leader of the union, severely criticized the International Brotherhood of Bookbinders for allowing its locals to impose upon the Government Printing Office rules which impeded efficiency, economy, and production.[58] Roosevelt himself continued, all the while, to explain his decision in terms of morality and justice. "The labor unions shall have a square deal," he assured Clarkson, "and the corporations will have a square deal, and in addition all the citizens will have a square deal." [59] The door of the White House, the President insisted, would swing open just as easily to labor as capital—"and not one bit easier." [60] Whatever other motives may have prompted his action in the Miller affair, Roosevelt was continually aware of its possible political effect. In a confidential letter to his old friend Senator Henry Cabot Lodge, he declared that "the country as a whole" was "well pleased" with his handling of the case, but he admitted that "from the political standpoint there is no use in disguising the fact that the country as a whole will probably forget all about it; while the labor union people who are angry will not forget." [61] Actually, Roosevelt saw to it that the "country as a whole" was not allowed to forget. In his own words, he used the Miller in-

[57] Memoranda by Cortelyou, July 21, 22, 23, 24, 1903, in Garfield Papers; Garfield Diaries, August 10, 1903, p. 222.

[58] W. P. Prescott, "The Miller Case," *Inland Printer*, XXXI (1903), 852–54; W. P. Prescott, "The Miller Case Again," *ibid.*, XXXII (1903), 207–209; "The Union Stint in the Government Bindery," *International Bookbinder*, IV (September, 1903), 172; "The Task in the Government Bindery," *ibid.*, IV (November, 1903), 208.

[59] Roosevelt to Clarkson, July 16, 1903, in Morison (ed.), *Roosevelt Letters*, III, 519.

[60] Owen Wister, *Roosevelt: The Story of a Friendship, 1880–1919* (New York: Macmillan, 1930), 217.

[61] Roosevelt to Lodge, September 3, 1903, in Lodge (ed.), *Roosevelt-Lodge Correspondence*, II, 51–52.

cident "as an illustration of the fairness with which the administration has tackled the two sides of the labor-capital question." [62]

Anxious about the growing popularity of Hearst with organized labor, Roosevelt worked closely with Cortelyou, Clarkson, and others who attempted to eradicate the ill will created by Miller's reinstatement. Although the President constantly related his action to the decision of the Anthracite Coal Strike Commission in an effort to demonstrate his genuine commitment to a Square Deal for all groups, he was not satisfied to deal merely in abstractions. Earlier in his administration he had made it clear that civil servants were not to participate actively in political campaigns and the situation created by the agitation over Miller prompted him to enforce that order. For example, he directed the postmaster general to "take prompt action" against all letter carriers responsible for the endorsement of Hearst by their national organization. "People in the classified service," he declared, "are not allowed to go as delegates to conventions or take offensive political action *for* the President, and they certainly shall not do so *against* the President." [63]

All the while, representatives of the International Brotherhood of Bookbinders pressed charges against Miller with a view toward persuading the President to change his mind about Miller's fitness for public service. Stockman and Barrett of Local No. 4 met with Cortelyou almost daily throughout July, 1903, in an effort to get from him a decision regarding Miller's ultimate fate.[64] They reminded him that the President had promised to withhold his final decision until Cortelyou's investigation had been completed. But from the beginning both Roosevelt and Cortelyou maintained that the union must not confuse the "several issues" raised by the Miller incident. They emphasized that since the Government Printing Office was in fact an open shop, there was no justification for Mill-

---

[62] Roosevelt to Jacob G. Schurman, August 31, 1903, in Morison (ed.), *Roosevelt Letters*, III, 581.

[63] Roosevelt to Henry C. Payne, July 16, 1903, in Morison (ed.), *Roosevelt Letters*, III, 518.

[64] Cortelyou, a trained stenographer and shorthand expert, kept a complete record of these conferences. Dozens of detailed memoranda describing his discussions with the spokesmen for the bookbinders appear in the Garfield Papers. The inclusive dates are July 20 to October 10, 1903.

er's dismissal, and his reinstatement was "a closed incident." Any charges that the bookbinders' union made against Miller constituted "a new case" and would be handled "in a routine manner." [65] Although such a stipulation required the union to file its charges with Palmer, it was obvious that the public printer would act upon them only with advice of Cortelyou and the committee which he had assigned to investigate the GPO. The union officials complied with this arrangement and assured Cortelyou that they would "do everything possible to keep the discussion within proper limits." In their view Palmer had erred in removing Miller because of his expulsion from the union since he "had ample grounds to dismiss him upon other charges of various sorts." [66]

Disturbed by the unfavorable publicity given their union, the bookbinders placed "great pressure" upon Barrett and Stockman to preserve its reputation by securing the permanent expulsion of Miller.[67] In an effort to achieve this end, they presented to Palmer numerous affidavits testifying to Miller's unfitness as a government employee. The union emphatically declared, "We have never attempted to dictate the policy or management of the affairs in the Government Printing Office, but we claim we have the right to punish a member when he makes efforts to persecute other members and uses his official position for the furtherance of personal ends." The union flatly denied any opposition to efforts designed to reduce expense and increase production in the GPO. In the case of Miller, its opposition was directed at his innovations which "reduced the quality of the product." [68] But the more sensational charges against Miller concerned his private life and treatment of subordinates. The affidavits of all witnesses generally agreed that his domineering attitude and "contemptuous treatment of his fellow union members" seriously impeded the "efficiency of government service." Sev-

[65] Roosevelt to Cortelyou, July 25, 1903, Cortelyou to Roosevelt, July 24, 25, 1903, in Garfield Papers; Roosevelt to Cortelyou, September 23, 1903, in George B. Cortelyou Papers, Manuscript Division, Library of Congress.

[66] International Brotherhood of Bookbinders to Cortelyou, July 22, 1903, in Garfield Papers.

[67] Memoranda by Cortelyou, July 24, 25, 1903, in Garfield Papers.

[68] International Brotherhood of Bookbinders to Cortelyou, July 22, 1903, in Garfield Papers.

eral witnesses claimed that Miller was "a foul-mouthed braggart" who practiced "favoritism of the worst sort." Others described him as "crazy after women," a lecher constantly in pursuit of the young women employed in the GPO. Allegedly, Miller selected those with whom he desired "to have sexual intercourse," then "went after them," threatening them with the loss of their jobs unless they submitted to his advances. The bookbinders' union also presented to the public printer documents which purported to prove that he was a thief and a bigamist. Various persons long acquainted with him claimed that he had been "run out of Minneapolis" because he stole gold leaf from his employer. The charge of bigamy was based upon marriage certificates and direct testimony; it was claimed that Miller had married three women, all of whom were living, and had never obtained a divorce from any of them.[69] When Palmer presented Miller with these charges, he at first refused to accept them on the grounds that they were merely ridiculous contrivances by an angry labor union. Although he finally accepted the charges when Palmer assured him of their serious nature, he was allowed to postpone his response. In fact, he refused to answer the specific charges and contented himself with leveling countercharges against Stockman and Barrett for absenting themselves from their jobs in the Government Printing Office in order to stir up strife among union members working under his supervision.[70]

Although Cortelyou appreciated the patience and "conservative action" of the union, both he and Palmer persisted in postponing a decision regarding the new charges filed against Miller. When the officials of the bookbinders' union pressed Cortelyou for a decision, he insisted that Palmer alone had jurisdiction in such matters. Palmer, however, made it clear that he could act only at the direction of "higher authorities." Clearly, he would render no decision until Cortelyou's investigation had been completed. Frustrated by what was considered an obvious run-around, the bookbinders in

[69] See affidavits by Felix J. Belvir, July 29, 1903, Henry Haiky, July 31, 1903, John D. Hasson, July 29, 31, 1903, Harry Perry, July 31, 1903, Robert T. Stack, July 29, 1903, in Garfield Papers.
[70] Memorandum by Cortelyou, August 17, 1903, Memorandum by Garfield, September 1, 1903, in Garfield Papers.

the GPO who were working with Miller "under protest" became increasingly restive and revived their threat to strike. Convinced that a walkout at this juncture would be disastrous for the union in view of Roosevelt's earlier dictum, Barrett and Stockman exerted every effort to alleviate the tension. But when it appeared doubtful whether they could control the situation, they called upon the International Brotherhood for assistance. The continued postponement of Palmer's decision finally prompted leaders of the AFL to take up the Miller case.[71]

At Gompers' request, Roosevelt agreed to meet with members of the AFL executive committee. At this conference in the White House on September 29, 1903, the President conferred with the labor leaders, including Gompers and Mitchell, on such topics as the eight-hour bill, anti-injunction legislation, and the case of Ephraim W. Clark, a union man imprisoned for almost twenty-eight years. But obviously the main topic was the Miller incident.[72] The President reiterated his reasons for reinstating Miller and declared that his decision in that aspect of the matter was final. "In the employment and dismissal of men in the Government service," he maintained, "I can no more recognize the fact that a man does or does not belong to a union as being for or against him than I can recognize the fact that he is a Protestant or a Catholic, a Jew or a Gentile, as being for or against him." [73] Impressed by the reasonableness of the delegation, Roosevelt explained that the new charges against Miller involving his "personal fitness" constituted a wholly different case and would be settled "in the routine of administrative detail." Such charges, however, could "not be allowed to conflict with or complicate the larger question of government discrimination for or against any other man because he is or is not a member of a union." Of especial importance to the labor leaders was the Presi-

[71] Memoranda by Cortelyou, August 18, 19, 24, 25, 26, October 10, 1903, in Garfield Papers.

[72] Samuel Gompers to Roosevelt, September 24, 1903, in Roosevelt Papers; New York *Times*, September 30, 1903.

[73] Roosevelt's statement to the AFL committee was largely the work of Garfield, William Moody, and F. P. Sargent. See Garfield Diaries, September 29, 1903, p. 272; White House press statement, September 29, 1903, in Garfield Papers; New York *Times*, September 30, 1903.

dent's assurance that his concern in the Miller case dealt "purely with the relations of the Government to its employees." Gompers was convinced that Roosevelt's statement would scotch the "miserable attempt" by employers to construe his reinstatement of Miller as an endorsement of the open shop in private industry.[74]

Some of those enthusiastic about his decision in the affair were greatly disturbed by his so-called concessions to the AFL delegation. "The general opinion of thinking men must be," the New York *Times* declared, "that President Roosevelt came out of the complications of the Miller incident with less credit than he would have done if he had said less and made less effort to sugar-coat the pill which Gompers and his associates found unpalatable." [75] The Atlanta *Constitution*, a Democratic paper, described the White House meeting as characteristic of Roosevelt's "two horse acts." "He has stood pat on the Miller reinstatement," it explained, "but he bunched and lunched the labor leaders at the White House and delivered to them a didactic avowal of his deep devotion to the cause of union labor, incidentally lamenting that the laws of the land prevented his display of it in the aforesaid Miller case. It is as plain as a pike-staff that the President did all this to coddle the labor element and prevent a situation that might lose him a large measure of its vote next year." [76] William Jennings Bryan predicted that

[74] See White House press statement, September 29, 1903, in Garfield Papers. Considerable controversy erupted over whether the President had granted the AFL representatives a "conference" or a "hearing." Roosevelt told Senator Lodge that "our friends of the wealthy and cultivated classes" got it "into their fool heads that as I was to hold a 'conference' with the labor men, this meant that I intended to weaken. They immediately fell into a panic that I *had* weakened. It was some time before I discovered that their trouble was the terminology of the affair. I happened to say to one shrill remonstrant that I certainly could not deny a hearing to anybody, whether it was the labor people or the trust magnates. He seemed immensely relieved, and said that so long as it was a 'hearing' and not a 'conference' it was all right. I did not attempt to find exactly what the distinction was in his mind; but whatever it was seems to have been widespread, for all my financial and intellectual friends have solemnly agreed that while it would be wicked to hold a conference it would be eminently proper to hold a hearing." See Roosevelt to Lodge, September 30, 1903, in Lodge (ed.), *Roosevelt-Lodge Correspondence*, II, 63.

[75] New York *Times*, October 1, 1903.

[76] Atlanta *Constitution*, October 5, 1903.

Roosevelt would even go so far as to have John Mitchell as his running mate in an effort to win back the support of organized labor which the Miller incident had cost him.[77]

Regardless of Roosevelt's motive, his statement strengthened the position of the labor spokesmen in their attempts to avert a motion of censure against him during the national convention of the AFL. Meeting in Faneuil Hall in Boston on November 9, 1903, the convention was confronted with several resolutions regarding the Miller case which set off a "sharp discussion." The resolutions committee obviously acted as a moderating influence to prevent the passage of any measure which Gompers and Mitchell considered indiscreet. The resolution finally accepted by the convention called upon the President to review the new charges against Miller and to dismiss him permanently if "the said charges . . . are sustained." As amended from the floor, the committee's resolution also included the declaration that "the American Federation of Labor places itself on record as being in favor of the union shop everywhere, as well in federal, state and municipal employment as in private enterprises." That the leaders of the AFL were able to prevent the passage of a harsher resolution directed at the President may well have resulted in part from the strategically timed pardon which Roosevelt granted to Ephraim W. Clark.[78] Although this act largely escaped the notice of the press, it obviously helped to mollify various representatives to the AFL convention agitated by his reinstatement of Miller. Within a week after the close of the convention Roosevelt further showed his good will toward organized labor by entertaining at the White House six well-known union leaders from Montana who had shown him courtesies during his western tour.[79]

[77] *Commoner*, III (October 9, 1903), 7.

[78] *Report of the Proceedings of the Twenty-third Annual Convention of the American Federation of Labor, 1903*, pp. 87–90, 115, 142, 209, 210–11; New Orleans *Daily Picayune*, November 13, 1903; New York *Times*, November 12, 13, 14, 1903. Ephraim W. Clark was a merchant seaman accused of mutiny whose death sentence had been commuted by President Grant. For the background on the Clark case see Samuel Gompers, *Seventy Years of Life and Labor: An Autobiography* (2 vols.; New York: Dutton, 1925), I, 521.

[79] Boston *Pilot*, December 5, 1903; "Mr. Roosevelt and the Butte Union," *Engineering and Mining Journal*, LXXVI (1903), 726.

Following the adjournment of the AFL convention, the International Brotherhood of Bookbinders was virtually alone in the fight to secure Miller's dismissal on charges of being a "bigamist, perjurer, and defaulter." And even the bookbinders were not united on the issue.[80] Finally, on February 6, 1904, Gompers, who was more or less obligated by the action of the AFL convention to assist in the struggle, presented to the public printer certified copies of documents which purported to show that Miller was guilty of bigamy, wife-beating, desertion of family, fraud, theft, and other crimes making him unfit for government service. Gompers concluded that "the protection of American women, the sanctity of the American home and the honor of American workmen are involved in this case." [81] As usual, Palmer delayed action, largely at the insistence of Cortelyou, whose committee found Miller a valuable source of information in its investigation of the GPO. When Gompers could not stir Palmer to action, he appealed to Roosevelt and reminded him of his promise that the matter would be "settled in the routine of administrative detail." [82] The President then directed Palmer to render a decision. After consulting Cortelyou, the public printer finally informed Gompers in June, 1904, that Miller would not be dropped from government service. He argued that charges of moral misconduct in the past had little relevance to Miller's "present fitness for public service," especially since "no victims of the crimes herein mentioned have appeared here as complainants." [83] Gompers apparently accepted Palmer's reply as final, for it marked the end of his activities in connection with the Miller affair. A final gesture by organized labor was made in June, 1904, by the International Brotherhood of Bookbinders. At its annual convention it censured Roosevelt for retaining Miller in the GPO as an act inimical to the

[80] Edward F. Hurd, a prominent official of the International Brotherhood of Bookbinders in Ohio, expressed the sentiment of a large number of his fellow unionists when he assured Roosevelt that his decision in the Miller case was "perfectly just." See Hurd to Roosevelt, January 2, 1904, in Roosevelt Papers.

[81] Gompers to Palmer, February 6, 1904, in Garfield Papers.

[82] Gompers to Roosevelt, May 28, 1904, in Garfield Papers.

[83] Palmer to Gompers, June [?], 1904, in Garfield Papers. See also Memorandum by Cortelyou, June 4, 1904, in Garfield Papers.

interests of decent workingmen and to the efficiency of the public service.[84]

The Miller incident, like other controversies involving organized labor, indicated that during his first term of office Roosevelt did not take the initiative in formulating labor policy but rather reacted to specific issues forced upon him. In the Miller affair, once the President had taken a position, he attempted to balance its political effects against his role in the anthracite coal strike. The two gave meaning to his campaign slogan, A Square Deal. In the words of a pro-Roosevelt paper, the President was "comfortably entrenched behind the Miller case and the anthracite arbitration." [85] Organized labor was not allowed to forget his role in the coal strike and was also constantly reminded of the "fairness" of his decision in the Miller case, whereas anti-unionists and others who feared his action in the coal strike found considerable solace in his determination "to stand up" to organized labor in the reinstatement of Miller. In instructing his campaign strategists in 1904 about the actions of his administration which should be emphasized, Roosevelt listed the first five in the following order of priority: (1) the investigation of the Post Office Department, (2) the Panama Canal, (3) the anthracite coal strike arbitration, (4) the Northern Securities suit, (5) the Miller case.[86] Two campaign biographies of the President provided detailed statements of the Miller incident as an example of Rooseveltian "fair play." [87] That the Republican campaign handbook of 1904 juxtaposed its accounts of the coal strike and the Miller case was indicative of how Roosevelt intended that they be used as political complements to rally all groups to his support. Although Hearst described the President as a "secret enemy of labor" and Alton B. Parker, who was ultimately chosen the Democratic presidential nominee, condemned his labor policies on different grounds, Roosevelt's overwhelming victory at the polls in November, 1904, sus-

[84] *International Bookbinder,* V (June, 1904), 110.

[85] *Independent,* LVI (February 25, 1904), 401.

[86] Roosevelt to Elihu Root, June 2, 1904, in Morison (ed.), *Roosevelt Letters,* IV, 810–11.

[87] Francis E. Leupp, *The Man Roosevelt: A Portrait Sketch* (New York: Appleton, 1904), 232–41; Jacob A. Riis, *Theodore Roosevelt: The Citizen* (New York: Outlook, 1904), 380–83.

tained the predictions of Cortelyou, Lodge, and others who had assured him that "sensible labor union men" and voters in general would fully appreciate the justice of his actions in both the Miller affair and the anthracite coal strike.[88]

Another aspect of the Miller incident largely obscured by politics was the investigation of the Government Printing Office that it prompted. Throughout the public controversy Cortelyou's investigation had quietly compiled a formidable indictment of the GPO administration which formed the basis of the changes that Roosevelt inaugurated after his election in 1904. The investigation team, headed by Cortelyou, included James R. Garfield, the son of a former President and the director of the new Bureau of Corporations; Frank P. Sargent, commissioner of immigration; and two experts from the Civil Service Commission, George W. Leadley and Harold N. Saxton.[89] Garfield, "a Rooseveltian Progressive" with a strong commitment to efficiency and economy in government, shouldered the burden of the investigation. A man of great poise and tact who was not opposed to labor unions per se, he nonetheless objected to some of the aims of unionism. His attitude toward the concept of the closed shop could scarcely be described as friendly.[90] Sargent, a former president of the Brotherhood of Locomotive Firemen, was obviously considered labor's representative on Cortelyou's committee. Held in high esteem by Roosevelt for his conservative views on labor questions, he was charged with the task of investigating the role of unions within the GPO. Leadley and Saxton were directed to study "all matters relating to appointment, promotion, removal and reinstatement." Secretary of the Navy Moody and Secretary of

[88] *Republican Campaign Text-Book, 1904* (Milwaukee: Press of the *Evening Wisconsin*, 1904), 358–61; Ray Stannard Baker, "Roosevelt and Parker on Labor," *McClure's Magazine*, XXIV (November, 1904), 48–52; Atlanta *News*, January 21, 30, 1904; *Outlook*, LXXVIII (1904), 509–11; *International Bookbinder*, V (September, 1904), 169.

[89] Roosevelt to Cortelyou, July 13, 1903, in Morison (ed.), *Roosevelt Letters*, III, 515; Cortelyou to George W. Leadley, July 16, 1903, in Garfield Papers. See also Garfield Diaries, July 11, 1903, p. 192.

[90] For a thorough study of Garfield see Jack M. Thompson, "James R. Garfield: Career of a Rooseveltian Progressive, 1895–1916" (Ph.D. dissertation, University of South Carolina, 1958).

War Elihu Root, though not officially a part of the investigating force, served in advisory capacities.[91]

By mid-August, 1903, the committee began to apprise the President of its findings. Since its preliminary investigation indicated that "the general charges of laxity in the administration [of the GPO] are found to be true," the investigators early reached the conclusion that Palmer should be replaced as public printer.[92] Garfield reported to Roosevelt that the relation of unions to other government agencies was "very gratifying" and that whenever disagreements over labor issues arose they were "settled amicably and quickly." He noted, "There is no instance other than the GPO where conditions such as exist there have been permitted to develop."[93] But scarcely any aspect of the operation of the government printery escaped criticism. The committee's disclosures regarding business methods practiced there appalled the President, even though he had come to expect the worst. According to the committee report, the procedure for handling paper and gold leaf was incredibly loose; no full audit of the office's accounts had been made since 1893; inventories, if made at all, were perfunctory; and the public printer regularly made unrealistic estimates of costs. The investigators assured the President that his suspicions about the excessive cost of public printing were only too valid. In fact, it was discovered that in some instances printing jobs by the GPO would have cost 85 percent less if done in private printeries. But, as the report of the committee emphasized, the absence of good business procedures in the GPO was compounded by the agency's "division of responsibility between the executive and legislative departments."[94] Whether by coincidence or design, the question of the administrative relocation of the printery became the subject of considerable discussion in the press shortly after the committee concluded its initial investigation. Both Cortelyou and Roosevelt were

[91] Cortelyou to Roosevelt, July 16, 1903, in Roosevelt Papers; Cortelyou to Leadley, July 16, 1903, in Garfield Papers.

[92] Garfield and F. P. Sargent to Cortelyou, August 10, 1903, in Garfield Papers.

[93] Memorandum by Garfield, August 21, 1903, in Garfield Papers.

[94] Cortelyou to Roosevelt, August 19, 1903, in Roosevelt Papers; Roosevelt to Palmer, August 22, 1903, in Garfield Papers.

understood to favor placing the GPO within the Department of Commerce and Labor.[95]

On August 22, 1903, President Roosevelt submitted to Palmer the findings of the Cortelyou committee. Among the changes which he directed the public printer to make immediately were an audit of all accounts, a thorough inventory of materials, the placing under bond of all employees "with the care and control of funds," and an effective, modern system of time-keeping. Roosevelt also insisted that every employee in the GPO, rather than merely clerks on annual salary, should be required to "take the ordinary oath of office." "It seems to reflect most seriously upon any Government officer," Roosevelt wrote Palmer, "that it should be necessary to make recommendations of this kind for the administration of his office." [96] On the same day that the President wrote Palmer he also apprised Senator Platt, chairman of the Joint Committee on Printing, of the lax administration of the GPO. Although the President was convinced that "Mr. Palmer ought not to be kept in office," he promised to await the advice of Platt's committee before taking any further action regarding the public printer.[97] Clearly Roosevelt did not desire to complicate matters either by prompting charges of executive usurpation or by antagonizing Palmer's politically influential friends in Congress. To eliminate the administrative ambivalence of the GPO by placing it within the Department of Commerce and Labor as the President desired would obviously arouse strong opposition. Although Roosevelt supported this innovation throughout his administration, he was never able to achieve it.

Upon receipt of the President's strong letter directing certain changes within the GPO, Palmer first carried out the recommendation regarding the oath of office for all employees. Not only was it the easiest for him to implement, but it might also act as a deterrent upon per diem bookbinders who at the time had revived their threat of a strike.[98] On September 10, 1903, Palmer sent to the

[95] New York *Times*, September 22, 1903.

[96] Roosevelt to Palmer, August 22, 1903, in Garfield Papers.

[97] Roosevelt to Thomas C. Platt, August 22, 1903, in Morison (ed.), *Roosevelt Letters*, III, 569.

[98] *International Bookbinder*, IV (September, 1903), 176; New York *Times*, August 27, 1903.

President a lengthy defense of his administration of the printery in which he explained what Cortelyou's committee described as the high cost of public printing. He cited the necessity for hasty production, the number of costly alterations in proof, and the higher wage scale enjoyed by federal employees. "The cost of any piece of work seems greater than for similar work in private establishments," he declared, "but the office contends that in the year's production it costs the government less than it would to have its printing and binding done by contract." Most of the elaborate exhibits presented by Palmer in connection with his defense of the efficiency and economy of his administration concerned the quality and "promptitude" of GPO production.[99] Since the investigating committee had made no criticisms regarding the quality of GPO publications or its "execution of hurried orders," his exhibits were largely irrelevant to the issues raised in the President's letter. In short, Palmer's defense merely sustained Roosevelt's view that the government printery was being grossly mismanaged.

While Palmer groped desperately to fend off his critics, Cortelyou's committee continued to uncover abuses within the GPO which compounded his difficulties. Through informants within the printery it learned that employees who profited from the passage of the Sundry Civil Appropriation Act of 1900, which increased the hourly wage to $.50, had been assessed $2.50 per month "until very recently." A search in the files of the GPO revealed that Palmer not only knew of "this fee for lobbying" imposed by the various unions but that he had given the scheme his approval. In mid-November, 1903, George W. Leadley's report disclosed numerous instances in which Palmer bowed to the will of unions in dismissing and reinstating personnel. The report also cited an impressive array of cases in which senators and congressmen exerted influence to secure appointments and promotions for political allies.[100]

Throughout the investigation Miller himself remained a constant source of information for Cortelyou's committee. He appears

[99] Palmer to Roosevelt, September 10, 1903, in Garfield Papers.
[100] Garfield Diaries, August 22, September 24, 1903; Memoranda by Z. L. Dalby, September 10, 11, 1903, Report by Leadley, November 14, 1903, in Garfield Papers.

to have become a special confidant of Garfield, with whom he conferred regularly in the fall of 1903 and in the spring of 1904. In letters to Garfield, which were frequently a dozen pages in length, Miller cited numerous examples of fraud and corruption currently existing in the Government Printing Office. He claimed that J. P. Byrne, the foreman of binding, continued as usual to receive a 10 percent "commission" on all machinery installed in the bindery division. The "payoff" allegedly was made to an intermediary by the name of Mamie Sullivan, one of Bryne's lady friends. Miller discovered this practice when he attempted to arrange for the installation of a gold-saving device distributed by the Haas and Mc-Clelland Company of New York. Miller's information to Garfield implicated Palmer too, in what were described as displays of blatant favoritism in the purchase of supplies. Miller also explained in detail the process by which gold leaf continued to be stolen regularly from the GPO. Nor did he omit references to the activities of labor unions. He assured Garfield that the bookbinders' union, notwithstanding the earlier agitation over his own reinstatement, persisted in interfering with the management of the bindery and in obstructing the introduction of labor-saving machines.[101] Despite the accumulation of evidence regarding "the sorry state of affairs in government printing," Roosevelt apparently decided to postpone any action which risked involving him in a struggle with Congress during an election year.

Shortly after his triumph at the polls in 1904, the President confronted a new controversy in the GPO which corroborated Miller's charges about the letting of contracts. Late in that year, the public printer finally allowed linotype and monotype machines to be installed on a trial basis. Charges of influence-peddling and favoritism surrounded the letting of "these fat contracts." One of the bidders, the Mergenthaler Linotype Company, maintained that Palmer had been "improperly influenced" in reaching a decision in favor of the

[101] Miller to Cortelyou, October 10, 1903, Memorandum by Miller, March 23, 1904, Miller to Garfield, March 28, April 2, 5, 1904, Garfield to Miller, April 14, 1904, Miller to Garfield, April 18, 22, 24, 26, May 2, 1904, Memorandum by Garfield, May 9, 1904, Miller to Garfield, May 29, June 12, 1904, in Garfield Papers.

machines manufactured by the Langston Monotype Company.[102] This new squabble added to the urgency of a plea by two members of Roosevelt's trusted Tennis Cabinet for a committee to investigate "departmental methods" in general. These two were Gifford Pinchot, who had streamlined the Division of Forestry and had aided in efforts to bring about efficiency and economy in other administrative areas, and Garfield, whose experience in organizing the Bureau of Corporations and in investigating the Miller case had awakened him to the need for numerous improvements in the practices of the executive departments. In June, 1905, Roosevelt responded to their suggestions by establishing the Committee on Department Methods, better known as the Keep Commission after its chairman, Charles H. Keep, assistant secretary of the treasury. One of the first assignments of this group was an investigation of the charges regarding the purchase of typesetting machines in the GPO.[103] While the investigation was in progress, Public Printer Palmer became embroiled in a dispute with Oscar L. Ricketts, the foreman of printing and a friend of Miller, who challenged his decision in the purchase of typesetting machines. Ricketts sided with the Mergenthaler Company and maintained that the Langston machines were not suitable for the type of work done in the government printery. The Palmer-Ricketts row, coupled with the Keep Commission report early in August, 1905, charging the public printer with "great partiality and bias" in the selection of the Langston machines, was more than the President would tolerate. He demanded Palmer's resignation effective September 15, 1905, but when Palmer proceeded to dismiss Ricketts for "insubordination," he was summarily discharged. Roosevelt made Ricketts acting public printer.[104]

[102] Memorandum by Cortelyou, August 10, 1903, in Garfield Papers; "The Government Printing Scandal," *Literary Digest,* XXXI (1905), 371–72; *100 GPO Years,* 84–85.

[103] See Harold T. Pinkett, "The Keep Commission, 1905–1909: A Rooseveltian Effort for Administrative Reform," *Journal of American History,* LII (1965), 297–312.

[104] New York *Times,* September 6, 9, 10, 1905; Roosevelt to Lodge, September 6, 1905, in Morison (ed.), *Roosevelt Letters,* V, 12–13; Charles H. Keep, Report to the President, August 4, 1905, Record Group 95, National Archives; William S. Rossiter, "The Problem of Federal Printing," *Atlantic Monthly,*

Throughout the period from 1902 to 1909 the Government Printing Office remained a problem child. Like many government agencies during this era, the GPO attempted to operate under antiquated procedures and often conflicting regulations. It was in fact an administrative floating mass more appropriate for the age of Grant than the age of Roosevelt. The reorganization and reform required by the twentieth century were all the more difficult because of the GPO's unusual nature and function. It was a government-owned manufacturing establishment which enjoyed virtual independence administratively. The Miller incident first exposed to public view the diverse problems which beset the GPO. Although the labor union feature of the incident was of paramount interest at first, Miller's challenge acted as a catalyst to set in motion a series of attempts by Roosevelt to introduce into this sprawling and expensive printing complex a degree of efficiency, economy, and administrative order. In his annual message of 1904 the President reiterated the principle of the open shop in government service which had originally been prompted by the Miller affair. Finally in 1905 Congress joined the President in his "search for efficiency." But evidence of the difficulties in achieving the desired reforms was the rapid turnover in public printers during the Roosevelt administration. Whereas only two men had headed the GPO between 1889 and 1901, there were five public printers between 1901 and 1909. The administrative and fiscal innovations inaugurated by Public Printer Charles A. Stillings in 1905, complemented by additional recommendations from the Keep Commission and the enactment of remedial legislation by Congress two years later, went far toward accomplishing the reforms demanded by Roosevelt. In his last annual message to Congress, the President requested the passage of legislation which would place the GPO under the jurisdiction of the Department of Commerce and Labor. But this recommendation, like most of the others made in 1908, was ignored. Nevertheless, at the end of his term in 1909, he could view the new order in the GPO with considerable pride. In his autobiography, published

XCVI (1905), 331–34; "The Great Government Printing Hopper," *World's Work*, XI (1905), 6924–25.

four years later, he described in some detail the Miller incident which initiated the events that led to this transformation.[105]

The fact that Roosevelt chose to grapple with the questions raised by the Miller incident was in itself significant. He could have refused to become involved in so sensitive an issue, which after all had been pending since the establishment of the GPO. Although his predecessor had steered clear of the closed-shop issue when the electrotypers created a stir in 1897, Roosevelt was convinced that further evasion would lead to serious consequences, especially in view of the prevailing relations between labor and capital. Therefore, he seized the opportunity afforded by the Miller case to establish the principle of the open shop in the federal service. Always skillful in combining good politics and "sound principles," Roosevelt utilized his action in the case to counteract the hostility manifested toward him by certain segments of the business community. At the same time he was extraordinarily successful in allaying the fears of the moderates in the organized labor movement. He shared many of their aspirations even though he opposed some of their tactics, and he was careful to assure them that his reinstatement of Miller had implications only for government employees. Even so, the fact that his action coincided with "the employers' mass advance" meant that it was put to effective use in the open-shop campaigns being waged by such organizations as the National Association of Manufacturers. Writing in 1958, Paul P. Van Riper concluded that as a result of Roosevelt's decision in the Miller case "the federal service has retained an open shop policy ever since." Ironically, William A. Miller, the stormy petrel of the government printery whose protests led to Roosevelt's pronouncement of the open-shop principle, was reinstated in the bookbinders' union in 1907.[106]

[105] Charleston (S.C.) *News and Courier*, August 28, 1907; Roosevelt to Charles B. Landis, February 6, 1908, Roosevelt to John S. Leech, November 20, 1908, in Morison (ed.), *Roosevelt Letters*, VI, 924, 1367–68; *100 GPO Years*, 85–93; "Investigation of Purchases and Employment of Cost-Accounting Services at the Government Printing Office," *House Documents*, 60th Cong., 1st Sess., No. 968.

[106] Van Riper, *History of the United States Civil Service*, 188; Greenberg, "Theodore Roosevelt and Labor," 213. See also A. Viallate, "Etats-Unis," *Annales des Sciences Politiques*, XVIII (1903), 815–17, for a perceptive foreign assessment of the significance of the Miller case.

VI

The Problem of "Dear Maria"

*Mrs. Storer is an awful trial. I wish to Heaven she would
either quit her professional sectarian business or get
Bellamy to leave public life!*

THEODORE ROOSEVELT

President Theodore Roosevelt's summary dismissal of a well-known diplomat early in 1906 brought to a climax an affair that was at once serious and comical. The President's extraordinary action was prompted largely by the activities of Maria Longworth Storer, wife of the American ambassador to Austria-Hungary, who was bent upon having Archbishop John Ireland of St. Paul made a cardinal. A zealous convert to Catholicism, Mrs. Storer assumed the role of a female Warwick and committed such gross indiscretions that Roosevelt finally removed her husband, Bellamy Storer, from the diplomatic service. The "dear Maria" affair, as it was described in the press following the publication of letters which revealed the intimacy between the Roosevelts and the Storers, raised questions about church-state relations and presidential veracity. The Storer-Roosevelt correspondence that appeared at various times in pamphlets and newspapers exposed to public view the extent to which both personal friendships and political obligations were involved in "this cardinal business." In describing the episode years later, Julia

Foraker, wife of the senator from Ohio, recalled that "it involved popes, presidents, cardinals and statesmen, ran through two administrations, provoked vast rages and many laughs, was a seven days' wonder in London, Paris, Rome and Berlin, talked to tatters in Washington, and ended most unhappily." [1] It was not the only occasion in which political pressures were applied to secure a cardinal's hat for an American,[2] but certainly it generated more controversy than any other.

The Storers, both natives of Cincinnati, were people of wealth and social prominence in the city founded by their forebears. A graduate of Harvard College, Bellamy Storer was the son of a famous jurist by the same name and a descendant of William Penn. As a successful lawyer in Cincinnati, he was active in Republican politics and served as a member of Congress from 1891 to 1895. His acquaintances included such well-known Ohio political figures as William McKinley, Mark Hanna, Joseph B. Foraker, and William Howard Taft. But Storer was known less for his political acumen than for his other qualities. Famous for his "manly beauty," he was an urbane, "noble-hearted," "high-minded" individual who espoused philanthropic causes and even occasionally struck off sentimental poems. One contemporary who was wholly unimpressed by such traits characterized him as "a dilettante, a dabbler in the arts and graces, but a man without striking force." [3] Although many

[1] Julia Foraker, *I Would Live It Again: Memories of a Vivid Life* (New York: Harper, 1932), 244. Frederick James Zwierlein, *Theodore Roosevelt and Catholics* (St. Louis: Victor T. Suren, 1956) provides the most complete account of Roosevelt's relations with Catholics in general and with the Storers in particular and is especially useful for its lengthy quotations from unpublished correspondence. For a detailed treatment of Bellamy Storer's diplomatic career in Belgium and Spain, see Mother Christopher Shonahan, R.S.H.M., "The Diplomatic Career of Bellamy Storer in Belgium and Spain, 1897–1902," *American Catholic Historical Society of Philadelphia Records,* LXXXVI (March, 1968), 50–64, and subsequent issues.

[2] See Anson Phelps Stokes, *Church and State in the United States* (3 vols.; New York: Harper, 1950), II, 403–405.

[3] "Bellamy Storer," *Dictionary of American Biography* (New York: Scribner, 1937), XVIII, 93; *The National Cyclopaedia of American Biography* (New York: James T. White, 1901), XI, 338; William D. Orcutt, *Burrows of Michigan and the Republican Party* (2 vols.; New York: Longmans, 1917), II, 46; Mark Sullivan, *Our Times* (6 vols.; New York: Scribner, 1926–35), III, 102–103; "The Storer Incident," *Current Literature,* XLII (1907), 25.

would have disagreed with such a harsh judgment, it was generally conceded that his wife's ambitions for him were disproportionate to his talents for statesmanship and diplomacy. Indeed Mrs. Storer more than compensated for whatever lack of ambition her husband may have had. As witty and charming as she was ingenious, she devoted her abundant energies to the advancement of his career.

The granddaughter of Nicholas Longworth, a founder of Cincinnati, and the aunt of another Longworth of the same name who later married the daughter of Theodore Roosevelt, Maria Storer considered herself "a decorator in pottery and metal." She originated the famous "Rockwood pottery," which won several gold medals at the Paris expositions of 1889 and 1900. A patron of the arts no less than an artist, she sponsored Cincinnati's music festival, which achieved considerable renown in American musical circles. Restless, ambitious, and strong-willed, she was inclined to stifle those whom she befriended with affection and generosity and to be devastatingly vindictive toward her enemies. Her great interest in the affairs of others caused some to consider her "an incorrigible gossip" whose chatter invariably involved stories about persons of importance in political, ecclesiastical, and diplomatic circles on two continents. At the age of nineteen Maria Longworth married George Ward Nichols, by whom she had two children, a son and a daughter. Her marriage to Bellamy Storer soon after Nichols' death in 1885 was regarded as an incomparable match, uniting two of the most prestigious families of the Midwest. Within a few years after her second marriage Mrs. Storer began to move beyond the confines of Cincinnati: her husband went to Congress in 1891, and four years later her daughter married the Marquis de Chambrun, the great-great-grandson of Lafayette. The considerable energy which she later expended in efforts to make her husband ambassador to France was explained in part by her desire to be near her daughter and grandchildren.[4]

---

[4] *The National Cyclopaedia of American Biography*, XI, 338–39; Clara Longworth de Chambrun, *Cincinnati: Story of the Queen City* (New York: Scribner, 1939), 150, 268; *Woman's Who's Who, 1914–1915* (New York: American Commonwealth, 1914), 789; Archie Butt, *Taft and Roosevelt: Intimate Letters of Archie Butt* (2 vols.; Garden City, N.Y.: Doubleday, 1930), I, 267;

The base of Mrs. Storer's activities shifted to Washington when her husband assumed his seat in the House of Representatives. Established in a mansion which quickly became a center of the city's social life, the Storers widened their circle of friends among figures of national prominence. A particular intimacy developed between them and Theodore Roosevelt, the young civil service commissioner. Mrs. Storer and Mrs. Roosevelt became fast friends. Both of the Storers lavished attention upon the Roosevelt children, and "dear Bellamy" became the godfather of Roosevelt's son, Archie. Mrs. Storer came to consider "dear Theodore" as "a younger brother" whose political career warranted her support and cultivation. Roosevelt himself reciprocated the affection which the Storers showed him and his family.[5] "You know very well," he wrote Mrs. Storer in 1895, "that there are but few people in the world as dear to us as you and Bellamy are."[6]

The generosity of the Storers was by no means limited to their new acquaintances in Washington. When their old friend Governor William McKinley of Ohio found himself with a large personal debt which threatened to wreck his political career, the Storers hastened to contribute $10,000 toward its payment. McKinley later admitted that such friends enabled him to go to the White House rather than to the penitentiary. Myron T. Herrick, who was in charge of collecting funds to pay off the debt, suspected that of all the donors only the Storers ever asked a favor in return.[7] At any rate, by the mid-1890's McKinley, no less than Roosevelt, was tied to the Storers by more than mere friendship.

A change in Mrs. Storer's religious life which occurred during her

---

Alice Roosevelt Longworth, *Crowded Hours: Reminiscences* (New York: Scribner, 1935), 125–26; Herbert Peck, "The Amateur Antecedents of Rockwood Pottery," *Bulletin of the Cincinnati Historical Society*, XXVI (1968), 317–37.

[5] Foraker, *I Would Live It Again*, 254–55; Theodore Roosevelt to Anna Roosevelt, December 17, 1893, in Elting Morison (ed.), *The Letters of Theodore Roosevelt* (8 vols.; Cambridge: Harvard, 1951–54), I, 343.

[6] T. Roosevelt to Maria Longworth Storer, October 30, 1891, in Morison (ed.), *Roosevelt Letters*, I, 495.

[7] T. Bentley Mott, *Myron T. Herrick, Friend of France: An Autobiographical Biography* (Garden City, N.Y.: Doubleday, 1929), 48–54, 72–73; Margaret Leech, *In the Days of McKinley* (New York: Harper, 1959), 58–59.

husband's tenure in Congress was to have a significant impact upon his political future and upon their relationship with McKinley and Roosevelt. She appeared to have become infatuated with Buddhism, and their Washington residence was for a time outfitted with an elaborate Buddhist shrine. Later, she was converted to Roman Catholicism, presumably through the influence of her friend Bishop John J. Keane, the liberal rector of the Catholic University of America. Through Keane, she became acquainted with some of the leading spokesmen of liberal Catholicism in America, including Archbishop John Ireland of St. Paul. The correspondence between Mrs. Storer and the archbishop in 1895, during her first visit to the Vatican, indicated "a well established friendship." [8] But her conversion to Catholicism posed political difficulties for her husband in his bid for renomination to Congress in 1894. The clamor of the strongly anti-Catholic American Protective Association, coupled with the opposition of "Boss" George B. Cox of Cincinnati, was sufficient to end his career in Congress.[9] Convinced that Storer was defeated by a "piece of dirty political trickery," Roosevelt tried in vain to persuade President Grover Cleveland to appoint Storer to the position on the Civil Service Commission which he was vacating to become head of the New York City police board.[10]

Although Mrs. Storer was already taking "a hand in church politics," her primary concern was to secure for her husband a public office worthy of his talents. The victory of their old friend McKinley[11] in the presidential election of 1896 provided her with an opportunity to advance three careers simultaneously—those of her husband, Roosevelt, and Archbishop Ireland. Even before the presidential election, the Storers began preparations aimed in this direction. In July, 1896, while they were visiting the Roosevelts at Oyster

[8] Washington *Evening Star*, December 13, 1906; J. H. Moynihan, *The Life of Archbishop Ireland* (New York: Harper, 1953), 345.

[9] Donald L. Kinger, *An Episode in Anti-Catholicism: The American Protective Association* (Seattle: U. of Wash., 1964), 149; M. L. Storer to Myron T. Herrick, March 19, 1897, in William McKinley Papers, Manuscript Division, Library of Congress.

[10] T. Roosevelt to Grover Cleveland, April 20, 1895, in Morison (ed.), *Roosevelt Letters*, I, 443.

[11] The Storers first became acquainted with William McKinley in 1886.

Bay, there was a frank discussion of politics. Arguing that his work on the police board was nearing completion, Roosevelt expressed a desire to become assistant secretary of the navy and made it clear that he would welcome the Storers' influence with McKinley in securing the appointment.[12] "I should rather have you speak in my behalf," he wrote a little later to Storer, "than anyone in the United States, and I think you could do most good." [13] The Storers seized upon the opportunity to advance his cause, while Roosevelt in turn promised to urge Storer's appointment to a cabinet post. McKinley's victory in November, 1896, was the signal for the launching of these respective missions. Roosevelt approached both McKinley and his chief adviser Mark Hanna about the possibility of appointing Storer to an important position. At one time or another he suggested Storer for secretary of war, secretary of the navy, secretary of the treasury, and ambassador to France. Both Hanna and the President-elect were receptive to his arguments; in fact, McKinley felt that Storer had "an earnest and eloquent advocate" in Roosevelt. A host of other influential voices were raised in behalf of Storer's claim for office. Having followed Mrs. Storer into the Catholic church, he received enthusiastic support from Archbishop Ireland, whose endorsement was all the more important because he was credited with swinging a sizable Catholic vote for McKinley. Fully cognizant of his debt to the Storers, McKinley assured Mrs. Storer that her "noble and distinguished husband" would receive "my very best consideration both from head and heart." [14] But Storer's standing in the Republican Party of Ohio figured significantly in determining whether he received an office which his wife considered worthy of him. As McKinley soon discovered, the Storers did not enjoy universal popularity in their native state. When Senator Foraker opposed his

[12] Maria Longworth Storer, "How Theodore Roosevelt Was Appointed Assistant Secretary of the Navy," *Harper's Weekly*, LVI (1912), 8–9.

[13] T. Roosevelt to Bellamy Storer, November 19, 1896, in Morison (ed.), *Roosevelt Letters*, I, 567. See also Roosevelt's letters to B. Storer, June 24, August 10, 1896, and to M. L. Storer, August 10, 1896, *ibid.*, 544–56.

[14] William McKinley to M. L. Storer, December 3, 1896, in McKinley Papers; T. Roosevelt to M. L. Storer, December 5, 1896, in Morison (ed.), *Roosevelt Letters*, I, 568. See also Henry F. Pringle, *Theodore Roosevelt: A Biography* (New York: Harcourt, 1931), 455.

appointment even as assistant secretary of state, President McKinley inquired whether he would consent to a foreign post for Storer. "Certainly, the foreigner the better," Foraker replied. Finally, on May 4, 1897, McKinley appointed his "noble-hearted" friend as minister to Belgium.[15]

In the meantime, the Storers had been more successful in their efforts to secure Roosevelt's appointment. They spoke to those close to McKinley and even traveled to Canton to plead Roosevelt's cause with the President-elect in person. Mrs. Storer, in particular, was bent upon making "McKinley like Theodore as much as we do." In spite of Roosevelt's contribution to the party, McKinley protested that he was "too pugnacious" for a responsible government position. "Give him a chance," Mrs. Storer urged him. Whether the Storers' influence was decisive in persuading McKinley to make him assistant secretary of the navy is open to question. Undoubtedly it carried some weight. But the Storers were convinced that they were wholly responsible for the appointment.[16] Roosevelt too seemed to have given them credit. "I am so very fond of you," he wrote Mrs. Storer, "that I don't mind being under obligations to you." [17] During the next decade this sense of obligation undoubtedly accounted in large part for Roosevelt's indulgent attitude toward Mrs. Storer's machinations.

Deeply grieved at the prospects of leaving Washington, the Storers took up their new residence in Belgium with grave misgivings. The legation in Brussels was scarcely what Mrs. Storer had in mind for "dear Bellamy." She never considered it more than a way station on his road to a prestigious post of ambassadorial rank. Nonetheless, she became an enthusiastic participant in the social life of the Belgian capital, where as usual she and her husband gravitated toward persons of prominence and power. Throughout their tenure in Brussels, the Storers kept up a frequent correspondence with

[15] M. L. Storer to Herrick, March 19, 1897, in McKinley Papers. The statement by Foraker is quoted in Sullivan, *Our Times*, III, 103.

[16] M. L. Storer, "How Theodore Roosevelt Was Appointed Assistant Secretary of the Navy," 8–9; de Chambrun, *Cincinnati*, 284–85.

[17] T. Roosevelt to M. L. Storer, December 5, 1896, in Morison (ed.), *Roosevelt Letters*, I, 569.

Roosevelt and Archbishop Ireland. Mrs. Storer's letters included detailed accounts of political and ecclesiastical happenings in Europe and gossip about her new acquaintances among royalty, statesmen, and church prelates.[18] Roosevelt, who considered her "the best letter writer I know," responded with letters filled with news and opinions about political affairs in the United States as well as observations regarding his own work in the Navy Department. "The Secretary is away," he reported in August, 1897, "and I am having immense fun running the Navy." He assured them of the importance of their diplomatic work, which in his opinion had the additional advantage of removing them from the sordid arena of Ohio politics.[19]

Unwilling to confine themselves to the routine activities related to the legation in Brussels, the Storers were bent upon becoming involved in affairs of larger import. Their visit to the Vatican in 1895, coupled with Storer's entry into the Catholic church the following year and their association with various papal diplomats during their residence in Europe, whetted their appetites for more important roles in diplomacy and ecclesiastical politics. The Spanish-American War also provided an opportunity for them to launch a full-scale campaign to win a red hat for Archbishop Ireland, whom they entertained lavishly during his visit to Belgium in April, 1899. They were convinced that the circumstances created by the war, especially the question of the church lands in the Philippines, necessitated Ireland's membership in the college of cardinals. Not only was he an intimate friend, but he also represented the liberal wing of the church with which they were identified. An opponent of German-Catholic separatism and the Cahensly view,[20] he was an eloquent

18 T. Roosevelt to B. Storer, August 19, 1897, *ibid.*, I, 655.

19 *Ibid.*

20 Maria L. Storer, "Archbishop Ireland and the Red Hat," *Dublin Review*, CLXVIII (1921), 203–204; Moynihan, *Ireland*, 348–49. The Cahensly view was so named because it originated with Peter Cahensly, a German businessman and pious Catholic layman who became alarmed over "the great losses to the Faith among immigrants to the United States." To counteract these losses, Cahensly attempted to persuade the Vatican to institute more foreign representation in the church hierarchy in America. See Robert D. Cross, *The Emergence of Liberal Catholicism in America* (Cambridge: Harvard, 1958), 92–94; Thomas T. McAvoy, *The Great Crisis in American Catholic History, 1895–1900* (Chicago: Regnery, 1957), 66–68.

spokesman of Americanism and a devoted friend of the Republican Party. His position as a champion of liberal Catholicism often pitted him against Archbishop Michael Corrigan of New York. For the Storers, Archbishop Corrigan was the "enemy" not only because he was a spokesman for conservative Catholicism and was the alleged leader of "the Democratic section of the American Catholics" but also because his claims for the cardinalate threatened those of their own candidate.[21] Their desire for Ireland's elevation to the college of cardinals, which assumed the proportions of an obsession by early 1899, became entwined in the negotiations following the Spanish-American War. Having become acquainted with the papal secretary of state, Mariano Rampolla, and other Vatican officials, the Storers never wearied of apprising Rome of Ireland's popularity among both Catholics and Protestants in the United States. Nor did they allow Republican leaders to forget the party's debt to him.

Failing in 1898 to forestall the war by his efforts to act as mediator between Spain, the Vatican, and the McKinley administration, Ireland had won additional plaudits in the United States for his loyal support of the American cause in a war with a Catholic country. The Storers, like many Americans, believed that the elevation to the cardinalate would be an invaluable asset to the United States in the postwar settlement in regard to church matters in the Philippine Islands. Because of his strong Americanist views, they reasoned, he was the most logical candidate. Their efforts in his behalf were undeterred by Pope Leo XIII's official condemnation of a doctrine called "Americanism" early in 1899. In their view Ireland's appointment was all the more essential in order to compensate for the misunderstanding created by the pope's letter on Americanism. There were undoubtedly present at the Vatican forces opposed to Ireland, and unquestionably many conservative Catholics in the United States preferred Corrigan as a recipient of the red hat. This is not to say that Ireland was in disfavor at the Vatican, because the controversy over Americanism apparently resulted only in a temporary loss of prestige for liberal members of the American hierarchy. Ire-

[21] For treatments of the Ireland-Corrigan relationship see Cross, *Emergence of Liberal Catholicism*, 26–27, 38–40, 49; Salvatore Cortesi, *My Thirty Years of Friendships* (New York: Harper, 1927), 192–93.

land, no less than Corrigan, had reason to believe that the cardinalate was within his reach.[22]

The rivalry between Ireland and Corrigan quickened the Storers' determination to fulfill their mission regarding Archbishop Ireland. In March, 1899, they made frantic appeals in his behalf to President McKinley and to Roosevelt, who had become governor of New York. They insisted that Spain favored Corrigan over Ireland and only strong letters to the Vatican from American political leaders would save their plans from utter shipwreck.[23] Reluctant to refuse

---

[22] Frank T. Reuter, *Catholic Influence on American Colonial Policies, 1898–1904* (Austin: U. of Tex., 1967), 8–11; Cross, *Emergence of Liberal Catholicism*, 188–205. The lengthy and acrimonious controversy within the Catholic church over what was described by the rather misleading label *Americanism* involved a conglomeration of teachings and attitudes. Essentially it was a "war of ideas" between conservative and liberal factions. As Pope Leo XIII recognized, those who embraced the false doctrines imputed to the American church were by no means confined to prelates in the United States. Nevertheless, two American archbishops in particular, John Ireland and John J. Keane, were closely identified with the liberal movement. The Americanist controversy grew more intense in 1897 with the appearance of a careless French translation of Walter Elliott's *Life of Father Hecker*, a biography of the American churchman who founded the Congregation of St. Paul (Paulists) and who was widely known for his liberal views. The disturbance created by this book reached such proportions that Leo XIII issued a papal letter on January 22, 1899, which summarized the false doctrines imputed to some members of the American hierarchy. The errors included the adaptation of the church to modern civilization, the relaxation of its ancient rigor, the indulgence to modern methods and theories, the de-emphasis of religious vows, and the granting of "greater scope for the action of the Holy Spirit on the individual soul." The pope affirmed his admiration for the political and social qualities of the American people, which were also called Americanism. Liberals and conservatives alike claimed that the letter vindicated their positions. But liberal American churchmen such as Ireland could scarcely have been oblivious to the fact that, however mild its tone and measured its phrases, the letter constituted a papal condemnation of doctrines called Americanism and was addressed to Cardinal James Gibbons of Baltimore rather than to a prelate in Europe. For brief treatments of the Americanism controversy, see John Tracy Ellis, *American Catholicism* (Chicago: U. of Chicago, 1956), 117–20; Cross, *Emergence of Liberal Catholicism*, 189–201. For a full study see McAvoy, *Great Crisis in American Catholic History*.

[23] B. Storer to T. Roosevelt (Cablegram), March 10, 1899, in McKinley Papers; T. Roosevelt to B. Storer, February 28, 1899, in Morison (ed.), *Roosevelt Letters*, II, 954.

any favor requested by the Storers, Roosevelt nonetheless had serious misgivings about becoming involved in their efforts to promote Ireland. He appreciated the archbishop's contribution to the Republican Party and counted him among his personal friends. In his opinion, it "would be a fortunate thing if we can have him made a cardinal, especially in view of what must occur in the Philippines." Despite such convictions, Roosevelt refused to heed the Storers' request for a cablegram to the Vatican. "It is very hard for me not to do anything you ask," he wrote Mrs. Storer, "but I cannot mix in this cardinal business." [24] But to pacify "dear Maria," Roosevelt did refer the matter to President McKinley and related to him advice from various Catholic friends who insisted that precedents for such endorsements had been established by Washington and Lincoln. Proclaiming his ignorance of "this thing," Roosevelt suggested that "if it is proper in any way to help Archbishop Ireland," he earnestly hoped "it can be done." [25] McKinley, though mindful of the party's debt to Ireland and his potential usefulness in solving the Philippine problem, flatly refused to take any action that would be "regarded as unwarranted intrusion." [26] For Roosevelt, the President's decision was final. There was nothing that he could or should do. Even the Storers, who had their own future to consider at this point, held the matter of Ireland's elevation in abeyance.[27]

As a prominent Catholic in the American diplomatic service, Bellamy Storer was a natural choice as minister to Spain following the restoration of Spanish-American relations after the war. The legation in Madrid may not have been "the blue ribbon post" that Mrs. Storer desired but at least it offered greater opportunities for involvement in important diplomatic and ecclesiastical affairs. Appointed minister to Spain in April, 1899,[28] Storer adequately performed the sundry tasks essential to the reestablishment of friendly

---

[24] T. Roosevelt to M. L. Storer, March 27, May 1, 1899, in Morison (ed.), *Roosevelt Letters*, II, 971–72, 1001.

[25] T. Roosevelt to McKinley, March 13, June 8, 1899, *ibid.*, II, 960, 1019–20.

[26] McKinley to T. Roosevelt, June 13, 1899, in McKinley Papers.

[27] T. Roosevelt to McKinley, June 17, 1899, in Morison (ed.), *Roosevelt Letters*, II, 1021.

[28] New York *Times*, April 12, 1899.

relations between two former belligerents.[29] Within a few months, however, Mrs. Storer wearied of Madrid. Not only did she find the climate disagreeable but also her husband's duties following the signing of treaties became unexciting and unimportant. Anyone with mediocre intelligence could, in her opinion, do the work. It was a waste of incomparable talent to keep "dear Bellamy" in such a post. She spelled out her grievances in a steady flow of correspondence to Roosevelt, who agreed that "Bellamy ought to be made an ambassador." He attempted to dissipate her despair by assurances that the disagreeable work in Spain would pave the way for the assignment of her husband to Paris. Roosevelt, in fact, urged Secretary of State John Hay to keep the Storers in mind in the event that a vacancy should occur in the embassies at Paris or Rome.[30] While waiting for their political friends to arrange for their transfer, Mrs. Storer continued to fret about her unhappy plight. In one of her numerous letters to President McKinley, she wrote that any diplomat, whether Protestant or Catholic, would be welcomed in Madrid so long as his wife was young and beautiful. "With the Spaniards," she declared, "the woman is the more important." That Mrs. Storer was no longer beautiful or young may well have contributed to her discontent.[31] As if to escape what she considered the humdrum existence of Madrid, she spent much time in Biarritz and Rome writing and speaking to influential persons in behalf of Archbishop Ireland.

Several developments in late 1899 and 1900 seemed to indicate success for her designs. Ireland became increasingly involved in the

[29] For Storer's performance as minister to Spain, consult Dispatches from United States Ministers to Spain, 1899–1902 (Microfilm copy in National Archives). William R. Carter, an acquaintance of Bellamy Storer for many years, was wholly unimpressed with his diplomatic accomplishments and complained to the President that Storer was "the most intensely narrow and bitter zealot in his religious views" he had ever known. Carter claimed he had heard Storer publicly state the desirability of a return of the Spanish Inquisition. See William R. Carter to T. Roosevelt, March 25, 1902, in Record Group 59, National Archives.

[30] T. Roosevelt to B. Storer, April 21, 1899, T. Roosevelt to M. L. Storer, December 2, 1899, T. Roosevelt to John Hay, December 6, 1899, in Morison (ed.), *Roosevelt Letters*, II, 992–93, 1101–1102, 1105.

[31] M. L. Storer to McKinley, January 27, 1901, in McKinley Papers.

settlement of the Philippine question in a way that won the gratitude of both the Vatican and the United States government. The Church was well aware of his assistance in securing a friendly commission to deal with the problem of the friars' lands, and the Republican administration appreciated his defense of its colonial policies against the attacks from various Catholic sources.[32] When Mrs. Storer's old friend from Cincinnati, William H. Taft, was appointed to organize the civil government in the Philippines, she hastened to assure him that "no one in the Catholic Church could so efficiently help both sides to a friendly and just solution of all the problems which you will find awaiting you—as Archbishop Ireland." She quoted at length from letters which she had received from "dear Theodore" testifying to his high regard for Ireland. As an old friend of the Storers whose official duties brought him into contact with the Holy See, Taft quickly became the object of their attention.[33] With some degree of success Mrs. Storer attempted to enlist his support for her campaign to make Ireland a cardinal. In the meantime, President McKinley had strengthened her belief that his administration could yet be persuaded to endorse her efforts by his selection of the archbishop to represent the United States at the unveiling of the statue of Lafayette in Paris in the summer of 1900.[34] Ireland traveled from Paris to Rome, where he had a highly satisfactory audience with the pope. Convinced that he was "in highest favor," the archbishop frankly encouraged Mrs. Storer in her campaign to win for him the cardinal's hat. At the same time he urged

---

[32] Cross, *Emergence of Liberal Catholicism*, 203. One of the most delicate problems confronting the United States in the Philippines centered around the powerful position occupied by the Spanish members of four religious orders. Although the controversy over the Spanish friars involved a variety of religious, political, and social issues, an important aspect of the conflict concerned the disposition of the extensive lands which they owned. As a result of prolonged and tedious negotiations, the Vatican was persuaded not only to create a new church hierarchy in the Philippines divorced of Spanish clerical authority but also to sell the friars' lands (410,000 acres) for $7,239,000. In December, 1903, William Howard Taft signed the preliminary contracts for the sale. See Reuter, *Catholic Influence on American Colonial Policies*, 88–103, 151–59.

[33] M. L. Storer to W. H. Taft, February 8, 1900, in McKinley Papers.

[34] Cross, *Emergence of Liberal Catholicism*, 203.

upon Roosevelt and President McKinley the desirability of having Bellamy Storer transferred to the embassy in Paris.[35]

In 1900, when the prospects of making Ireland a cardinal seemed bright, Mrs. Storer tried again to gain a direct endorsement from Roosevelt. Her insistence obviously annoyed him. Roosevelt flatly refused to make further overtures to McKinley in the matter. Repeatedly, he affirmed his high regard for the archbishop and his opinion that Ireland's elevation to the cardinalate would assist in the solution of the problems in the Philippines. But with no less persistence Roosevelt rejected her entreaties to become directly involved in "this cardinal business." [36] "You want me to do all kinds of things that I cannot possibly do," he wrote Mrs. Storer, "and that I ought not to do." Whatever may have been his ignorance of Roman Catholicism or his misconceptions of what constituted the loyalty that "good Catholics" gave the Holy See, he fully understood the zeal of a politically conscious recent convert such as Mrs. Storer. He reminded her that "there are many other people who feel about *their* religion just as you feel about *yours*." [37] His forthright refusal to intrude himself into ecclesiastical matters, despite affirmations of his affection for the Storers, probably would have been sufficient to cause anyone else to quit seeking his help. But Maria Storer was amazingly immune to Roosevelt's plain language. She merely bided her time for a more opportune moment to approach him again.

Although the Storers remained in Europe during the presidential campaign of 1900, they attempted to exert an influence that would at once aid in the election of the Republican ticket headed by McKinley and Roosevelt and advance the cause of Archbishop Ireland. For them secular and ecclesiastical politics had become one. During several visits to Rome in the summer and fall of 1900, they discussed both questions with the pope and high-ranking papal officials.

[35] John Ireland to M. L. Storer, August 5, 1900, Ireland to B. Storer, October 21, December 20, 1900, in Maria L. Storer, *In Memoriam: Bellamy Storer, with Personal Remembrances of President McKinley, President Roosevelt, and John Ireland* (Boston: Merry Mount Press, 1923), 46–48, 51–54, hereinafter cited as M. L. Storer, *In Memoriam.*

[36] T. Roosevelt to M. L. Storer, February 26, April 30, 1900, in Morison (ed.), *Roosevelt Letters*, II, 1201–1202, 1272.

[37] T. Roosevelt to M. L. Storer, May 18, 1900, *ibid.*, 1298–99.

Though Storer had apparently been commissioned to speak about American policies in the Philippines, there is considerable evidence that he did not limit himself to this issue. Shortly after the McKinley-Roosevelt victory in November, 1900, Mrs. Storer wrote the President, "We did what we could do on this side of the ocean by going to Rome and talking with the Pope and Cardinal Rampolla—telling them that it was for the interest of the church that all good Catholics should vote for you and your administration in the new colonies." [38] By the same token, she again suggested, it would be to the advantage of all Americans to have Ireland made a cardinal "because in that position he will have immense advantage and influence with the Vatican which will help our country in every way." [39] But the Storers did not even await the outcome of the election to offer their mansion in Washington rent-free to Roosevelt. Suffering a financial strain at the time of his election as Vice President, he accepted their offer on the condition that he pay them the relatively low rent which he would have to spend for a smaller, less adequate house.[40]

Despite the generosity of the Storers, some of their activities had begun to disturb Roosevelt. During the presidential campaign he first learned that in her correspondence with others Mrs. Storer had quoted extensively from letters which he had written to her regarding Ireland and the cardinalate. For an astute politician like Roosevelt, the danger inherent in Mrs. Storer's practice of invoking his name in Ireland's behalf was all too obvious. "I understand absolutely, oh warmest of friends and staunchest of supporters," he wrote her, "what your motives are!" [41] Nevertheless, his letter was clearly

[38] M. L. Storer to McKinley, November 25, 1900, in McKinley Papers.
[39] *Ibid.*
[40] T. Roosevelt to B. Storer, July 27, 1900, in Morison (ed.), *Roosevelt Letters*, II, 1366. See also B. Storer to T. Roosevelt, April 1, 1901, in Theodore Roosevelt Papers, Manuscript Division, Library of Congress. Roosevelt never lived in the Storers' house because he became President a month before he was scheduled to occupy it. See Maria L. Storer, *Theodore Roosevelt: The Child* (London: W. Straker, 1921), 48 n.
[41] T. Roosevelt to M. L. Storer, November 23, 1900, in Morison (ed.), *Roosevelt Letters*, II, 1437–38. Roosevelt maintained that what had disturbed his political friends was an allusion to "Protestant fanaticism" in his letter to Mrs. Storer on March 27, 1899.

a warning to Mrs. Storer, however mild its wording, that excerpts from his private letters were not to be bandied about freely in her maneuverings to gain the red hat for Ireland. Bellamy Storer at least appeared to be sensitive to Roosevelt's remonstrance and attempted to smooth over any difficulties created by his wife. Roosevelt, obviously hoping that his reprimand had produced the desired effect, hastened to assure Storer that he could not possibly "be such an ungrateful fool as to become angry with your dear wife." [42] With this source of friction quickly dispelled, the Storers lost little time in renewing their pressures upon the new Vice President to aid them in the fulfillment of their various ambitions. Still keenly aware of his obligation to them, Roosevelt wrote them in April, 1901, "My dear friends, you cannot imagine how badly I have felt at times for fear you would feel that I was ungrateful or was not trying to do what I ought to in reference to you." [43] Although he protested that his office of Vice President was without power or influence, he did join with Archbishop Ireland to secure from McKinley a commitment to have Storer sent as ambassador to either France or Austria as soon as it could be arranged.[44]

If Mrs. Storer's plans for her husband seemed near success in 1901, her efforts on behalf of Archbishop Ireland received a serious setback. The consistory which took place in that year failed to result in his elevation to the cardinalate. Both of the Storers were disappointed and saddened by what they considered an obvious slight caused by evil influences at work at the Vatican.[45] Bellamy Storer even predicted that Ireland "would never receive the cardinal's hat." [46] His wife, however, was anything but discouraged. At this juncture she decided to play her trump cards by placing in the hands of her special friend at Rome, Cardinal Rampolla, two letters from

[42] T. Roosevelt to B. Storer, November 27, 1900, *ibid.*, 1445.
[43] T. Roosevelt to B. and M. L. Storer, April 17, 1901, *ibid.*, III, 56.
[44] T. Roosevelt to M. L. Storer, March 6, 11, April 25, 1901, *ibid.*, 4–5, 10, 68; Ireland to M. L. Storer, May 2, 1901, in M. L. Storer, *In Memoriam,* 54–56.
[45] Ireland to M. L. Storer, May 2, 1901, in M. L. Storer, *In Memoriam,* 54–56; Taft to M. L. Storer, May 19, 1901, in *Letter of Bellamy Storer to the President and the Members of the Cabinet, November, 1906* (n.p., n.d.), 9–10, hereinafter cited as *Letter of Bellamy Storer.*
[46] Quoted in Moynihan, *Ireland,* 351.

Roosevelt in which he had expressed his personal pleasure at the possibility of Ireland's elevation. These letters assumed a new importance in the fall of 1901 when McKinley's death suddenly placed Roosevelt in the White House.

Rumors soon reached Washington to the effect that Vatican officials possessed documentary evidence of President Roosevelt's endorsement of Ireland. Such rumors treated the position of cardinal as if it were an important postmastership or some other bit of patronage to be used as a reward for services rendered to the Republican Party. Roosevelt himself was profoundly disturbed by the whole turn of events, and he was especially disturbed to learn that Cardinal Rampolla had "at least one letter" which he had written to Mrs. Storer while he was governor of New York.[47] The source of this information is not known, but in all probability it was Eugene A. Philbin, an old friend and a prominent New York Catholic, who had little sympathy with Mrs. Storer's intrigues. Roosevelt was well aware that any publicity of his involvement in Mrs. Storer's campaign would not only alienate those Catholics favoring Corrigan but would also create an uproar in Protestant circles. The effect might well jeopardize the final settlement of the friars' lands in the Philippines, not to mention his own political standing. Early in January, 1902, President Roosevelt informed Mrs. Storer of the grave mischief which her use of his letters might conceivably cause and urged her to get back into her possession all correspondence from him. "A most resolute effort has been made," he declared, "to mix up facts and try to show that, as president, I have been endeavoring to interfere with ecclesiastical matters." [48] Mrs. Storer, suspicious that "someone was trying to make trouble between herself and Roosevelt," protested loudly that the only object of her activities was to help her country and her church by making sure that the reactionaries in her church did not sabotage Ireland's claim to the cardinalate.[49] Her penitence and Roosevelt's indulgence again prevented

[47] T. Roosevelt to B. Storer, January 16, 1902, in Morison (ed.), *Roosevelt Letters*, III, 218.

[48] T. Roosevelt to M. L. Storer, February 17, 1902, *ibid.*, 232.

[49] M. L. Storer to T. Roosevelt, January 30, 1902, in Roosevelt Papers. Cardinal Rampolla returned Roosevelt's letters to Mrs. Storer, who offered to

any rupture in their relationship. In the spring of 1902 the Storers were guests at the White House during a brief visit to the United States. Although their discussion with the President regarding Archbishop Ireland was not altogether satisfactory to Mrs. Storer, the bonds of friendship were as firm as ever.[50] Roosevelt, in fact, went to considerable trouble in arranging for them to be transferred from Madrid. At first he considered the Berlin embassy but later decided to make Storer ambassador to Austria-Hungary. "Theodore," Henry Adams declared in April, 1902, "has upset the whole diplomatic service in order to make the Bellamy Storers an embassy." They were destined for Vienna rather than Berlin, according to Adams, because of the "Kaiser's deadly fear of Mrs. Bellamy." [51]

If Roosevelt believed that either the reprimand regarding the use of his letters or the transfer to Vienna would in any measure affect Mrs. Storer's behavior, he was sorely disappointed. In fact, her activities in behalf of Ireland assumed more serious proportions when they became involved with the diplomatic mission which Roosevelt dispatched to Rome in 1902 for the purpose of negotiating directly with the Vatican for the purchase of the friars' lands in the Philippines.[52] For several years Mrs. Storer had maintained a lively interest in the settlement of the land question. She regularly offered advice to Governor Taft and took it upon herself to save her friend Papal Secretary Rampolla from being misled by his own emissary on the American position regarding the Philippines. She also corresponded frequently with Ireland, who figured prominently in the preliminary discussions of the mission to the Vatican. Although the archbishop was unable to prevail upon Roosevelt to place Bellamy Storer at the head of it, he and Mrs. Storer were wholly satisfied

---

give them back to the President. But Roosevelt assured her, "That is all right. You need not bring the letters. All I want you to do is keep them *yourself.*" See *Letter of Bellamy Storer,* 14–15.

[50] Ireland to M. L. Storer, March 29, 1902, in M. L. Storer, *In Memoriam,* 65–67; M. L. Storer to T. Roosevelt, March 28, 1902, in Roosevelt Papers.

[51] Henry Adams to Elizabeth Cameron, April 20, 1902, in Worthington C. Ford (ed.), *Letters of Henry Adams* (2 vols.; Boston: Houghton, 1938), II, 389.

[52] For a treatment of the Taft mission to Rome see Reuter, *Catholic Influence on American Colonial Policies,* 137–59.

with the selection of Taft.[53] When Taft failed to accomplish the specific aim of his mission, some observers interpreted it as the result of animosities between "the Ireland and Corrigan factions." Even Taft himself saw this rivalry as a factor but also maintained that the "opposition to Archbishop Ireland among the monastic orders added zeal to those who opposed our purpose." [54] Roosevelt learned that Mrs. Storer had distributed to various papal officials Taft's letters to her "about Ireland for the cardinal's hat." "Apparently," he wrote Taft, "they were used to some effect to help beat negotiations and were certainly used to arouse feeling against them among Catholics in this country." [55]

The linking of Ireland's name to the Taft mission revived rumors about Roosevelt's endorsement of him for the cardinalate.[56] Stories about Mrs. Storer's use of the names of Roosevelt and Taft in connection with her campaign in Ireland's behalf were no longer confined to official circles. So widespread had they become by the fall of 1902 that the Chicago *Northwestern Christian Advocate*, a Methodist publication, editorialized about the President's involvement in Catholic politics. Shortly afterward the Wisconsin Methodist Conference called upon the President to refute allegations that "he had asked Rome to make Archbishop Ireland a cardinal." [57] The pro-Roosevelt press dismissed such rumors as "a silly newspaper fiction" and assured disturbed Protestants that the President "has too keen a sense of propriety to make such a mistake." [58] Fortunately

[53] M. L. Storer to Taft, February 8, 1900, in McKinley Papers; Ireland to B. Storer, December 3, 1901, March 26, 1902, Ireland to M. L. Storer, March 29, 1902, in M. L. Storer, *In Memoriam*, 58–60, 62–65; Philip C. Jessup, *Elihu Root* (2 vols.; New York: Dodd, 1938), I, 364–67.

[54] Salvatore Cortesi, "The First American Mission to the Vatican," *Independent*, LIV (1902), 1942–45; Cortesi, *My Thirty Years of Friendships*, 182–96; Taft to T. Roosevelt, September 13, 1902, in Roosevelt Papers.

[55] T. Roosevelt to Taft, in Morison (ed.), *Roosevelt Letters*, III, 303.

[56] One reason for the linking of Ireland's name with the Taft mission to the Vatican was that Bishop Thomas O'Gorman of Sioux Falls was a member of the delegation. O'Gorman was an intimate friend of Ireland. See Cortesi, "The First American Mission to the Vatican," 1942–45.

[57] Atlanta *Constitution*, September 16, 1902; Chicago *Tribune*, September 17, 1902.

[58] Chicago *Tribune*, September 17, 1902.

for Roosevelt, Mrs. Storer's preoccupation with the move to Vienna at this juncture temporarily interrupted her pursuit of the cardinal's hat for Ireland, causing a lull in the rumors.

The Storers, at last ensconced in a diplomatic post of ambassadorial rank, became "reconciled" to Vienna, though it was their third choice after Paris and Berlin. Archbishop Ireland, ever a faithful correspondent of his chief advocate, advised Mrs. Storer, "Lift up your head: be proud of your title—ambassadrice à Vienne." He added, "Don't forget me amid the splendors of the 'Saison Viennoise.' " [59] He also provided her with the names of various individuals in Rome who would look with favor upon his elevation to the cardinalate and assured her that Roosevelt, "as regards Catholic matters," was "becoming better and better each day." [60] Although Mrs. Storer was searching for a suitable "palazzo" and busy establishing herself in "Austrian high life," the promotion of the archbishop was never far from the center of her interests. New friends acquired in Vienna, where she quickly became a favorite at the imperial court, as well as the growing circle of her acquaintances at the Vatican, served to enhance her crusade. Nor did she fail to call upon politically influential friends in the United States.

By the summer of 1903 the Storers were again deeply involved in the prosecution of their "cardinal business." At last, it appeared to them, Roosevelt was ready to lend direct support to their cause. During a leave of absence from Vienna in the summer of 1903, they visited the President and his family at Oyster Bay. A lengthy conversation regarding Archbishop Ireland which took place during this visit later became a matter of much dispute. The Storers insisted that Roosevelt, though refusing to put anything in writing, directed them "to go to Rome and say, *viva voce*, to the Pope" how much the archbishop's elevation would be appreciated by him. A little later, Ireland himself reported that the President had told him of his commission to the Storers. It was also Ireland who first informed them that earlier in the year Roosevelt had authorized

[59] Ireland to M. L. Storer, September 28, 1902, in M. L. Storer, *In Memoriam*, 73–74.
[60] Ireland to M. L. Storer, April 5, July 28, September 11, 1903, *ibid.*, 74–81.

Bishop Denis O'Connell, a close friend of the archbishop, "to say the same thing to the Pope." According to one of the Storers' journalistic acquaintances at Rome, O'Connell arrived at the Vatican at a "very unpropitious moment," because Pope Leo lay on his death bed, and O'Connell's message from Roosevelt had to be delivered to the new pontiff, Pius X, who "was not well acquainted with many church questions." Nevertheless Pope Pius reportedly was favorable to the President's suggestion and declared that "his wishes in regard to Mgr. Ireland will most probably be fulfilled." When a news service reported that an American prelate had visited the new pope in Ireland's behalf at the request of the President, the White House flatly denied that Roosevelt had authorized anyone to speak for him.[61]

Lest the denial do their cause harm at Rome, the Storers were anxious to perform their "commission" immediately. Haste was all the more necessary because of rumors that a consistory was to take place early in 1904. Archbishop Ireland again apprised them of those whom he considered his friends in Rome so that preliminary contacts with them might pave the way for a favorable response to their mission. Although his role in settling the church lands dispute in the Philippines—a settlement nearing completion—had earned him the enmity of the friar cardinals, others of importance, especially Cardinal Francesco Satolli, were well disposed toward him. The Storers, in the meantime, "made friendly advances to the new papal secretary," Rafael Merry del Val, the successor to Rampolla and a Spaniard who was not expected to be sympathetic toward Ireland. On December 2, 1903, in a lengthy audience with Pope Pius, they delivered the message regarding Ireland's elevation which Roosevelt had supposedly authorized. According to Mrs. Storer, the pope responded, "I will consider what you have said to me on the part of President Roosevelt." Despite the fact that this reply was substantially less encouraging than the one given O'Connell, Ireland hastened to assure the Storers that their visit was "a masterpiece of diplomatic art." And Bellamy Storer claimed that imme-

[61] Ireland to M. L. Storer, October 23, 1903, in M. L. Storer, *In Memoriam*, 81–84.

diately afterward he sent Roosevelt "a personal and confidential letter, giving a full account of what occurred."[62] Despite efforts to keep the visit confidential and secret, it was the subject of a news dispatch which reported that the pope had been urged to give Ireland the red hat. Protestant reaction to the news was sharp. The New York *Christian Advocate*, a Methodist publication, denounced Storer for "running after popes and cardinals" in order for the Republican Party to pay its debts to Ireland. The Loyal Orange Institution, a strongly anti-Catholic society, described the ambassador as "a disgrace" who "played with the national honor in the furtherance of the justifiable ambition of an ecclesiastic to whom he owes his advancement." *Leslie's Weekly* characterized the whole incident as a dangerous precedent in church-state relations.[63]

Roosevelt's reaction to the news, coupled with his previous denial of sending any message to the pope by Bishop O'Connell, seemed to raise doubt as to whether either the bishop or the ambassador had been authorized to speak for him in Ireland's behalf. The President never attempted to hide his personal admiration and friendship for the archbishop and repeatedly stated that his elevation to the cardinalate no less than the promotion of his other clerical friends, both Catholic and Protestant, would give him great satisfaction. Undoubtedly his preoccupation in 1903 with insuring his own nomination and election in the following year quickened his appreciation of the archbishop's influence with Catholic voters. But Roosevelt was far too sophisticated a politician to be oblivious to the potential dangers of any direct involvement in this "cardinal business." There were too many good Republicans who would not brook such "coquetting with Rome." And if he decided to become involved, his previous experience with the Storers would apparently have been sufficient to make him wary of entrusting them with such a delicate mission. It may well have been that Bishop O'Connell and the

[62] *Letter of Bellamy Storer*, 15–19; Ireland to B. Storer, November 11, 1903, Ireland to M. L. Storer, November 13, 1903, Ireland to B. Storer, November 24, December 6, 1903, January 5, 1904, in M. L. Storer, *In Memoriam*, 84–94.

[63] John F. Lemmon to Hay, December 24, 1903, including a clipping from the New York *Christian Advocate*, in Roosevelt Papers; *Leslie's Weekly*, XCVII (1903), 610.

Storers allowed their devotion to Ireland's cause to mislead them into believing that what the President said in private conversations was intended as an official endorsement. Even if Roosevelt waxed enthusiastic about the archbishop's promotion, as he undoubtedly did, Ireland's advocates could scarcely have been wholly unaware of the need for discretion in using his name. Indiscretion on their part was almost certain to defeat their quest for the red hat.[64]

Regardless of whether Roosevelt did or did not authorize anyone to speak to the pope, he appeared shocked to learn that his utterances in regard to Ireland had been quoted at the Vatican. In the latter half of December, 1903, the President wrote Storer three letters expressing his grave concern about the use of his name in connection with Ireland's elevation. On December 19, 1903, he informed Storer that although he had expressed to Bishop O'Connell his high regard for Ireland and had indicated that his elevation to the cardinalate would be most welcomed, he "could not as President in any way try to help any clergyman of any denomination to high rank in that denomination."[65] Then, after Storer's own visit to Rome created a stir in the press, Roosevelt ordered him "not to quote me in any way or shape hereafter." The President declared,

> What has occurred shows clearly that it is hopeless for you to expect that people will appreciate the differences between what you, as an American Catholic, in your private capacity, say, and what you, as an American ambassador, say. I take it for granted that you supposed you were speaking merely in your private capacity, to people who would not misunderstand you, and who would not repeat what you said. Your faith has evidently been misplaced. In view of what has occurred I must ask you, while you are in the United States service, to take no part either directly or indirectly in such a matter as this, and hereafter to repeat to no man what I have said to you concerning the subject.[66]

Although Roosevelt as usual sent his "love to Maria," his letter was

---

[64] For Henry F. Pringle's assessment of the affair see his *Roosevelt: A Biography*, 454–58.

[65] T. Roosevelt to B. Storer, December 19, 1903, quoted in Zwierlein, *Theodore Roosevelt and Catholics*, 98.

[66] T. Roosevelt to B. Storer, December 27, 1903, in Morison (ed.), *Roosevelt Letters*, III, 683.

unmistakably a rebuke. In a fit of frustration at what appeared to her as the President's determination to foil all their efforts in Ireland's behalf, Mrs. Storer resolved to "retire from diplomatic relations with the Vatican, leaving all that *business* to Bellamy." [67] But Archbishop Ireland's entreaties soon persuaded her to abandon such notions. Neither she nor her husband was willing to admit that her activities "as a private citizen" had any relationship to his position as an official of the United States government. Interestingly enough, however, her husband never for a moment entertained any notions of forsaking Ireland. A "rather fatuous incapacity to recognize an imperative order" characterized his reaction to the presidential rebuke.[68] Storer not only defended his action but also appealed to Roosevelt to recognize the real value of it. The purpose of all their efforts in behalf of Ireland, Storer explained, was to insure the Republican Party the support of Catholic voters.[69]

Roosevelt had reasons for being dissatisfied with the ambassador other than his visit to the Vatican and his response to an executive reprimand. Much to his dismay Storer took up the cause of Carlton B. Hurst, the son of a Methodist bishop who had been dismissed as consul general in Vienna. Convinced that the young man had been treated shabbily by the State Department, Storer attempted to intercede in his behalf by writing directly to Senator Hanna. Secretary of State Hay was "exceedingly indignant" over his presumptuousness and recommended that the ambassador be given "some official rebuke." Instead Roosevelt wrote him a personal letter apprising him of the impropriety of commenting to an "outsider" upon a removal directed by the President on the advice of the State Department. Storer's assurance that he no longer had "the slightest personal interest in Hurst" seemed to satisfy Roosevelt.[70] That the

[67] Ireland to M. L. Storer, January 9, 1904, in M. L. Storer, *In Memoriam*, 95.

[68] Sullivan, *Our Times*, III, 115.

[69] B. Storer to T. Roosevelt, January 10, 1904, in *Letter of Bellamy Storer*, 21–24.

[70] *Ibid.*; T. Roosevelt to B. Storer, December 30, 1903, in Morison (ed.), *Roosevelt Letters*, III, 685–86; B. Storer to Mark Hanna, May 9, 1903, in Record Group 59, National Archives. Although Carlton Bailey Hurst described the Storers as "the most cultivated and distinguished people that ever graced our Foreign Service," he omits any mention of the circumstances sur-

convention and election of 1904 were in the offing may well have figured in Roosevelt's decision to patch up any rift with the Storers. Certainly he desired to avoid anything likely to have an adverse effect upon his popularity among Catholics. "It is absolutely all right," Roosevelt wrote Storer in January, 1904. "We will treat the incident as closed. Nothing could persuade me to accept your resignation, old fellow." [71] By the spring of 1904 cordial relations, overtly at least, had been reestablished between the President and the Storers.

Although Archbishop Ireland was at first elated by the Storers' visit to Rome in his behalf, he too came to have misgivings about further activities on their part. Undoubtedly he recognized that publicity of the type prompted by their visit would hardly improve his chances of gaining the red hat. He had probably heard rumors then in circulation to the effect that Mrs. Storer's "meddling" had annoyed both the pope and Cardinal Merry del Val. Furthermore, Ireland was worried about the activities of others who championed his cause, such as Senator Nathan B. Scott and T. St. John Gaffney, the American consul at Dresden, whose machinations merely complicated matters. Still dubious of Merry del Val, the archbishop preferred to entrust his case to Cardinal Satolli and the two brothers, the Cardinals Vannutelli.[72] "All that should have been done to influence the Vatican has been done," Ireland wrote Mrs. Storer early in April, 1904, "—anything else would be *de trop*. If the Vatican does not now yield, 'tant pis pour lis.' I will not for my part take another hand's turn to sway it—neither should my friends." [73] Yet he continued to send the Storers strange assurances that Secretary of War Taft as well as President Roosevelt considered them their spokesmen at Rome.

Even if Ireland was "quite reconciled to the outcome, whatever it

---

rounding his dismissal from the Vienna post. See his *The Arms above the Door* (New York: Dodd, 1932), 79–80.

[71] T. Roosevelt to B. Storer, January 29, 1904, in *Letter of Bellamy Storer*, 24–25.

[72] Ireland to M. L. Storer, January 9, 1904, Ireland to B. Storer, February 4, 1904, in M. L. Storer, *In Memoriam*, 94–101.

[73] Ireland to M. L. Storer, April 5, 1904, *ibid.*, 103.

may be"—and he was scarcely as reconciled as his letters indicated—the Storers were as unrelenting as ever in their quest. Mrs. Storer in particular courted the favor of Merry del Val, and by the summer of 1904 she appeared to be convinced that the papal secretary was sympathetic to her schemes to get Ireland the red hat.[74] All the while she persuaded certain friends acquired at the Austrian court to take part in her crusade. One of these, Princess Alexandrine Windisch-Graetz, provided a valuable contact with the pope himself, whom she had known as Patriarch of Venice. On March 25, 1904, when the princess had an audience with Pope Pius, she read him a letter from Mrs. Storer "concerning Archbishop Ireland." The Holy Father responded, "I have studied the question—it will be done." At last the matter seemed to be settled. Princess Alexandrine reported that Ireland would "be made a cardinal at the next consistory," which would probably meet late in 1904 or sometime in 1905.[75] Mrs. Storer immediately transmitted these glad tidings to the archbishop, who interpreted this triumph as the result of her "ceaseless planning and working." He wrote her, "Take all the credit yourself, yourself including my dear Bellamy." [76] With Cardinal Merry del Val "well in hand" and the pope committed to Ireland, the Storers seemed near to achieving their long-sought goal. Their main concern was to make sure that nothing went askew before the consistory took place. At the moment their only anxiety was caused by reports that the pope was displaying some interest in Archbishop John Farley, Corrigan's successor in New York. News that John D. Crimmins, a friend of Roosevelt and a former Rough Rider, was in Rome to press Farley's claim to the red hat was disturbing. Although Ireland was certain that Crimmins had used his friendship with Roosevelt in promoting Farley, he assured the Storers that nothing would come of his efforts.[77]

Roosevelt was aware of Mrs. Storer's activities even if her letters to him were less frequent. He was kept informed by Secretary Taft,

[74] See Ireland to M. L. Storer, February 2, 1904, *ibid.*, 99.

[75] Alexandrine Windisch-Graetz to M. L. Storer, April 1, 1904, in *Letter of Bellamy Storer*, 55–56.

[76] Ireland to M. L. Storer, April 24, 1904, in M. L. Storer, *In Memoriam*, 107.

[77] Ireland to B. Storer, April 25, 1904, *ibid.*, 110.

with whom she corresponded regularly. Whether Taft was her "truest friend," as Ireland reported, it does appear that he went even further than Roosevelt in endorsing her various schemes.[78] Certainly he received advice from her on a wide range of topics, from how to solve the Philippine question to how Merry del Val should be handled. Exasperated by her persistent "meddling," the President wrote Taft in July, 1904, "Mrs. Storer is an awful trial. I wish to heaven she would either quit her professional sectarian business or get Bellamy to leave public life!" He encouraged Taft to "pay no attention to her." [79] Despite his pique, the President invited the Storers to the White House in the autumn of 1904 when they made their annual trip to the United States. As usual, Archbishop Ireland became a chief topic of conversation. What the President said about him on the evening of October 20, 1904, so impressed Mrs. Storer that she made it the subject of a memorandum. According to her account, Roosevelt told her of a conversation with Cardinal Satolli in which he expressed his admiration for Ireland as a churchman and as a force for civic good. Satolli apparently reported his remarks to the Vatican. To Mrs. Storer, according to her memorandum, the President said, "I do most sincerely hope that Archbishop Ireland may be made a Cardinal at the next Consistory. Nothing could help me more in matters connected with the Church here and in the Philippines. I have done everything and said everything which it is possible for me to say and do in the matter. I certainly said enough to Cardinal Satolli (without mentioning the cardinal's hat which of course I could not do) to show my wishes and desires should the Pope see fit to gratify them." [80] The Storers interpreted this statement as an endorsement of the very intrigues for which they previously had been rebuked. Actually, Roosevelt said

---

[78] Zwierlein, *Theodore Roosevelt and Catholics*, 56. See also de Chambrun, *Cincinnati*, 287. Clara Longworth de Chambrun suggests that the breach which later developed between Taft and Roosevelt was related to their differences over the handling of the "dear Maria" affair.

[79] T. Roosevelt to Taft, July 11, 1904, in Morison (ed.), *Roosevelt Letters*, III, 853–54. Roosevelt suggests in this letter that Mrs. Storer's meddling may have caused him some concern regarding its political consequences during the campaign of 1904.

[80] Quoted in *Letter of Bellamy Storer*, 27.

nothing more in the conversation than he had been saying for five years. In view of what had happened in the previous year, anyone other than the Storers might well have detected a note of exasperation in the President's comments, and even they should have been able to comprehend what he meant by saying that there was nothing more that he could do for Ireland. But the reprimand of the previous year seems to have been forgotten.

The Storers returned to Vienna convinced that all was well between them and the President. That such was not the case became evident early in 1905, when Mrs. Storer again pleaded with Roosevelt to make her husband ambassador to Paris or, if that embassy was not available, to send him to Berlin or London. The President pointedly removed all hopes of gaining the Paris post because the French government had indicated that political conditions did not make the appointment of a Catholic advisable. As a formality Storer submitted his resignation after Roosevelt's election in November, 1904. The President's rather strange reply, which was not altogether lost upon the Storers, stated that "dear Bellamy" would either be reappointed or his resignation would not be accepted, depending upon what Secretary Hay advised. He held out virtually no hope for Storer's transfer and indicated that he might have to give up the Vienna post within three years. Clearly it was no longer a question of the Paris embassy but either Vienna or nothing—and possibly Vienna for only three more years.[81] Several weeks after receipt of Roosevelt's letter, Mrs. Storer learned indirectly from acquaintances in Paris that the President was "hurt" by her accusation that he had treated her husband unfairly by refusing him an appointment to a more prestigious post. She hastened to ask forgiveness for any "hurt" that her unwarranted remarks may have caused him and explained them as merely the expressions of a devoted and disappointed wife. But she reminded Roosevelt, "I have cared for you as if you were a younger brother." Apparently she was forgiven, because Roosevelt promised to grant her request that "dear Bellamy" be appointed

[81] T. Roosevelt to M. L. Storer, January 9, 1905, in Morison (ed.), *Roosevelt Letters*, III, 1095–96; T. Roosevelt to B. Storer, January 9, 1905, in *Letter of Bellamy Storer*, 28.

special ambassador to Madrid "in the event of the marriage of the King of Spain." [82]

Mrs. Storer's disappointment over having to remain in Vienna in no way dampened her enthusiastic support of Archbishop Ireland. Until late in the autumn of 1905 she assumed that his elevation to the cardinalate was settled. Presumably the meeting of the consistory in December would bring to fruition her years of labor. Then, quite suddenly, rumors were revived that Ireland's elevation was in doubt primarily because of efforts by friends of Archbishop Farley to secure for him a red hat.[83] Panic-stricken, Mrs. Storer made inquiries of Cardinal Merry del Val, whose response confirmed her worst fears. "I must inform you that, as far as I know," the Cardinal wrote, "there will be no American cardinal named at the next Consistory." He also informed her that the names of two "very distinguished prelates" other than that of Ireland were being urged upon the Holy Father. Despite Merry del Val's insistence that "any attempt to bring pressure to bear in such a delicate matter" would be harmful,[84] Mrs. Storer sought to persuade President Roosevelt and Secretary Taft to intercede in order to save Ireland's chances to become a cardinal. Her actions at this point were those of a desperate woman frantically attempting to save years of scheming and negotiation from utter defeat.

The President first learned of her latest effort from Taft, who showed him a letter from her. Upon inquiry he found that Mrs. Roosevelt had also received a letter from "dear Maria" addressed to him. Mrs. Roosevelt had treated this letter as she had treated others from Mrs. Storer which she knew would make the President indignant: she simply had not delivered it to him. Roosevelt was shocked and infuriated by Mrs. Storer's latest correspondence. In it she reviewed Ireland's chances of becoming a cardinal and repeated rumors that Eugene A. Philbin had been dispatched to Rome with a request from Roosevelt that Archbishop Farley also be given a red hat. In support of these rumors she quoted Cardinal Merry del Val

[82] M. L. Storer to T. Roosevelt, April 30, 1905, in Roosevelt Papers.

[83] M. L. Storer to T. Roosevelt, November 20, 1905, in *Letter of Bellamy Storer*, 29–30.

[84] Rafael Merry del Val to M. L. Storer, November 23, 1905, *ibid.*, 55–56.

as saying, "The President of the United States has asked for the elevation of two archbishops, therefore he cannot care very much for either." [85] She explained to the President what a disaster it would be for "the reactionary element" represented by Farley to receive recognition at the expense of Ireland. Convinced that Ireland's chances would be destroyed by the movement in behalf of Farley, she begged Roosevelt to send a cable to the pope denying any endorsement of the New York archbishop. "I could take a cable from you to Rome myself," she pleaded, "and put it directly in the Pope's hand without Cardinal Merry del Val's knowledge or interference. You can trust me really." [86] Her plea for Roosevelt not to be angry was of no avail whatsoever. His reaction was immediate and stated "in the plainest kind of plain language."

Roosevelt's reply to Mrs. Storer was enclosed in a letter to her husband. Clearly he was serving notice on the ambassador. In fact, his communication was more than a warning; it was a threat. Roosevelt dismissed as absurd Mrs. Storer's request that she be "authorized to go to Rome to take part in . . . an ecclesiastical intrigue." He reviewed what he considered her extraordinary record of indiscretion, which not only compromised her husband's career but also threatened to put the American government in a "false and wholly improper position." The President wrote, "For the last couple of years, I have continually been hearing of your having written one man or the other about such matters. I find that you are alluded to by foreign members of the diplomatic body in Washington, Paris and Berlin as the 'American ambassadress to Rome.' I was unofficially informed on behalf of both Berlin and Paris that because of these actions of yours it would not be agreeable to them to have Bellamy come as ambassador to either place." Roosevelt requested that all his letters be returned lest the Storers continue to quote "isolated sentences" from them in their advocacy of Ireland. He also demanded that "so long as her husband remained in the diplomatic service" Mrs. Storer promise to refrain from involvement in "this cardinal's hat business." Roosevelt wrote her, "I must ask you to

[85] Quoted in M. L. Storer, *In Memoriam*, 111.
[86] M. L. Storer to T. Roosevelt, November 20, 1905, in *Letter of Bellamy Storer*, 29–30.

give this promise in writing if Bellamy is to remain in the service."
Under the circumstances he did not feel that Storer could be sent
to Madrid as the special ambassador at the royal wedding.[87]

The President's stern rebuke struck home. The Storers were indignant and felt that they had been insulted by a man whose political success owed much to the same kind of "intrigues" which they
employed in Ireland's behalf. In spite of Roosevelt's request for a
reply, they chose to ignore his letter altogether. At the time their
whole world seemed to be collapsing. Not only had they fallen from
official favor in Washington but also Ireland was again passed over
at the consistory which took place in mid-December. Disheartened
and humiliated, the Storers canceled plans to attend the wedding of
the President's daughter Alice and Mrs. Storer's nephew Nicholas
Longworth. Instead they embarked upon a lengthy visit to Egypt.[88]
Their failure to respond to Roosevelt's directive prompted another
letter, dated February 3, 1906, in which the President again demanded a reply. When his second letter was also ignored, Roosevelt
cabled Storer on March 5, 1906, that he had been relieved of his post
as ambassador to Vienna. Although the official reason given for
Storer's summary recall was his failure to answer letters from the
President, the real reason of course was what Roosevelt considered
their indiscreet, improper use of a public office to advance an ecclesiastical cause. But other aspects of Storer's conduct had long been
a source of irritation to the State Department. These included his
interference in the Hurst affair and his tendency to remain away
from his post on lengthy leaves of absence, as well as Mrs. Storer's
incessant "meddling" in affairs within the jurisdiction of the American ambassadors to Italy and France.[89] Whatever the reasons for
Storer's dismissal, it has been described by a recent scholar as "the

[87] See Roosevelt's lengthy letter to Maria L. Storer enclosed in a brief letter
to Bellamy Storer, both dated December 11, 1905, in Morison (ed.), *Roosevelt
Letters*, V, 107–11.

[88] M. L. Storer, *In Memoriam*, 113–15; *Letter of Bellamy Storer*, 41.

[89] T. Roosevelt to B. Storer, February 3, March 5, 1906, in Morison (ed.),
Roosevelt Letters, V, 145, 171–72; Chicago *Tribune*, March 28, 1906. See also
Jessup, *Elihu Root*, II, 109; Elihu Root to Comte Galuchowski, March 26,
1906, U. S. Department of State, Notes to Foreign Legations in the United
States from the Department of State (Microfilm copies in National Archives).

most striking example of summary recall in the annals of American diplomacy." [90]

The effect of Roosevelt's action was immediately evident in Washington social circles. The socially elite there, formerly referred to as "the Roosevelt-Storer crowd," divided into two mutually hostile camps, "the Roosevelt partisans and the Storerites." [91] Archbishop Ireland's efforts to salvage the friendship between the two families were wholly unsuccessful.[92] After a brief visit to the United States in the spring of 1906, at which time they expressed their displeasure with Roosevelt in several well-publicized interviews, the Storers took a house in Versailles and set to work compiling documents to vindicate themselves.[93] The more Ireland tried to "pour oil on troubled waters," the more irritated Maria Storer became. She was disappointed at what she considered the equanimity with which he viewed her husband's public humiliation. A long letter from her in February, 1907, ended their regular correspondence as well as their long-standing friendship.[94]

Roosevelt too rebuffed all efforts to mediate the differences between him and the Storers on the grounds that he had already shown them "every possible consideration." He assured friends of Ireland as well as the archbishop himself that the "extraordinary indiscretions" of the Storers left him no alternative but to remove them as representatives of the United States government. According to Roosevelt, the most tragic aspect of "the trouble with the idiot Storers" was "Ireland's possibly having his feelings hurt." [95] The

[90] Graham H. Stuart, *American Diplomatic and Consular Practice* (New York: Appleton, 1952), 266.

[91] Foraker, *I Would Live It Again*, 255.

[92] Ireland to M. L. Storer, April 6, 12, 1906, in M. L. Storer, *In Memoriam*, 115–19.

[93] Chicago *Tribune*, April 1, 2, 1906; Washington *Evening Star*, March 29, April 1, 1906; Longworth, *Crowded Hours*, 125; B. Storer to Root, August 3, November 8, 1906, Robert Bacon to B. Storer, September 10, 1906, in Record Group 59, National Archives.

[94] Moynihan, *Ireland*, 353.

[95] William M. Laffan to T. Roosevelt, April 8, 1906, in Roosevelt Papers; T. Roosevelt to Ireland, February 21, 1906, T. Roosevelt to Laffan, March 15, 1906, T. Roosevelt to Thomas O'Gorman, March 27, 1906, in Morison (ed.), *Roosevelt Letters*, V, 161, 180–82, 200.

President, as Mrs. Storer claimed, may well have been furious when Ireland's name was not presented at the consistory in 1905; but, contrary to her charges, his disappointment at the archbishop's failure to win the red hat was not the reason for the dismissal of her husband. Such explanations convinced Roosevelt that she had become "slightly unbalanced." He wrote a friend "that Mrs. Storer had gotten to feel so violent a hatred of Archbishop Corrigan as to make her transfer no small part of her feeling to his successor, Archbishop Farley, and she was almost as much engaged in intrigue against Archbishop Farley as in supporting Archbishop Ireland, and she dragged Storer in with her." [96] Farley and his supporters of course fully approved of Roosevelt's disposal of the Storers.[97] Bishop Charles A. McCabe, a Methodist from Philadelphia, also endorsed his action but for wholly different reasons. "These Catholics," he pointed out to the President with obvious relish, "will deceive you every time." [98]

The Storer-Roosevelt quarrel quickly became the subject of numerous headlines, editorials, and cartoons and was "talked to tatters." Although Roosevelt sought to use his influence with newspapers to soft-pedal publicity of the affair, it was too good as copy to remain off the front pages. In most instances the news stories rested largely upon a minimum of facts interspersed with much speculation based upon old rumors about Mrs. Storer's campaign in behalf of Archbishop Ireland. About the only documentary evidence relating to the background of Storer's dismissal was a letter written by Roosevelt while governor of New York which Mrs. Storer had released to the press during her visit to the United States in the spring of 1906.[99] The paucity of other direct evidence in no way deterred journalists from piecing together the details of the Storer-Roosevelt relationship or from rendering judgments. The anti-Roosevelt press was quick to interpret the "mournful affair" as a product of the President's penchant for impulsive actions or as an-

[96] M. L. Storer, *In Memoriam*, 112–13; T. Roosevelt to Ernest Harvier, April 18, 1906, in Morison (ed.), *Roosevelt Letters*, V, 213.

[97] Eugene A. Philbin to T. Roosevelt, April 6, 8, 1906, in Roosevelt Papers.

[98] Charles A. McCabe to T. Roosevelt, April 22, 1906, in Roosevelt Papers.

[99] Washington *Post*, April 1, 1906.

other example of his playing fast and loose with the truth. Some editorial opponents even suggested that his action revealed an anti-Catholic bias.[100]

Late in 1906, just as the Storer-Roosevelt quarrel began to fade from the front pages, public interest in it was suddenly revived when Storer published a lengthy pamphlet in his own defense. This document, which contained much of the correspondence exchanged between Roosevelt and the Storers since the 1890's, was mailed to various high-ranking government officials. The burden of Storer's defense was that if any indiscretion had been committed or if anyone had tampered with the truth, Roosevelt was the culprit and he, as ambassador, had merely carried out presidential instructions. Delivered into the hands of reporters by Senator Shelby Cullom of Illinois, Storer's document quickly assumed the proportion of a national sensation. Lengthy excerpts from the Storer-Roosevelt correspondence which were reprinted in many newspapers provided readers with a full confirmation of the rumors so long in circulation. The agitation finally reached such dimensions that the President presented a rebuttal in the form of a public letter to Secretary of State Elihu Root. In this document Roosevelt largely reiterated what he maintained on many occasions previously about the impropriety of his becoming involved in ecclesiastical politics. He emphasized that the Storers had been sufficiently warned about their own involvement.[101]

Opinion diverged sharply on various aspects of the "dear Maria" affair. Some criticized Roosevelt's peremptory dismissal of Storer as a punishment "absurdly disproportionate" to the offense. Others questioned why the President had allowed him to remain in the diplomatic service so long. In the view of many Americans, the most deplorable aspect of the Storer-Roosevelt controversy was the revela-

[100] "The Bellamy Storer Lesson," *Literary Digest*, XXXII (1906), 471–72; "Recall of Ambassador Storer," *Independent*, LX (1906), 761–62; Baltimore *Sun*, March 22, 1906.

[101] *Letter of Bellamy Storer*; B. Storer to T. Roosevelt, November 18, 1906, in Roosevelt Papers; Sullivan, *Our Times*, III, 100–101; Washington *Evening Star*, December 10, 1906.

tion that "diplomacy and ecclesiastical affairs have been, for a time at least, disastrously entwined." [102] According to the Washington *Evening Star*, the quarrel "warned afresh against any sort of union between church and state." [103] While the affair was being discussed in terms of its implications for church-state relations, some editors insisted upon treating it as a comedy. Voicing the sentiments of a sizable segment of the American press, the Philadelphia *North American* maintained that the busybody activities of an American wife which caused all the fracas proved nothing so much as the validity of the Catholic notion of celibacy. Whether treated seriously or humorously, public opinion seemed inclined to believe that Mrs. Storer's intrigues had "wrecked the hopes of those dearest to her," namely her husband and Archbishop Ireland.[104] In fact, sympathy was divided between the archbishop, whose elevation to the cardinalate had been sabotaged by the "perfervid zeal" of a recent convert, and Storer, whose career as a diplomat was discredited by the "gushing intriguer" whom he had had the misfortune to marry. Rather ironically, Ireland was generally absolved from any complicity in the schemes of Mrs. Storer, and Secretary of War Taft was regarded by the Storers as having been their chief advocate in the Roosevelt administration throughout the disturbance. As for Bellamy Storer, his reputation suffered as a result of his publication of the Storer-Roosevelt correspondence, an act which tended to corroborate charges that he was irresponsible and indiscreet. Although many Americans were not convinced that Roosevelt was as innocent as he proclaimed, Storer's efforts at self-vindication tended to focus guilt upon him rather than the President.[105]

The activities of the Storers following their removal from public life filled Roosevelt with a feeling of "shame and indignation on behalf of my country." In his words, the former ambassador was

[102] A review of the press reaction is found in *Current Literature*, XLII (1907), 21–25.

[103] Washington *Evening Star*, December 11, 1906.

[104] See *Current Literature*, XLII (1907), 21–22.

[105] *Ibid.*, 23–24; "The Storers," *Collier's*, XXXVIII (December 22, 1906), 15; "The Case of Mrs. Bellamy Storer," *Outlook*, LXXXIV (1906), 901–902; de Chambrun, *Cincinnati*, 287.

clearly demonstrating "what a vile creature he is." [106] Although the President preferred to keep the affair out of the press, he was unwilling to show much charity toward the Storers once it had become the subject of headlines. He adamantly stood his ground regarding his own position in the crusade to win a cardinal's hat for Ireland. He argued that he had always believed that the archbishop deserved the honor but that he had consistently refused the Storers' entreaties to become a party to their intrigues. The Storers themselves admitted that the only letters of his which they had used were two written while he was governor of New York. Roosevelt, like many others, believed that the episode was all the more unfortunate because its chief victim was Archbishop Ireland, who never was to receive the red hat.[107] As regrettable as the President considered the dispute, he admitted that some of it was "delicious." Later, in 1906, when his daughter and her new husband, Nicholas Longworth, visited the Storers at Versailles, he facetiously inquired of them whether there was any new letter from him to "dear Maria" ready for publication. In later years Roosevelt liked to tell a story about reading two volumes entitled *Indiscreet Diplomatic Correspondence* and his disappointment in finding that they "did not compare in interest or indiscretion with the Storer correspondence." One of his favorite cartoons also involved "dear Maria." It was a drawing of him and Taft in a touring car racing down the road amid fragments of the Philippines, trusts, and railroads, with an old hen in midair marked "Maria," which had barely escaped the wheels.[108]

The "dear Maria" affair, for all its comic aspects, offered a glimpse into the state of the American diplomatic service in the early twentieth century. The wealthy, charming Storers were in many respects typical of diplomats who occupied the most important embassies in

[106] T. Roosevelt to John St. Loe Strachey, December 21, 1906, in Morison (ed.), *Roosevelt Letters*, V, 531–32.

[107] See Roosevelt's letters to Harvier, April 18, 1906, and to Strachey, December 21, 1906, *ibid.*, V, 213, 531–32; Washington *Evening Star*, December 11, 1906.

[108] Arthur Wallace Dunn, *From Harrison to Harding: A Personal Narrative Covering a Third of a Century, 1881–1921* (2 vols.; New York: Putnam, 1922), II, 16–17; Butt, *Taft and Roosevelt*, I, 288.

the era. Their advancement obviously depended less upon Bellamy Storer's diplomatic achievements than upon his personal relationship with Presidents McKinley and Roosevelt. Despite his overt criticism of the spoils system, Roosevelt felt obligated to the Storers to such an extent that he put up with actions from them which, by his own admission, he would not have tolerated from other diplomats. There was an element of irony in Storer's whole diplomatic career: as a congressman he was a spokesman of a movement to reform the foreign service; yet the very spoils system which he had tried to correct made possible his appointment to various diplomatic posts.[109] In the final analysis, he was a victim of that system. Unquestionably the Storers had "intrigued daringly" in an effort to gain a red hat for Ireland and the Paris embassy for themselves. In the words of Julia Foraker, "so much passion had been spent on these ambitions, so many grand wires pulled, there were such heartburnings." [110]

If Mrs. Bellamy Storer "swept into history on the arm of the archbishop," she was swept out by the swift action of a President whose early career she had helped to advance. She never wearied of complaining about Roosevelt's ingratitude. It was a persistent theme in her various publications after 1906, which were designed to vindicate the dismissal of her "dearest Bellamy." Taking up residence in France, she and her husband spent their remaining years among the nobility, church prelates, and other Europeans of prominence who had figured in what Ireland once described as their "romance-like, intensely interesting, almost 'irrealisable' letters." [111] But their Versailles chateau was as near as Mrs. Storer ever got to gracing "with her undeniable distinction the American Embassy in the French capital." In 1923, after most of the participants in the Storer-Roosevelt quarrel were dead, she published a book, *In Memoriam: Bellamy Storer*, as a final vindication of her husband. Bitterness mingled with a note of forgiveness characterized her ref-

---

[109] See Warren F. Ilchman, *Professional Diplomacy in the United States, 1779–1939* (Chicago: U. of Chicago, 1961), 66.

[110] Foraker, *I Would Live It Again*, 255.

[111] Ireland to M. L. Storer, January 9, 1904, in M. L. Storer, *In Memoriam*, 95.

erences to Roosevelt, "our dead friend," who had fascinated his generation because he forever remained a child.[112]

The Storer-Roosevelt controversy involved more than "a tale of intrigue in which one ambitious and energetic woman" wrecked "the hopes of those dearest to her." It was actually a tale of mutually obligated friends—McKinley, Roosevelt, Ireland, and the Storers—whose political and ecclesiastical ambitions ultimately reached a point of irreconcilable conflict. The Storers' self-appointed role as kingmakers succeeded so long as it was confined strictly to the sphere of secular politics. But their reliance upon friends from this sphere in the promotion of an eminent churchman at the Vatican, even though the end according to Storer was the advancement of the Republican Party, ran afoul of the American ideal of separation of church and state. In fact, their activity violated one of the basic principles of the very "Americanism" of which Archbishop Ireland was an outspoken advocate. One historian has described the Storer-Roosevelt controversy as "an illuminating incident in American church-state relations" which should "serve as a lesson not only to future presidents and diplomats, but to all American public men—and women!" [113]

---

[112] See M. L. Storer, *In Memoriam* and M. L. Storer, *Theodore Roosevelt: The Child.* Mrs. Storer also published excerpts from her correspondence with Roosevelt in the Springfield (Mass.) *Republican* in 1910, in *Harper's Weekly* in 1912, and in the *Dublin Review* in 1921.

[113] Stokes, *Church and State*, II, 403.

VII

The Struggle for
an Artistic Coinage

*Saint Gaudens gave us for the first time a beautiful coinage,
a coinage worthy of this country .... The first few thousand of the Saint Gaudens gold coins are, I believe, more
beautiful than any coins since the days of the Greeks.*

THEODORE ROOSEVELT

For almost eight years the White House was a "bully pulpit" from
which Theodore Roosevelt instructed his countrymen on an infinite
variety of topics. Adept at dispensing the gospel of fair play and at
chastising big business, he was also ready with pronouncements regarding art and aesthetics. Nor was Roosevelt content merely to deliver homilies in the field of art. His words were followed by action.
In fact, his achievements as a patron and promoter of "governmental
aesthetics" were sources of considerable personal pride. As President he was largely responsible for the beautification of the capital
city, the restoration of the White House, the creation of a national
art gallery, and the production of artistic coins and medals. If historians have rarely emphasized his contributions in this area, artists
of his day were lavish in their praise of his efforts. They described
him as the greatest friend of art to reside in the White House since

213

Thomas Jefferson and considered his administration a remarkable "epoch in our art history."[1]

Roosevelt's interest in the arts appeared all the more dramatic because of the attitudes manifested by his predecessors. During the previous seventy-five years no President, save perhaps John Quincy Adams, utilized the presidential office to promote and encourage artistic endeavors. As a result, the official registers of the nation's taste such as the coinage and the national capital bore many signs of neglect. Virtually all coins in circulation were inferior numismatic creations by employees of the mint rather than objects of beauty designed by the nation's most eminent artists. The capital city had become a sprawling metropolis with little evidence of any regard for the original L'Enfant plan. In fact, the extent of its squalid alley-dwellings was far more impressive than the number of its art galleries. Numerous government buildings, both in architecture and location, clearly reflected the lack of any official concern for aesthetic values. For years various individuals and organizations had been waging a crusade to compel the government to seek "expert judgment" in its activities relating to art and art works. But not until Roosevelt's elevation to the presidency in 1901 did they win a sympathetic ear at the White House.

That the Rough Rider and advocate of the strenuous life should display a perceptive and sensitive appreciation of the fine arts testified both to the complexity of his character and to the breadth of his interests. Roosevelt was, to be sure, a layman in the field of the graphic arts. But he was not a layman complacent in the conviction that he "knows what he likes." His widely acclaimed review of the International Exhibition of Modern Art (the Armory Show) of 1913 offers sufficient evidence of his sophistication as a lay critic. As might well be expected, the strident nationalism that shaped so many of his attitudes also affected his artistic predilections. For example, he roundly condemned the emigration of American artists to Europe and heaped praise upon those who chose to remain in America to

[1] See Royal Cortissoz, *American Artists* (New York: Scribner, 1928), 327–40; Glenn Brown, "Roosevelt and the Fine Arts," *American Architect*, CXVI (1919), 711–19; Edward Wagenknecht, *The Seven Worlds of Theodore Roosevelt* (New York: Longmans, 1958), 81–84.

produce works that gave expression to "our inmost national life." Nor was he reticent to abandon classical artistic symbols for those more distinctly American. At his insistence, the State Dining Room of the White House was decorated with buffalo heads rather than the heads of lions. "Art," the President maintained, "must follow the marked trails of a people, must express the blossoming of a nation."

Roosevelt rejected the idea of art as an esoteric preoccupation or as the property of an elite "to be cultivated aloof from the ordinary affairs of man." Instead he related it to the public welfare and to what he called "Lincoln's plain people." He strongly endorsed the idea that the American democratic ideal was "Brahminism in manners and tastes, not in sympathies and ideas." For him, art was a vehicle for enhancing the "beauty of living and therefore the joy of life." To train the people to appreciate artistic beauty contributed to their welfare as surely as actions of a strictly economic and political nature. Thus, the creation of "durable" objects of beauty was a legitimate function of the national government. Although Roosevelt himself "could not have been an aesthete if he had tried," an instinct "for the charm of aesthetics was in his blood." Such an instinct, coupled with his flair for homiletics, enabled him to achieve an extraordinary record in promoting public projects of an artistic nature.

The President readily admitted the "immense gaps" in his knowledge of art, and he sought diligently to surmount the restrictions imposed by such deficiencies. In art as in politics he was determined to achieve "a high standard." His pursuit of excellence in politics, the field of his own greatest ability, prompted him to seek the counsel of "really first class men" such as Gifford Pinchot and James R. Garfield. Similarly, his concern for a high standard in art led him to "surrender to the guidance of those who really do know what they are talking about." Therefore, a group of famous sculptors, architects, and painters including Augustus Saint-Gaudens, Charles F. McKim, and Francis D. Millet, all personal friends of the President, formed an executive consultative body whose service in the field of art paralleled that of others in politics. Early in 1909, at the suggestion of the American Institute of Architects, Roosevelt formalized this body of experts by creating the Fine Arts Council to advise executive departments in all matters of an artistic nature. Although the President generally accepted the advice of his artistic experts, circumstances occasionally forced him to modify some of their recommendations and to ignore others. In some instances he, rather than the experts, suggested artistic innovations. But regardless of the origin, once the President had endorsed an artistic enterprise, he transformed it into a cause and endowed it with all the elements of high drama.[2]

One such enterprise which Roosevelt himself listed among the notable accomplishments of his administration was the issuance of a new gold coinage designed by his favorite American sculptor, Augustus Saint-Gaudens. The sculptor had come into the Roosevelt circle in 1901 as a member of a commission of famous artists and architects created to assist in restoring the city of Washington to the original plan of L'Enfant. An intimate friendship soon developed between the shy, retiring sculptor and the effervescent, demonstrative President. Roosevelt found much about the works of this imaginative and versatile artist which appealed to his aesthetic instincts. But the two qualities of Saint-Gaudens' sculpture which elicited the President's greatest enthusiasm were what he called its "distinctly American spirit" and its "soaring imagination" restrained by a self-mastery which eliminated "all risk of the fantastic and the overstrained." In Saint-Gaudens, he recognized a kindred soul who shared his "almost Greek horror of extremes." [3]

After the election of 1904, Roosevelt commissioned Saint-Gaudens to design the inauguration medals customarily struck for each new President. He was delighted with the product and compared it to the commemorative objects of fifth-century Greece. He

[2] The preceding paragraphs constitute a summary of my essay "Theodore Roosevelt: Champion of Governmental Aesthetics," *Georgia Review*, XXI (1967), 172–83.

[3] Theodore Roosevelt, *An Autobiography* (New York: Macmillan, 1913), 434; Homer Saint-Gaudens, "Later Works of Augustus Saint-Gaudens," *Century*, LXXV (1908), 695–714; Constance M. Green, *Washington: The Capital City, 1879–1950* (Princeton: Princeton, 1963), 133–35; Theodore Roosevelt, "Augustus Saint-Gaudens," in Hermann Hagedorn (ed.), *The Works of Theodore Roosevelt* (24 vols.; New York: Scribner, 1924–26), XII, 562–65.

was especially impressed by its "simplicity of inscription" and "dignity of arrangement." He wrote the sculptor, "I thank heaven we have at last some artistic work of permanent worth, done for the Government." [4] The success of the inauguration medal led the President to approach Saint-Gaudens about a project for the improvement of the artistic quality of American coins.

In December, 1904, the President discussed with his secretary of the treasury, Leslie M. Shaw, the possibility of doing something about the "artistically atrocious hideousness" of the present coinage. "Would it be possible, without asking permission of Congress," he asked the secretary, "to employ a man like Saint-Gaudens to give us a coinage that would have some beauty?" [5] When Shaw approved the legality of such a course, Roosevelt took up the question with Saint-Gaudens during a dinner at the White House in the winter of 1905. He described the coinage as his "pet" project for bringing art "to bear upon public welfare." In his opinion the low-relief coinage in circulation was unworthy of a civilized people. Roosevelt saw no reason why the United States should not have coins "like the Greeks" and promised that if Saint-Gaudens would design some artistic coins, he would force the mint to stamp them "in spite of itself." In full agreement with Roosevelt's desire to use the coins of ancient Greece as models, Saint-Gaudens consented to undertake new designs for the one-cent piece, the ten-dollar gold piece (eagle), and the twenty-dollar gold piece (double eagle). [6]

For two and a half years the President found time, even at the height of political and diplomatic struggles, to promote his coinage project. He followed every step in Saint-Gaudens' work with a critical eye and made numerous suggestions. It mattered not that Secretary Shaw thought him "a cracked-brained lunatic on the subject."

[4] Joseph B. Bishop, *Theodore Roosevelt and His Time* (2 vols.; New York: Scribner, 1920), I, 359.

[5] Theodore Roosevelt to Leslie M. Shaw, December 27, 1904, in Elting Morison (ed.), *The Letters of Theodore Roosevelt* (8 vols.; Cambridge: Harvard, 1951–54), IV, 1088.

[6] *The Reminiscences of Augustus Saint-Gaudens*, edited and amplified by Homer Saint-Gaudens (2 vols.; New York: Century Co., 1913), II, 329–30; "Roosevelt and Our Coin Designs: The Letters between Theodore Roosevelt and Augustus Saint-Gaudens," *Century*, XCIX (1920), 724–25.

Although Roosevelt wanted a high-relief coin, he cautioned the sculptor against making the relief too high lest the "mercantile classes" openly rebel against it. Probably the major innovation of an artistic nature instigated by the President concerned the design of the head of Liberty on the ten-dollar gold piece. At his request the sculptor replaced the traditional Phrygian cap which adorned Liberty's head with an Indian feather headdress. Saint-Gaudens readily agreed with Roosevelt's argument that "American Liberty should, if possible, have something distinctly American about her." And Roosevelt saw nothing American about the Phrygian cap. The President of course approved all preliminary designs and assisted the sculptor by providing answers to questions about legal and technical requirements. Both agreed that the dignity and simplicity of the ancient Greek coins could be recaptured only by keeping inscriptions at a minimum.[7] Therefore, when Saint-Gaudens suggested that the traditional motto "In God We Trust" would be an "inartistic intrusion," Roosevelt sanctioned its omission after a review of relevant statutes convinced him that there was no legal mandate for its inclusion.[8]

The President's major contribution to the execution of the new coinage lay primarily in his effort to remove or circumvent obstacles which in any way threatened the success of the project. From the outset, Saint-Gaudens' commission encountered serious opposition from the officials of the mint, who considered it an encroachment upon their traditional prerogatives. Fully aware of this hostility, Roosevelt impressed upon the director of the mint the necessity of allowing the sculptor "an absolutely free hand" even though his coins might require extensive modifications of the minting process. When his suggestions and requests failed to achieve the desired results, the President resorted to "dictatorial" orders in an attempt to overcome the obstructionist tactics of the mint. In spite of this exer-

[7] "Roosevelt and Our Coin Designs," 724–28; Bishop, *Theodore Roosevelt and His Time*, I, 359–61; Roosevelt to Augustus Saint-Gaudens, January 6, 1906, in Theodore Roosevelt Papers, Manuscript Division, Library of Congress.
[8] *The Reminiscences of Augustus Saint-Gaudens*, II, 332.

tion of executive pressure, the mint was able to force substantial alterations in the coin designs.[9]

Scarcely less menacing to the coinage project was the rapid deterioration of the sculptor's health. Roosevelt was aware of his illness, and he also knew that Saint-Gaudens was working on several assignments other than the coins. Employing the utmost tact, the President occasionally gave him a gentle nudge in the hope of bringing the coin designs to an early completion. Among other considerations was the schedule for the appearance of the coins. From the beginning, Roosevelt had feared congressional intervention and therefore wanted them to appear while Congress was not in session. He calculated that if Congress were inclined to intervene, such a schedule would at least permit several thousand coins of the original design to be in circulation before any alterations could be made. He originally planned to release the coins during the congressional recess in 1906, but the weakened physical condition of Saint-Gaudens and the tedious negotiations with the mint delayed the project for many months.[10]

Early in 1907 the idea of a new one-cent piece was abandoned, and all efforts were concentrated upon the completion of the double eagle and the eagle. Saint-Gaudens repeatedly modified his designs at the insistence of the mint officials, who maintained that his high-relief coins could not be struck by a single blow. So ill had he become by the summer of 1907 that his assistant, Henry Hering, actually altered the models under his direction and negotiated with officials of the Philadelphia mint. When Saint-Gaudens died on August 3, 1907, Hering assumed full responsibility for the new coinage and was able to conclude the project with the active intervention of Roosevelt and the new director of the mint, Frank A. Leach. Upon Leach's order the mint installed a special device for striking the coins. Largely because of Roosevelt's manipulation of the schedule,

[9] Roosevelt to Shaw, January 16, 1905, in Morison (ed.), *Roosevelt Letters*, IV, 1103–1104; "Roosevelt and Our Coin Designs," 728–29; Saint-Gaudens to Roosevelt, January 9, 1906, in Roosevelt Papers.
[10] Roosevelt to Saint-Gaudens, December 20, 1905, in Roosevelt Papers; "Roosevelt and Our Coin Designs," 728–33.

the mint issued the first of the new coins in November, 1907, less than a month before Congress reconvened.[11]

The President manifested great pride in the success of this "artistic enterprise." He considered the initial issues of the coins among the most valuable and beautiful objects of art in his possession. Much about the new coins appealed to his particular artistic tastes: the ten-dollar piece bore the head of Liberty in an Indian headdress on one side and a majestic standing eagle on the other; the twenty-dollar piece possessed a full-length figure of Liberty with the Capitol in the background on the obverse side and a soaring eagle on the reverse.[12] Roosevelt himself had contributed more to the composition of the ten-dollar coin, but the twenty-dollar piece, distinctly Saint-Gaudens', stole all his attention. "The $20 piece," he wrote a friend, ". . . is far better than any modern coin and ranks close alongside the best and most beautiful of the old Greek coins." [13]

Many prominent art critics shared the President's estimate of the new coinage, but they generally regretted the "depreciation" which Saint-Gaudens' designs had suffered at the hands of the mint's die-makers. For example, Kenyon Cox proclaimed that for the first time the United States had a coinage worthy of a civilized nation. Talcott Williams, who shared Cox's enthusiasm, was nevertheless depressed by the failure of the public to appreciate Saint-Gaudens' "masterpieces." He concluded that the coins would have the same "reception which a great portrait would receive in a land where no man ever looked on aught but a village photograph." [14] Such diverse persons as the King of Italy and Whitelaw Reid, American ambassador to England, expressed their admiration of Roosevelt's success in

[11] Henry Hering, "History of the 10 and 20 Gold Coins of 1907 Issue," *Numismatist*, LXII (1949), 455–59; Frank A. Leach, *Recollections of a Newspaperman* (San Francisco: Samuel Levinson, 1927), 374–80.

[12] Roosevelt, *An Autobiography*, 434. See also Rilla E. Jackman, *American Arts* (New York: Rand McNally, 1928), 329–30; *Catalogue of Coins, Tokens, and Medals in the Numismatic Collection of the Mint of the United States at Philadelphia* (Washington: Government Printing Office, 1912), 35, 39; E. G. Bradfield, "Theodore Roosevelt and Our Coinage," *Numismatist*, LXXI (1958), 1283–85.

[13] Roosevelt to Lawrence F. Abbott, November 27, 1907, in Roosevelt Papers.

[14] "The Saint-Gaudens Coins," *Century*, LXXV (1908), 799; Talcott Williams, "Augustus Saint-Gaudens," *International Studio*, XXXIII (1908), 138.

bringing artistic qualities of Greek proportion to modern numismatics.[15] "I hope," Lawrence Abbott wrote the President, "you will keep right on and give us some more helpful, practical object lessons in governmental aesthetics." [16]

Such praise, however, paled before the outburst of protest which accompanied the issuance of the new coins. The New York *Sun*, one of the President's most persistent critics, described the coins as "a bit of modern barbarism" which represented the crudities of Theodore Roosevelt rather than the artistry of Saint-Gaudens. The *Sun* editorialized at length about the manner in which the sculptor had suffered constant embarrassment as a result of presidential commands and suggestions.[17] Equally agitated was the *Bookman*, "a magazine of art and life," which singled out the ten-dollar gold piece for special criticism. It described the coin as a "blasphemy against numismatic art." [18] The *Wall Street Journal* fully agreed that the new coins were "lacking in artistic attractiveness" but directed its criticism primarily at their high relief, which made stacking impossible. The business community in general echoed the *Journal*'s sentiments about "the impracticality of the coins for commercial purposes." [19]

Neither the artistic quality of the coinage nor the difficulties that it presumably posed for banking houses was the source of the major disturbance. The real controversy involved the removal of the motto "In God We Trust," which in the public mind ranked high among the "age old" national traditions. Any tampering with it therefore was likely to be considered unpatriotic and unchristian. Actually, in 1907, the coinage motto was of relatively recent vintage. The idea of placing a sacred inscription on coins originated with a Pennsylvania clergyman in 1861. In the event the United States de-

---

[15] Lloyd C. Griscom to Roosevelt, February 10, 1908, in Roosevelt Papers; Royal Cortissoz, *The Life of Whitelaw Reid* (New York: Scribner, 1921), II, 379; Jules J. Jusserand, *What Me Befell: Reminiscences* (Boston: Houghton, 1933), 342–43.

[16] Abbott to Roosevelt, November 26, 1907, in Roosevelt Papers.

[17] New York *Sun*, November 15, 16, 1907, March 17, 1908.

[18] "In God We Trust," *Bookman*, XXVI (February, 1908), 1.

[19] *Wall Street Journal*, November 13, December 11, 1907. See also New York *Times*, December 8, 1907.

stroyed itself in the Civil War, he argued, such coins would provide "antiquaries of succeeding generations" with concrete evidence that Americans had been a Christian people. Impressed by his plea, Lincoln's secretary of the treasury, Salmon P. Chase, caused the phrase "In God We Trust" to be stamped upon certain coins. Congress specifically authorized the use of the motto in 1865 and 1873. But the section of the law authorizing its use was omitted in the Revised Statutes of 1874.[20] On the basis of this evidence Roosevelt concluded that the motto could be legally omitted.

Regardless of its legality, the removal of the inscription subjected the President to a barrage of criticism. One observer noted that he was "suffering criticism even in the humblest homes." [21] Local chapters of the Grange, the Women's Christian Temperance Union, the Junior Order of the United Mechanics of America, and the Christian Endeavor Union were quick to condemn the President and to demand the restoration of the motto. "What was a motto for Our Country when it was in dire distress," declared the Cottekill (New York) Council No. 68 of the Junior Order, "we consider good enough for us in time of peace and prosperity." [22] The protest was probably loudest and most widespread in Pennsylvania, the home of the clergyman who had originally suggested the use of the motto in 1861. Pennsylvanians apparently felt obligated to defend the tradition initiated by one of their very own. Frederick Carroll Brewster, a prominent Philadelphia attorney and Episcopal layman, spearheaded a movement throughout the East designed to force the restoration of "In God We Trust" to the coins. The arguments he set forth in a widely distributed pamphlet contended that the removal of the inscription by executive order was unconstitutional, since Congress alone had jurisdiction over all matters relating to the

[20] "Annual Report of the Secretary of the Treasury for the Year 1896," *House Documents*, 54th Cong., 2nd Sess., No. 8, pp. 260–61; Joseph Coffin, *Our American Money: A Collector's Story* (New York: Coward, 1940), 66–67; "The Motto on the Coinage," *Outlook*, XCIX (1907), 707.

[21] Joseph Hampton Moore, *Roosevelt and the Old Guard* (Philadelphia: Macrae-Smith, 1925), 199.

[22] Resolution of Cottekill Council No. 68, Junior Order, United Mechanics of America, December 30, 1907, in Records of the Senate Committee on Finance (Record Group 46, National Archives).

coinage. Brewster therefore maintained that Congress should reclaim its jurisdiction and restore the motto.[23]

Many of those incensed over the new coins accused the President of a formidable list of sins. Either he was guilty of premeditated assault upon religion or he had displayed a reckless and impulsive disregard for the religious sentiments of the majority of Americans. Actually he was guilty of neither. He merely approved the removal of the motto at the suggestion of Saint-Gaudens, who believed that it would detract from the artistic arrangement of the coins. That the removal of a single phrase could unleash a controversy of such proportions may be explained by several factors. Obviously the issue involved a peculiar combination of piety and patriotism whose potentially explosive ingredients had been set off by the spark of a single presidential act. A second factor was the particular time at which the coins appeared. Their appearance coincided with a swell of anti-Roosevelt sentiment. About to enter his last full year in office, Roosevelt had begun to reap the harvest of criticism which naturally followed six years of his vigorous leadership. Unfortunately for him, the first issues of the new coins began to circulate at the very peak of the panic of 1907, which his opponents insisted upon calling the "Roosevelt panic." Under such circumstances the coins provided additional ammunition for the anti-Roosevelt forces. The removal of the motto could be turned to good use by those seeking evidence of the President's impulsiveness and penchant for Caesarism.[24]

Rare was the newspaper that failed to take a definite stand in the coinage controversy. The New York *Sun* and the *Wall Street Jour-*

[23] F. Carroll Brewster to the Senate, April 27, 1908, Brewster to [?], April 27, 1908, Brewster to Bishops and Clergy, May 2, 1908, Brewster to the Senate Judiciary Committee, May 2, 1908, in Records of the Senate Committee on Finance (Record Group 46, National Archives); Moore, *Roosevelt and the Old Guard*, 199.

[24] "Those Coins," *Collier's*, XL (December 28, 1907), 5; "Is Roosevelt Hurting Prosperity?" *Current Literature*, XLIII (1907), 351–58; "The Roosevelt Panic," *Harper's Weekly*, LI (1907), 1787–88; Moore, *Roosevelt and the Old Guard*, 198–99. Among those who maintained that the removal of "In God We Trust" from the coins was another evidence of Rooseveltian impulsiveness was Mark Twain. See Mark Twain, *Mark Twain in Eruption*, ed. Bernard De Voto (New York: Harper, 1922), 49–50.

nal, hostile to the coins for other reasons, also objected to the President's arbitrary removal of a legend so dear to "a majority of the people." [25] The New York *Evening Post* interpreted the act as another evidence of the President's "habit of acting hastily without due foresight of the consequences." The Philadelphia *Press* called on Roosevelt "to halt a movement" distasteful to "so large a proportion of the American people." [26] The issue, as stated by the Atlanta *Constitution*, was whether the American people would choose "God or Roosevelt." [27] Other journals, such as the Chicago *Tribune* and the Cleveland *Plain Dealer*, leaped to the President's defense. They generally echoed the argument used by the President himself which maintained that linking the name of the deity with "filthy lucre" suggested sacrilege rather than piety. The New York *Times* and the Kansas City *Journal* approved the omission of the motto on the premise that a holy religious expression ought not to be needlessly exposed to jest and ridicule.[28]

Quite naturally the liveliest discussion of the new coinage took place within ecclesiastical circles. Clergymen throughout the nation were quick to align themselves in the debate, and "In God We Trust" soon became a favorite sermon topic.[29] Religious bodies framed resolutions and laymen expressed their views in speeches and letters-to-the-editor. The vestrymen of St. John's Church in Richmond, the scene of Patrick Henry's famous revolutionary oration, filed their protest with the President. Cardinal James Gibbons, careful to avoid involvement in the agitation, stated his concern over the President's action by resorting to a subtle proverb about the dangers of dismissing tradition lightly. Several Catholic papers were less circumspect and boldly rebuked the President for his "act

[25] New York *Sun*, March 17, 1908; *Wall Street Journal*, November 3, 1907.

[26] Quoted in *Literary Digest*, XXXV (1907), 788, and in *Current Literature*, XLIV (1908), 69–70, respectively.

[27] Atlanta *Constitution*, November 17, 1907.

[28] "In God We Trust," *Literary Digest*, XXXV (1907), 788; New York *Times*, November 15, 1907.

[29] Thomas K. Cree to Nelson W. Aldrich, May 2, 1908, in Records of the Senate Committee on Finance (Record Group 46, National Archives); *Madison Avenue Reformed Church Pulpit*, I (November 24, 1907), 1–12; New York *Sun*, November 29, 1907; Atlanta *Journal*, November 18, 1907.

of irreverence." In the meantime, on November 14, 1907, the Presbyterian Brotherhood of America passed a resolution requesting Congress to restore the sacred motto.[30] On the same day the Convention of the Episcopal Diocese of New York officially protested the elimination of the inscription and urged the secretary of the treasury to order its restoration. Among the lay delegates to this Episcopal gathering was J. P. Morgan, the Wall Street banker, who was "indignant" and "very much worked up" about the new coinage. There were suggestions that the convention's resolution reflected Morgan's indignation.[31] On the other hand, the leading Episcopal paper, the *Churchman*, edited by Roosevelt's friend Silas McBee, endorsed the removal of the legend from the coins and reminded Episcopalians that "the robust Christian faith of this nation needs no such clinking asseveration." [32] "I am glad," McBee later confided to Roosevelt, "that I defended your religion about the motto on the coins before I saw the ten-dollar coin itself." The editor described the coin as a classic case of "bad art." Only with the appearance of the twenty-dollar gold piece was he convinced that the President's efforts to produce an artistic coinage had not been in vain.[33]

Unlike McBee, most ecclesiastical spokesmen displayed little interest in the artistic qualities of the new coinage. Rather they concentrated upon determining the implications of the President's removal of the inscription. Their speculations produced a wide variety of opinions. Some dismissed the omission of the motto as an act of little consequence; others saw it as an ominous "sign of the times." Several influential church papers, including the *Baptist Commonwealth*, the *Catholic Citizen*, and the *American Hebrew*, attached little religious significance to the incident and disclaimed the existence of any presidential challenge to organized religion. The *Westminster*, a Presbyterian journal, complimented the Presi-

[30] Atlanta *Constitution*, November 13, 15, 1907; New York *Sun*, November 16, 1907; "Religious Press on the Coinage Motto," *Literary Digest*, XXXV (1907), 869–70.

[31] New York *Times*, November 15, 1907; *Wall Street Journal*, November 16, 1907; New York *Sun*, November 14, 1907.

[32] "The Motto on the Coins," *Churchman*, November 23, 1907, p. 3.

[33] Silas McBee to Roosevelt, December 6, 21, 1907, in Roosevelt Papers.

dent for omitting the sacred motto until the ethical level of business in the United States warranted the use of God's name as "the symbol of commerce." [34] A few churchmen viewed the removal of the inscription in terms of the American tradition of the separation of church and state. The *Independent* reminded its readers that the teaching of religion, by coinage inscriptions or otherwise, was "no business of the State." Another paper declared, "It is a little strange that the motto was not dropped long ago." [35]

A majority of the church spokesmen accepted none of these views and preferred to label the omission of "In God We Trust" as evidence of the secular spirit of the age. "To get God off the coins," they argued, reflected the same irreligious climate which spawned movements "to get the Bible out of the schools." [36] A few critics went so far as to suggest that the President's action smacked of rank atheism. "It seems too much like the first step toward ruin," observed a Massachusetts layman, "and not too far removed from the act of France in the revolution of 1790 when they decreed that God did not exist." [37] George Harvey, editor of *Harper's Weekly*, intimated that the godless money had been created "in deference to the arguments" of a national agnostic society.[38] The strong support given the President and his coinage by the *Truth Seeker*, "a journal of free thought," seemed to lend credence to this idea. And the endorsement of the "ungodly" coins by the Bohemian Free Thought Federation of America only confirmed the suspicions of those inclined to view the whole project as a deep-laid atheistic plot.[39]

[34] See "Religious Press on the Coinage Motto," 869–70; "The President and the Motto on Our Coins," *Current Literature*, XLIV (1908), 68–70.

[35] "What Makes a Christian State?" *Independent*, LXIII (1907), 1263–64; "In God We Trust," *Literary Digest*, 788. See also Christian F. Reisner, *Roosevelt's Religion* (New York: Abingdon, 1922), 248–49; Anson Phelps Stokes, *Church and State in the United States* (3 vols.; New York: Harper, 1950), III, 601–605.

[36] New York *Sun*, November 29, 1907.

[37] Quoted from a letter by N. W. Merrill of Springfield, Mass., which was only one of numerous documents read into the *Congressional Record* on January 7, 1908, by Congressman Morris Sheppard of Texas. See *Congressional Record*, 60th Cong., 1st Sess., 513–16.

[38] "In God We Trust," *Harper's Weekly*, LI (1907), 1714.

[39] See *Congressional Record*, 60th Cong., 1st Sess., 3288; Memorial of the Bohemian Free Thought Federation of America, Chicago, Ill., February 22,

At the height of the controversy the President found that some of his oldest and most steadfast friends were among the critics of his coins. Perhaps the most notable of these was Lyman Abbott, editor of the *Outlook*, who seriously doubted whether "the aesthetic reasons for the removal of the motto are strong." The editor believed that Roosevelt had shocked the American people without "adequate compensating advantage." Abbott's chief regret was that church assemblies failed to show half as much interest in child labor and other practical "moral issues" as they had demonstrated over the elimination of "In God We Trust" from two coins.[40]

Although Roosevelt had anticipated criticism of the new coinage, he apparently had not expected it to focus upon the removal of the sacred inscription. The religious overtones of the agitation troubled him and probably accounted for his extraordinary restraint throughout the controversy. He considered the whole discussion unfortunate and unnecessary and earnestly desired a quick termination of it by any means short of abject surrender. On more than one occasion, he attempted to prevent actions which would intensify the disturbance. When Saint-Gaudens' son, Homer, mentioned the removal of the motto in an article which he prepared for the *Century*, Roosevelt prevailed upon the editor to delete the reference before publishing the manuscript. In his opinion Homer Saint-Gaudens was "an awfully nice young fellow" who "simply does not understand the undesirability of arousing the people to attack the coinage." [41]

The President confided to his friend Owen Wister that the controversy over the coinage motto had become a source of considerable worry. Apparently his insomnia had worsened as a result of it. Yet, the President remained convinced that he had acted wisely. "Whether wise or not from the standpoint of politics," he wrote Wister, "I cannot help feeling that it [the removal of the motto] was the right action from the standpoint of good taste, and indeed a little

---

1908, in Records of the Senate Committee on Finance (Record Group 42, National Archives).

[40] "The Motto on the Coinage," 707–708.

[41] Roosevelt to Richard Watson Gilder, December 18, 1907, in Roosevelt Papers.

more than good taste." [42] On the contrary, Secretary of Commerce
Oscar S. Straus gained the impression that Roosevelt "was not the
least perturbed" by the controversy. But the mere fact that he had
discussed the matter at length with Straus during a White House
dinner at least indicated his concern. During the conversation Roosevelt assured the secretary that "it was sometimes a good thing to
give people some unimportant subject to discuss, for it helped put
through more important things." [43]

Perturbed or not, the President felt compelled to issue a public
statement to justify the omission of the traditional legend from the
new coins. He began by proclaiming that the inclusion of the motto
was not legally mandatory. At the same time he conceded that it had
become a well-established custom, and therefore he "would have
felt at liberty to keep the inscription" if he "had approved of its
being on the coinage." His disapproval rested primarily on the premise that the use of the sacred motto on money was a sacrilegious
association of God and mammon. The President described the
phrase "In God We Trust" as a "beautiful and solemn sentence"
suitable for use on public buildings and monuments, where it would
"imply a certain exaltation of spirit." To place the legend on coins
or postage stamps invited irreverence and levity rather than "lofty
emotions." Roosevelt asserted, "In all my life, I have never heard
any human being speak reverently of this motto on the coins." Instead the inscription had occasioned only "jest and ridicule" as
demonstrated by such common jokes as "In God We Trust for the
Short Weight" and "In God We Trust for the Other Eight Cents."
The President sincerely hoped that the "religious sentiment of the
country" would not force the restoration of the motto. He clearly indicated, however, that if Congress passed a law restoring the motto,
he would bow to its wishes.[44]

[42] Owen Wister, *Roosevelt: The Story of a Friendship, 1880–1919* (New York:
Macmillan, 1930), 268.

[43] Oscar S. Straus, *Under Four Administrations: From Cleveland to Taft*
(Boston: Houghton, 1922), 262–63. For a more extensive discussion of the same
subject see Oscar S. Straus Diary (MS in Oscar S. Straus Papers, Manuscript
Division, Library of Congress), 123–24.

[44] Roosevelt to the Reverend Roland C. Dryer, November 11, 1907, in Roosevelt Papers. The President's statement appeared in the press on November 14,

The President's explanation, however ingenious, utterly failed to calm the agitation. His critics especially seized upon his suggestion that the pious phrase on coins inspired irreverence rather than "lofty emotions." "It is an irreverence," replied the Philadelphia *Public Ledger*, "to flout the reverential attitude of the Republic." [45] The Atlanta *Journal* pointed out that the President's act had prompted far more irreverence than the motto itself. Shortly after this display of pious concern, the *Journal* suggested that perhaps the "President was thinking of the irreverence of his colored friends in shooting craps when he was induced to strike the motto from the coins." [46] The *United Presbyterian* wondered whether Roosevelt would also favor "the expunging of the Decalog because some men treat it with lightness and irreverence." [47]

The agitation over the removal of the sacred inscription was by no means confined to editorial pages or to church conventions. Ordinary citizens were deeply disturbed. Some considered the elimination of the motto as "an act of blasphemy"; others interpreted it as "a backward step" or as "a menace to our institutions." Still others, displaying less piety, suggested that the eagle on the coins should be replaced by a teddy bear over the inscription "In Theodore We Trust." [48] Citizens of a poetic bent resorted to verse in expressing their displeasure with the President. One of these, who used the pseudonym "Anti-Trust," wrote:

> In God We Trust
> Oh, no we don't
> That is, we mustn't say so;
> Such sentiment is out of date
> At least so says the potentate
> And He's the country and the State
> > > Our Teddy.

1907. See New York *Times*, November 14, 1907. Secretary of Commerce Straus claimed that he suggested the contents of Roosevelt's public statement on the coinage. Straus Diary, 124.

[45] Quoted in *Literary Digest*, XXXV (1907), 870.

[46] Atlanta *Journal*, November 17, 30, 1907.

[47] Quoted in *Literary Digest*, XXXV (1907), 870.

[48] *Congressional Record*, 60th Cong., 1st Sess., 513–15; Augusta (Ga.) *Chronicle*, November 16, 1907; New York *Sun*, November 18, 19, 1907, February 2, 1908; New York *Times*, November 16, 1907.

In God We Trust
Upon Our Coins!
Oh, sacrilegious people!
God is not needed in this nation;
We have the great Administration;
And he's enough for all creation
                    Our Teddy.[49]

By the time that Congress reconvened on December 2, 1907, the public outcry against the new coinage had become loud and menacing. Constituents inundated their congressmen with demands for a law to restore "In God We Trust" to the coins. Within a few days after the opening of Congress, six bills, sponsored largely by Democrats, had been introduced in compliance with the popular demand. The first flurry of activity in the new Congress indicated that the Democrats intended to capitalize on the coinage controversy; but Republicans, no less than Democrats, who had smarted under the President's strong leadership were inclined to support virtually any measure designed to humble him.[50]

Few were more vocal than Democratic Congressman Morris Sheppard, "the boy orator from Texas" and the author of a bill requiring the restoration of the sacred inscription. On January 7, 1908, he lodged the first protest against the "godless coinage" from the floor of Congress in what amounted to a half-hour sermon. Interrupted seven times by loud applause, the young Texan lived up to his reputation in an eloquent defense of the motto as "a sentence summarizing the history and reflecting the character of the American people." He, like "all patriots," deeply regretted that the President had allowed the sacred symbol on the coins to be replaced by a design "which shows on the one side a woman in savage headdress and on the other a Roman eagle in predatory flight—the one side a degradation of woman and the other an eulogy of war." Sheppard pleaded with his colleagues to erase this presidential sacrilege by restoring appropriate recognition to the "God of Washington, of

[49] New York *Sun*, November 17, 1907.
[50] Moore, *Roosevelt and the Old Guard*, 198–200.

Lincoln, and of Lee." [51] Only Congressman Henry S. Boutell, a Republican from Illinois, rose to the defense of the President and his coinage. Resorting to the Scriptures, he reminded the House that Christ himself had had to deal with issues similar to those in the coinage controversy and that Christ had advised men to render "unto Caesar those things which are Caesar's, and unto God those things that are God's." Boutell concluded, "This doctrine was sufficient warrant for the course pursued by the President, who has displayed good judgment, discriminating taste, and a proper reverence." [52]

Fearful lest the Democrats turn "In God We Trust" to party advantage, Republicans in the House hastened to gain control of the matter. When the Committee on Coinage, Weights, and Measures met to consider the various bills providing for the restoration of the motto, the Republican majority quickly agreed to give preference to a bill sponsored by a member of the President's own party. The obvious choice was a measure introduced on December 21, 1907, by Congressman J. Hampton Moore of Pennsylvania, who counted himself among the President's friends in Congress. Actually one of Moore's constituents, Frederick Carroll Brewster, a Philadelphia attorney who acted as spokesman for the opponents of the new coinage, had drafted the bill, and Moore had introduced it at his request. The Republicans, however, wished to ascertain the President's attitude before recommending any measure. Their purpose was "to avoid a veto if possible." Since the chairman of the Coinage Committee, William B. McKinley of Illinois, was "not the closest friend of Roosevelt," Moore agreed to approach the President about the restoration of the motto. Rumors that Roosevelt was "in no conciliatory mood" led the Pennsylvania congressman to believe that he had been assigned the job of "bearding the lion in his den." Convinced that "the President must yield" eventually, Moore believed "that he would take a suggestion from me as from a friend." [53]

When the Pennsylvanian arrived at the White House, he found

[51] *Congressional Record,* 60th Cong., 1st Sess., 511–16.
[52] *Ibid.,* 516.
[53] Moore, *Roosevelt and the Old Guard,* 199–200.

it crowded with senators and congressmen waiting to see the President. Ushered into the executive offices ahead of the others, Moore at first believed that the rumors about Roosevelt's intransigent attitude had been wholly accurate. Mention of the bills in Congress requiring the restoration of "In God We Trust" prompted the President to remark, "I don't see that legislation is necessary." Then, when Moore referred to the unfavorable comments in the press and called his attention to a recent article in the New York *Sun*, Roosevelt exploded. "Don't mention that paper to me," he shouted. "I don't want to hear from that sheet." After the President calmed down, the congressman quietly explained that the coinage episode had placed Roosevelt in a "false light" and had profoundly "shaken" the religious community. He implied that the popular notion of a White House challenge to religion might be eradicated if the President sanctioned the passage of a law restoring the motto. When Moore concluded his explanation, the President summoned Senator Thomas Carter, a Republican from Montana, from the corridor to hear his answer to the congressman, so that the Senate as well as the House might be informed of his attitude. Addressing himself to the senator, Roosevelt declared,

> The Congressman says the House Committee [on Coinage, Weights, and Measures] wants to pass a bill restoring the motto to the coin. I tell him it is not necessary; it is rot; but the Congressman says there is a misapprehension as to the religious purport of it—it is so easy to stir up a sensation and misconstrue the President's motives—and that the Committee is agitated as to the effect of a veto. I repeat, it is rot, pure rot; but I am telling the Congressman if Congress wants to pass a bill re-establishing the motto, I shall not veto it. You may as well know it in the Senate also.[54]

Moore hastened back to Capitol Hill to assure his colleagues of the President's acquiescence in the movement to restore the motto.

Chairman McKinley of the Committee on Coinage, Weights, and Measures appointed a subcommittee headed by Congressman George A. Pearre of Maryland to study the numerous petitions dealing with the removal of the motto. Pearre's group unanimously recommended the restoration of the inscription as an "outward and

54 *Ibid.*, 202.

visible" symbol of "the Christian patriotism" of the American people. In the meantime, McKinley had introduced a slightly modified version of the Moore bill, which required "In God We Trust" upon certain coins "as heretofore." On February 26, 1908, the full committee unanimously recommended the passage of the McKinley measure. In its report, the committee exonerated the President of any illegal exercise of power but maintained that the bill was designed to clarify the legal status of the coinage inscription in the future.[55]

On March 8, 1908, the McKinley bill reached the floor of the House. The proponents of the measure displayed great feeling in their defense of the right of a "Christian, God-fearing, God-loving" people to place "In God We Trust" upon their coinage. Two Democratic orators, Charles C. Carlin of Virginia and Ollie M. James of Kentucky, described in detail the history of the sacred inscription and traced the use of such mottoes to the Roman emperor Constantine. "The country is to be congratulated," James declared, "that our trust is again to be restored in God." Congressman Charles Edwards of Georgia fully agreed with such sentiments but refused to join those who classified the President as an infidel or atheist. He preferred to think of Roosevelt as a "God-fearing man" who had "virtually admitted his mistake" in eliminating the motto. Washington Gardener of Michigan favored the pious inscription primarily as a gesture to register his opposition to anarchism and "the purpose of the anarchists." [56] Among those who opposed the restoration of the motto were Gustav Küstermann, a Wisconsin Republican, and George Gordon, a Tennessee Democrat. Küstermann doubted the validity of any religion whose survival depended upon such "advertising." And he wondered whether the "fine sentiments" expressed by his colleagues in defense of a godly coinage had not been motivated less by their "Christian patriotism" than by their fear of offending the religious prejudices of their constituents. Gordon suggested that the House might satisfy its yearning for the public display of the sacred phrase by placing it on the walls of the

[55] *House Reports*, 60th Cong., 1st Sess., No. 1106, pp. 1–3.
[56] *Congressional Record*, 60th Cong., 1st Sess., 3384–88.

chamber in plain view of all congressmen, including Speaker Joseph G. Cannon. But the efforts of Küstermann and Gordon were futile. The measure passed the House by the overwhelming vote of 259 to 5.[57]

In the Senate the bill encountered even less vocal opposition than in the House. Frederick Carroll Brewster, the persistent critic of the new coins, made certain that the senators fully appreciated the popular clamor for the restoration of the motto. The shrewd management of the measure in the Finance Committee by Senator Nelson W. Aldrich of Rhode Island eliminated any obstacles that might have impeded it. The Senate passed it without debate on May 13, 1908, and the President signed it six days later. In accordance with the new law, "In God We Trust" reappeared on all coins struck after July 1, 1908.[58]

The disturbance over the "ungodly St. Gaudens coins" quickly subsided after Roosevelt affixed his signature to the McKinley bill. To the end, however, the President considered the agitation "pure rot" and the law restoring the motto an unnecessary interference by the "coordinate branch" with a work of art. Perhaps the most puzzling aspect of the episode was the absence of the usual Rooseveltian pugnacity in behalf of a "pet" project. Many interpreted his readiness to acquiesce in the restoration of the motto as a tacit admission that he had erred in omitting it. Others were considerably less generous. The New York *Sun*, for example, accused him of displaying rank political opportunism in "true Roosevelt fashion" and reversing himself solely because the omission of the inscription proved to be extremely unpopular.[59]

Such interpretations scarcely did justice to the President. To be sure, he regretted the outburst occasioned by the removal of "In God We Trust" and resented the insinuations about his motives.

---

[57] *Ibid.*, 3386, 3389–90, 3391.

[58] Brewster to United States Senate, April 27, 1908, Alexander Henry to Aldrich, May 9, 1908, in Records of the Senate Committee on Finance (Record Group 42, National Archives); *Congressional Record*, 60th Cong., 1st Sess., 3423, 6114, 6189, 6893; *Annual Report of the Secretary of the Treasury, 1908* (Washington: Government Printing Office, 1908), Appendix, 279–80, 283.

[59] New York *Sun*, March 17, 1908.

But at no time did he seek to escape the onus of the popular reaction by shifting the blame to Saint-Gaudens, who had actually suggested the omission of the pious motto and who was safely in his grave when the coins appeared. The currying of popular favor played little role in his calculations. Roosevelt ultimately approved the Mc-Kinley bill because he wished to end an acrimonious controversy which might jeopardize a more important, long-range objective. He viewed the work of Saint-Gaudens as merely the beginning of a "great reform," which others would continue. Thus, a strategic retreat on the motto might enhance the success of a more comprehensive project for the artistic improvement of the coinage. Regardless of the motives that prompted him to compromise, Roosevelt set the stage for subsequent reforms in the artistic quality of American coins. He focused public attention on the issue and shattered tradition by employing the nation's most famous sculptor to perform a task usually delegated to an employee in the mint. And "in spite of itself," the mint was forced to surrender its prerogative. The coins by Saint-Gaudens provided the precedent for James E. Fraser's buffalo nickel, Victor D. Brenner's Lincoln penny, Bela Pratt's half- and quarter-eagles, and Adolph Weinman's dime and silver half-dollar. All of these artists, save Brenner, had been students of Saint-Gaudens.[60] But their coinage, like that of their mentor, was part of the Rooseveltian legacy.

[60] See Cortissoz, *American Artists*, 331; *Annual Report of the Secretary of the Treasury, 1908*, pp. 43–44.

VIII

The Secret Service Controversy

... the provision about the employment of secret service men will work very great damage to the Government in its endeavor to prevent and punish crime. There is no more foolish outcry than this against "spies"; only criminals need fear our detectives.

THEODORE ROOSEVELT

On January 8, 1909, the galleries of the House of Representatives were jammed to capacity. The throng was so great that the wives of several congressmen had to sit on the steps. The business before the House was another round in the struggle between President Roosevelt and Congress over the Secret Service.[1] The crowd had gathered in the House galleries to hear the report of a committee appointed to recommend an appropriate response to a portion of the President's annual message and to a special message dealing with the restrictions placed upon the Secret Service during the previous session of Congress. Members of Congress had taken offense at Roosevelt's suggestion that the restrictions had been imposed because

[1] For accounts of Roosevelt's struggle with Congress during his closing months in office see George E. Mowry, *The Era of Theodore Roosevelt and the Birth of Modern America, 1900–1912* (New York: Harper, 1958), Chap. 11; Henry F. Pringle, *Theodore Roosevelt: A Biography* (New York: Harcourt, 1931), 328–48; William Henry Harbaugh, *Power and Responsibility: The Life and Times of Theodore Roosevelt* (New York: Farrar, Straus, 1961), 363–73.

236

congressmen "were afraid of being investigated themselves." Some even talked privately of impeachment. Evidence of the prevailing mood in the House was the wild applause from both sides of the aisles which greeted every sarcastic or barbed reference to the President.

In the midst of the heated debate, in which only a handful of congressmen spoke in Roosevelt's defense, the doorkeeper announced, "Mr. Speaker, a message from the President of the United States." The announcement precipitated so much laughter and jeering that Speaker Cannon cracked the edge of his desk with his gavel in an attempt to restore order. After seven hours of debate, the House voted overwhelmingly to lay on the table that portion of the President's annual message concerning the Secret Service and the entire special message on the same topic. Not since Andrew Jackson had a President incurred this particular form of congressional chastisement. The wife of a Texas congressman, who witnessed these events in the House from the gallery steps, described it as "T. R.'s being metaphorically 'thrown to the lions.' " When the Senate joined in the assault, a widely respected journalist accused Congress of succumbing to "an orgy of malice" against the President. And few denied that the closing months of Roosevelt's administration constituted "one long lovely crackling row between the White House and the Capitol." [2]

Observers generally described this orgy as a release of pent-up hostility which had accrued during the seven and a half years of Roosevelt's tenure. Roosevelt was, as historians have noted, an especial victim of the traditional diminution of executive power which Presidents seem destined to experience.[3] He himself recognized that Congress was bent upon settling some old scores with him during the lame-duck phase of his administration.[4] His revitaliza-

---

[2] *Congressional Record*, 60th Cong., 2nd Sess., 645–83; Ellen Maury Slayden, *Washington Wife: Journal of Ellen Maury Slayden from 1897–1919* (New York: Harper, 1962), 116; Walter Wellman in the Chicago *Herald*, January 10, 1909; Alice Roosevelt Longworth, *Crowded Hours* (New York: Scribner, 1935), 160.

[3] Mowry, *Era of Roosevelt*, 212.

[4] Theodore Roosevelt to Kermit Roosevelt, January 14, 1909, in Elting

tion of the executive office, coupled with what some interpreted as his shift to a more radical political position, had alienated conservatives who were jealous of the prerogatives of the legislative branch and its preeminence within the federal government. Convinced that Roosevelt had usurped power and eroded legislative prestige, many congressmen were intent upon striking "some particularly vicious blow at the President" for the purpose of recapturing some of the authority he had taken from them.[5]

The dispute over the appropriations for the Secret Service provided an opportunity for anti-Roosevelt partisans to deliver their retaliatory blow. In one way or another, the Secret Service had been linked with virtually all controversial activities of the Roosevelt administration, including the antitrust campaigns, the crusades against peonage, and the exposure of land frauds.[6] But more important, in the view of many congressmen, were persistent rumors that Roosevelt had used Secret Service agents to harass and intimidate those who opposed his legislative program. Such rumors, which fed upon assorted gossip, tended to corroborate the view of those who charged Roosevelt with aspiring to become a despot. Since the ordinary citizen made few distinctions between Secret Service personnel and numerous other investigative and inspection agents in the various executive departments, it was relatively easy for the President's enemies to talk in terms of an enormous "sleuthing fund" and to warn against the pernicious activities of his "army of spies." The disturbance over the Secret Service which erupted in 1908 not only prompted a hostile confrontation between the Congress and the President; it also raised serious questions about the place and role of a secret detective force within a democratic state. Furthermore, the debate over the issue exposed the spectacular growth of federal investigative functions since the opening of the twentieth century. Nor was the controversy devoid of the personal equation: it brought

Morison (ed.), *The Letters of Theodore Roosevelt* (8 vols.; Cambridge: Harvard, 1951–54), VI, 1475–76.

[5] Atlanta *Constitution*, January 11, 1909.

[6] See Walter S. Bowen and Harry E. Neal, *The United States Secret Service* (Philadelphia: Chilton, 1960), 49–83.

to a climax the long-standing feud between Roosevelt and Senator Benjamin R. Tillman.

By the very nature of its operations the Secret Service was shrouded in mystery. The popular view of the agency as a network of government sleuths busily engaged in mysterious activities was nourished by romantic tales rather than factual accounts describing their actual duties.[7] The Secret Service traced its origins to the year 1857, when the Treasury Department received an appropriation for use in detecting counterfeiters; but the formal Secret Service Division was not created within the department until eight years later.[8] Like other government agencies, it came into being under an appropriation act and continued to exist from year to year on the basis of such legislation. In 1865 William P. Wood became the first chief of the division, whose primary function was "detecting and bringing to trial and punishment persons engaged in counterfeiting." Late in the nineteenth century, Secret Service agents assumed, on an informal basis, the additional duty of protecting the President. Not until 1907, however, was the scope of their work legally broadened to include "the protection of the person of the President." Despite the specific nature of the Secret Service's duties, rumors early began to circulate about its extralegal activities. During the early 1870's a scandal was exposed which allegedly proved that government detectives had been used to "shadow" congressmen. Fear that such an agency might act irresponsibly unless confined to specific tasks helps

[7] For example, see Louis Bagger, "The Secret Service of the United States," *Appleton's Journal*, X (1873), 360–65; Waldron Fawcett, "Secret Service and the Big Black Cabinet," Portland *Oregon Sunday Journal*, December 27, 1908.

[8] During the Civil War there was another organization popularly known as the "Secret Service." Actually it was an intelligence agency created in 1861 for the Commanding General of the Army, Winfield Scott, but within the year came under the direction of the State Department. In 1862 it was transferred to the War Department, where it continued to perform various types of detective work including some investigations in regard to counterfeiting. This detective force went out of existence in 1865 and some of its employees may have been incorporated in the new Secret Service Division formally organized in the Treasury Department in that year. See Norman Ansley, "The United States Secret Service: An Administrative History," *Journal of Criminal Law, Criminology and Police Science*, XLVII (May–June, 1956), 93–94.

explain why Congress was reluctant even to expand its functions to include protection of the President.[9]

Technically, there were no secret service agents in any federal department except the Treasury. Actually, however, investigative agents charged with detecting crime were also found in other departments, such as the Post Office and Interior departments. In 1871, the year after the organization of the Justice Department and six years after the formal establishment of the Secret Service in the Treasury Department, Congress provided the attorney general with a "lump-sum appropriation" for "the detection and prosecution of crimes" against the United States. The Justice Department at first relied primarily upon private detectives, especially those from the Pinkerton Agency; but when Congress prohibited this practice in 1892, the attorney general sought assistance from customs house inspectors, bank examiners, agents of the Interior Department, and particularly members of the Secret Service in performing the investigative functions of the department. By the beginning of the twentieth century the detailing of agents from the Secret Service Division for use by other departments was a well-established practice. In the absence of any other federal agency with comparable training and experience, the Secret Service came to act as an interdepartmental detective bureau.[10]

The activities of the division expanded considerably under the direction of Chief John E. Wilkie. Before his appointment in 1898, Wilkie possessed a wide reputation as a crime reporter on the Chicago *Tribune*.[11] Described by his contemporaries as a famous

[9] Bowen and Neal, *The United States Secret Service*, 11–17, 125–26; "Inquiry Pursuant to Resolution Authorizing Investigation of Secret Service . . . ," *Senate Report*, 60th Cong., 2nd Sess., No. 970, pp. 2–7, hereinafter cited as "Inquiry . . . of Secret Service"; "Strange Stories of the Secret Service," *Bookman*, XXXIII (June, 1911), 381–89; "Secret Service Work," New York *Tribune*, December 20, 1908.

[10] Homer C. Cummings and Carl McFarland, *Federal Justice: Chapters in the History of Justice and the Federal Executive* (New York: Macmillan, 1937), 365–74. See also Ansley, "The United States Secret Service," 93–106; Joseph G. Cannon as Told to L. White Busbey, *Uncle Joe Cannon* (New York: Holt, 1927), 230.

[11] *Who's Who in America, 1903–1905* (Chicago: Marquis, 1903), 1614.

"criminologist," he introduced into the Secret Service a degree of discipline and efficiency which had previously been lacking. From his office in Washington, Wilkie directed the operations of agents located in various cities throughout the country. The main force of detectives was composed of ten men, who were permanent employees under the classified civil service. In addition, there were per diem agents whose names were on the eligible lists of the Civil Service Commission. As the need arose, such individuals were called into service by Wilkie either for work within the Treasury Department or for assignment to some other department. Their identity, insofar as possible, remained secret, but Wilkie recruited primarily young men with experience as policemen or as claims agents for railroads. It was this auxiliary force of per diem agents paid from funds provided in the Sundry Civil Appropriation bills which later became the focus of the so-called Secret Service controversy.[12]

Under Wilkie the Secret Service became increasingly involved in investigations which attracted national publicity.[13] His efficient operation of the division elicited a mixed reaction. Critics recalled earlier troubles with the Secret Service and feared that he was building an empire which might well become an uncontrollable monster in the future.[14] Among those who looked with favor on the streamlined Secret Service was President Theodore Roosevelt, who counted Wilkie among the nation's most valuable public servants. From the outset of the Roosevelt administration the investigative activities of the Secret Service assumed a new importance and dimension. Roosevelt's war on corruption accelerated the use of Secret Service agents by departments other than the treasury.[15] In practice, whenever a department requested the service of an operative,

[12] "Secret Service Work," New York *Tribune*, December 20, 1908; "How the Secret Service Does Its Work," clipping, December [?], 1908, in Secret Service Scrapbook, Record Group 87, National Archives; New York *Evening Post*, December 19, 1908.

[13] Bowen and Neal, *The United States Secret Service*, 50–55.

[14] Chicago *Inter-Ocean*, January 3, 1904.

[15] Although Roosevelt considered the Secret Service agents detailed to the White House a "necessary thorn in the flesh," his objections were of a purely personal nature and in no way reflected discredit upon the value of the Secret Service in general.

Wilkie merely detailed him to that department. But the agent's reports were made to Wilkie, who referred them to the head of the department for which the investigation was done. Although the agent rendered the bill for his service to Wilkie, it too was forwarded to the disbursing clerk of the appropriate department. Since most departments received appropriations for investigative work, the agent was paid from such funds rather than from the appropriation made specifically for the Secret Service. Because Secret Service agents remained under Wilkie's jurisdiction even while on loan, some of his critics expressed concern over the dangers inherent in "a secret service force under one particular head to make all classes of investigations." [16]

The hostility which came to be directed toward Wilkie was often meant as much for the President as for the head of the Secret Service. Many congressmen and senators viewed Wilkie as a kind of Fouché, whose "army of sleuths" moved at the direction of Roosevelt, an American version of Napoleon. The increasing use of the Secret Service in various investigations ordered by the President tended to support this interpretation. The role of Wilkie's men in the probe of the beef trust aroused considerable hostility, and southern congressmen complained bitterly about the involvement of Secret Service personnel in Roosevelt's campaign against peonage.[17] During the prolonged controversy over the Brownsville incident, Roosevelt's chief antagonist, Senator Foraker, made much of the use of Secret Service agents in "hounding" the Negro troops accused of shooting up the Texas town. Foraker was also convinced that he himself had been kept under constant surveillance at Roosevelt's direction.[18] By early 1908 the most sensational new disclosure involving the Secret Service concerned the use of one of its agents by

[16] Cummings and McFarland, *Federal Justice*, 373; "Inquiry . . . of Secret Service," 5–9.

[17] New York *Evening Post*, December 19, 1908; Chicago *Inter-Ocean*, January 3, 1904; Charleston *News and Courier*, April 2, 1908; Fawcett, "Secret Service and the Big Black Cabinet," Portland *Oregon Sunday Journal*, December 27, 1908; Washington *Evening Star*, April 2, 22, 1908.

[18] Julia B. Foraker, *I Would Live It Again: Memories of a Vivid Life* (New York: Harper, 1932), 287–89; Baltimore *American*, December 18, 1908; Washington *Post*, December 17, 18, 1908.

the secretary of the navy to investigate a naval officer charged with abducting the daughter of a prominent society matron in Washington. Much of the corridor talk about the Secret Service referred to its manufacture of evidence, reliance upon paid informants, and use of intimidation in acquiring confessions.[19]

More important in triggering the controversy over the Secret Service was the use of its operatives in the land fraud investigations. When the Roosevelt administration launched its war against "land thieves" as a part of its conservation program, Secret Service agents regularly assisted in gathering evidence. Convinced that the General Land Office was "largely under the control of land thieves," Secretary of the Interior Ethan A. Hitchcock came to rely upon Secret Service men, especially William J. Burns, in carrying out investigations.[20] More common, however, was the practice whereby the Justice Department borrowed Secret Service operatives, who were in turn assigned to land fraud cases. "Thus," as was later observed, "there was the situation of agents from one department [Treasury] loaned to another [Justice] to investigate violations of laws under the administration of still another department [Interior] and reporting back to the Secret Service Division, which had nothing to do with the administration of the laws violated or with the prosecution of the violators." [21] Virtually all responsible officials recognized that this procedure was administratively cumbersome. Apparently for this reason Roosevelt early advocated a centralization of all detective forces in one bureau, and Wilkie, who agreed with this idea, suggested that the bureau be placed under the attorney general. When James R. Garfield became secretary of the interior in 1907, he dispensed with the services of Wilkie's agents detailed directly to his department because of the friction that had developed be-

[19] *Congressional Record*, 60th Cong., 1st Sess., 5536.

[20] Don Wilkie, *American Secret Service Agent* (New York: Stokes, 1934), 60–65; "Special Message of the President of the United States, January 4, 1909," *House Documents*, 60th Cong., 2nd Sess., No. 1255, p. 13, hereinafter cited as "Special Message of the President"; H. S. Brown, "Punishing Land Looters," *Outlook*, LXXXV (1907), 427–39; Gene Caesar, *Incredible Detective: The Biography of William J. Burns* (Englewood Cliffs, N.J.: Prentice-Hall, 1968), 106–107.

[21] "Inquiry . . . of Secret Service," 5.

tween them and investigators in his own department. He worked out an arrangement with Attorney General Charles J. Bonaparte "whereby agents of the Interior Department were to have sole charge of land fraud matters until the cases were worked up and ready for prosecution." [22]

While Garfield worked toward perfecting the efficiency of the Interior Department in land fraud matters, the Justice Department was undergoing a reorganization in an effort to improve the performance of its investigative chores. Beginning in 1905, Secret Service agents detailed to the department for work in land fraud and antitrust cases were usually assigned to the chief examiner. The appointment of Charles J. Bonaparte as attorney general a year later accelerated the movement for a corps of competent investigators exclusively under the control of the Justice Department. At Bonaparte's insistence in 1907 Congress allotted funds "for the collection, classification and preservation of criminal identification records," which were to be "exchanged with state officials." [23] In his annual report of that year the attorney general called the attention of Congress "to the anomaly that the Department of Justice has no executive force, and more particularly no permanent detective force under its immediate control." He urged that such a force was not only necessary for the performance of his duties but would also lead to "economy and better assurance of results." A "small, carefully selected and experienced [detective] force" at the command of the attorney general would eliminate the wasteful and expensive practice of having federal marshals appoint large numbers of deputies to perform investigative functions. "A Department of Justice with no force of permanent police in any form under its control," Bonaparte concluded, "is assuredly not fully equipped for its work." Although he indicated that the Secret Service might well be transferred

[22] "Hearings before Subcommittee of House Committee on Appropriations," *House Reports*, 60th Cong., 2nd Sess., No. 2205, I, 126; John E. Wilkie, Memorandum on House Debate of January 8, 1909, in Theodore Roosevelt Papers, Manuscript Division, Library of Congress.

[23] Cummings and McFarland, *Federal Justice*, 374–76. See also Albert Langeluttig, *The Department of Justice* (Baltimore: Johns Hopkins, 1927); Frank Buckley, "The Department of Justice—Its Origin, Development and Present Day Organization," *Boston University Law Review*, V (1925), 177–85.

to his jurisdiction, he was confident that the implementation of his plans for a "force of permanent police" within the Justice Department need not necessarily disturb the Secret Service, which presumably would continue to concentrate on counterfeiting and protection of the President.[24] When Bonaparte appeared before the House Appropriations Committee during the hearings on the Sundry Civil Appropriation Bill in March, 1908, he reiterated his ideas about a permanent detective force in the Department of Justice. Again, he justified his plan on the grounds of economy and efficiency. Implicit in his arguments was the recognition of the necessity for congressional approval of his plan.[25]

The interplay of several factors at this particular juncture in the history of the Roosevelt administration precluded the granting of such approval. One was the hostility of Congress toward the President, which was manifested in its increasing tendency to ignore or reject his recommendations. Much of the congressional agitation over the Secret Service was related to the convictions of well-known political figures for violations of the public land laws on the basis of evidence collected by its agents on loan to the Justice and Interior departments. Those either convicted or discredited as a result of the land fraud investigations included most of the Republican leaders in Oregon.[26] Coinciding with the conviction of public officials in land fraud cases and the reorganization of the Justice Department was a heightened interest in annual outlays for "secret service" work of all kinds. Beginning in 1906, the Appropriations Committee chairman, James A. Tawney, an old-guard Republican from Minnesota and a persistent critic of the Roosevelt administration, requested the attorney general to make available complete lists of all inspectors and special agents employed by the Justice Department since 1896. The information furnished by Bonaparte indi-

[24] *Annual Report of the Attorney General of the United States for the Year 1907* (Washington: Government Printing Office, 1907), 9–10.

[25] "Hearings before Subcommittee of House Committee on Appropriations," April 2, 1908, *House Reports*, 60th Cong., 1st Sess., No. 2205, I, 773–81.

[26] See John Messing, "Public Lands, Politics, and Progressives: The Oregon Land Fraud Trials, 1903–1910," *Pacific Historical Review*, XXXV (1966), 35–66; J. O. O'Callaghan, "Senator Mitchell and the Oregon Land Frauds, 1905," *Pacific Historical Review*, XXI (1952), 255–61.

cated that there had been a steady increase in the number of special agents, largely as a result of the department's involvement in antitrust and land fraud investigations. As a member of "the ruling clique" in the House, Tawney was generally disturbed by the proliferation of federal investigations and particularly objected to the use of Secret Service personnel in the investigation of "business arrangements." Tawney, no less than the public, classified all federal employees engaged in investigative and inspection work as "secret service" agents. Such a definition enabled Roosevelt's critics to cite the growth in the Secret Service as tangible evidence of his pursuit of a centralized and unhampered executive power.[27]

During the hearings on the Sundry Civil Appropriation Bill in March and April, 1908, Tawney and other members of the committee, including Walter I. Smith of Iowa, Swagar Sherley of Kentucky, and John J. Fitzgerald of New York, made clear their misgivings about the expanded secret service work of the government. They questioned at length W. H. Moran, the assistant chief of the Secret Service, about the extent to which agents from his division had been lent to other departments and reminded him that this practice was itself a violation of the law. When Attorney General Bonaparte appeared before the committee, his plea for the authorization of a special corps of detectives in the Justice Department met with a cool reception. Ignoring his request, the committee proceeded to prohibit the Justice Department from borrowing detectives from the Secret Service.[28] Largely at Tawney's insistence, the committee inserted in the Sundry Civil Appropriation Bill the following restriction: "No person employed in the Secret Service Division of the Treasury Department or under the appropriation for suppressing counterfeiting and other crimes, who is detailed, furloughed, granted leave of absence, dismissed or otherwise temporarily or finally separated from the service of such division and is thereafter employed under any branch of the public service shall be restored

[27] Cummings and McFarland, *Federal Justice*, 375–76. See especially Tawney's lengthy speech in the *Congressional Record*, 60th Cong., 2nd Sess., 660–68.

[28] "Hearings before Subcommittee of House Committee on Appropriations," March 24, April 2, 1908, *House Reports*, 60th Cong., 1st Sess., No. 2205, I, 185–93, 773–81; Washington *Evening Star*, April 2, 22, 23, 1908.

or paid compensation for service or expenses in the Secret Service Division for two years after the termination of his employment under such other branch of the government." [29] The practical effect of this strangely worded restrictive clause was to prohibit the detailing of Secret Service agents for special assignments in the various executive departments.

President Roosevelt was alarmed at the possibility that Tawney's amendment would pass Congress. He immediately lodged his objections to it with Speaker Cannon, who shared Tawney's apprehensions about the use of the Secret Service as an interdepartmental agency. The President assured the Speaker that the passage of the committee's proposed amendment would "materially interfere with the administration of justice" and would "benefit only one class of people—and that is the criminal class." He pointed out that the State Department would be deprived of means of protecting foreign visitors and the work of the Justice Department would be "very seriously hampered" in several fields. Roosevelt suggested that if Congress insisted upon the restrictive amendment, the Justice Department "would have to try to organize a [detective] corps of its own which under existing legislation it could do but imperfectly." He urged the Speaker not to be misled by all the loose talk about government "spies," which in his opinion was an "outcry of a peculiarly cheap sort." [30] Cannon was wholly unimpressed by the President's appeal.[31]

Various cabinet members joined the President in seeking to prevent the adoption of the Secret Service restriction. Secretary of the Treasury George B. Cortelyou voiced strong opposition to the amendment in letters to Tawney and Senate President William B. Allison. He recited a long list of important investigations undertaken by the Secret Service which had nothing to do with counterfeiting or the protection of the President but which had aided in

[29] *Congressional Record*, 60th Cong., 1st Sess., 5554.

[30] T. Roosevelt to Joseph G. Cannon, April 29, 30, 1908, in Roosevelt Papers. Professor William H. Harbaugh, in explaining Roosevelt's opposition to the amendment, declared that the President not only felt the "Secret Service was needed to combat anarchists" but also "to investigate corporation executives who had violated the law." See his *Power and Responsibility*, 365.

[31] Cannon, *Uncle Joe Cannon*, 232.

achieving justice and in saving substantial sums of money for the federal government. He emphasized that the Secret Service was the only corps of competent, experienced detectives at the disposal of the government. Tackling the issue from a legal angle, Cortelyou denied that use of Secret Service personnel by the Treasury Department or other departments for purposes other than those stated in the appropriations acts violated any law. He reasoned that the traditional restrictions upon these agents applied only to the "expenditure of money." Therefore, they could be employed by other departments to make investigations "so long as they are not reimbursed from the appropriation for suppressing counterfeiting." Since such personnel detailed to the Justice Department were paid from a lump-sum appropriation made specifically to that department for the detection and prosecution of federal crimes, the practice involved no violation of any law. Cortelyou also called attention to the fact that Secret Service agents were used by the Treasury Department for investigations of customs, of the Marine Hospital Service, and of other matters under the jurisdiction of his department which were unrelated to counterfeiting. Such use of the Secret Service, he argued, was consistent with the provision in the Revised Statutes (166) which permitted "each head of a department . . . [to] alter the distribution among the various bureaus and offices of his department of the clerks allowed by law as he may find it necessary and proper to do." The secretary, therefore, took the position that the Tawney amendment was in effect a restriction upon his statutory authority as head of the treasury.[32]

When the matter came up for debate in the House on May 1, 1908, several old-guard Republicans and Democrats vigorously defended the limitation upon the use of the Secret Service. Challenging the legality of using the Secret Service as an interdepartmental detective agency which was in effect answerable to no one save Wilkie, Tawney attempted to demonstrate that such a procedure was as uneconomical as it was illegal. Representatives Sherley and Smith, also members of the Appropriations Committee, discussed

[32] George B. Cortelyou to William B. Allison, May 5, 1908, in "Special Message of the President," 26–29.

the actual, as well as potential, abuses inherent in the unrestricted use of Secret Service agents. Sherley reviewed at length the role played by one such agent detailed to the Navy Department to investigate a naval officer charged with abducting the daughter of a "very estimable lady of Washington." When he expressed fears that the practice of spying by government detectives would be extended to include members of Congress, several of his colleagues joined in supporting the amendment. Pressing the point, Sherley asserted that the Secret Service had already been used for "looking into the personal conduct" of at least one congressman. While the advocates of Tawney's amendment were quick to emphasize the abuses of a government spy system, they were hesitant to deny that such a system in some form was necessary for the executive departments to perform their statutory duties. The alternative, which Tawney himself seemed to favor, was for the departments to have available the "eligible roll" of per diem agents kept by the Secret Service and to employ an individual from that roll for a specific job on a temporary basis. Apparently his objection to the prevailing arrangement of lending Secret Service agents focused upon the supervision which Chief Wilkie exerted over them even when they were on loan. Suspicions that Wilkie was an ambitious empire-builder who enjoyed the full confidence of Roosevelt underlay much of the congressional hostility toward the Secret Service.[33]

Despite the obvious popularity of Tawney's amendment, several congressmen did challenge it. Michael E. Driscoll of New York insisted that the arguments offered by Tawney and Sherley constituted a weak basis for enacting restrictions upon the Secret Service. In his opinion economy and administrative efficiency required the government to have access to a central bureau of trained detectives such as those provided by the Secret Service Division. Even more effective than Driscoll in opposing the restrictive amendment was William S. Bennet of New York, a friend of the President, who challenged it on technical grounds. In an effort to prevent House approval of it, Bennet raised a point of order regarding its legal propriety. He argued that the regular appropriation for the permanent personnel

[33] *Congressional Record*, 60th Cong., 2nd Sess., 5554–59.

of the Secret Service Division was authorized by the Judicial, Legislative, and Executive Appropriations Act rather than the Sundry
Civil Appropriation Bill then under discussion. The former legislation provided the sole legal foundation for the division, whereas
the latter was concerned only with per diem agents kept on the
Secret Service rolls and called into action by the chief as the need
arose.[34] When the Speaker sustained Bennet's point of order, Tawney hastened to recast his amendment to read as follows: "No part
of any money appropriated by this act shall be used in payment of
compensation or expenses of any person detailed or transferred
from the Secret Service Division of the Treasury Department, or
who may at any time during the fiscal year 1909 have been employed
in or under said Secret Service Division." [35] For reasons which are
not clear, Cannon overruled Bennet's point of order on the revised
version of the restrictive clause, which was incorporated in the Sundry Civil Appropriation Bill passed by the House.

Congressional consideration of restrictions upon the Secret Service elicited slight interest. In fact, the charge was later made that the
Tawney amendment had been "slipped through." Among those
newspapers which took note of the House debates were the Chicago
Inter-Ocean and the Washington Star, which rejoiced that Congress
had at last put an end to the free-wheeling activities of the government's notorious "black cabinet." [36] Taking an opposite view, the
New York Times reminded its readers of the utility of the Secret
Service in restoring "more than a million acres of the public domain
fraudulently obtained by a powerful 'ring' of land thieves." The
Times concluded that the representatives had "unwittingly become
the tool of thieves" and urged the Senate to reject the Tawney
amendment.[37] Upon reading the Times editorial, Henry L. Stimson, United States attorney for the Southern District of New York,
assured the attorney general that restrictions on the Secret Service
"would have a most serious and detrimental effect upon our work."

[34] Ibid.

[35] Ibid., 5558.

[36] Chicago Inter-Ocean, undated clipping, in Secret Service Scrapbook; Washington Evening Star, April 21, 1908.

[37] New York Times, May 6, 1908.

He declared, "I should feel as if the fighting power of my office were almost crippled by such a statute." [38]

Although the restrictive clause was not a part of the Sundry Civil Appropriation Bill originally passed by the Senate, it was included in the version which came out of the conference committee. In effect, the Senate acquiesced in the wishes of the House. Despite the President's objections to the restrictive clause, he signed the bill rather than jeopardize the appropriations for so many key agencies provided in the act. The New York *Tribune*, whose stories were often inspired by the White House, reported that the restriction upon the Secret Service was the work of congressmen "whose sympathies have been enlisted by men prosecuted for public land and timber frauds, although it is realized that certain business and transportation interests who could greatly augment their profits by wholesale violations of the law are overjoyed." [39]

At least in the case of one ardent advocate of the restriction, Congressman Smith of Council Bluffs, Iowa, Roosevelt did have in his possession data which conceivably could have been the source of the *Tribune*'s accusation. A report by Chief Wilkie, which was reviewed by Roosevelt as well as Cortelyou, Garfield, and Bonaparte, revealed that Smith had close connections with railroad companies in Iowa interested in various public lands and that he was "a personal friend and associate" of Charles T. Stewart of Council Bluffs, who was then under indictment for conspiracy to defraud the government of public lands. Wilkie's report on Smith, compiled in connection with the investigation of Stewart, also disclosed that the congressman was

[38] Henry L. Stimson to Charles J. Bonaparte, May 6, 1908, in File 44–3–11–3, Department of Justice. A month later Stimson wrote the attorney general, "The local Secret Service force [in New York] under Chief [William J.] Flynn has been invaluable during the past two and a half years, and it will be of the greatest possible misfortune to the interests of the Government to proceed with a less efficient force of men. Flynn is a man of exceptional ability and he has kept his force free from political and other influences. . . . Their service in connection with this office [United States Attorney] in preparation of evidence and location of witnesses has been in my opinion distinctly superior to that of any other detective force with which I have ever had to work." Stimson to Bonaparte, June 5, 1908, *ibid.*

[39] New York *Tribune*, May 6, 1908.

"interested in a number of land tracts in western Nebraska." [40]
There seems to be little doubt about the interpretation placed upon
these findings by Roosevelt and his chief advisers. Although there
was no concrete evidence that Smith had violated any law, his vigorous protests on the floor of Congress regarding the abuses of the
Secret Service tended to confirm their suspicions that he was attempting either to protect himself from exposure or to aid his friend
Stewart.

No sooner had Congress placed the restriction upon the Secret
Service than Roosevelt began to search for means to continue the
work previously done by its agents. The Justice Department in
particular was affected because it had come to rely heavily upon
"borrowed" agents to collect evidence against those charged with
violating various federal statutes. Other departments employed Secret Service men less often and usually only one or two at a time.[41]
As soon as the Appropriations Committee made public its intention
to limit the activity of the Secret Service, there were widespread
rumors that the Justice Department would create its own "secret
service." Stanley W. Finch, chief examiner in the department, saw
no alternative but to establish a detective bureau "for the purpose of
doing the work heretofore done by the people borrowed from Mr.
Wilkie." [42] Earlier, when Bonaparte and Roosevelt had broached
the subject of such a bureau, both had indicated that its establishment would require congressional approval. But the passage of the
Tawney amendment, as well as the recalcitrant attitude of Congress
in general, apparently helped persuade them that some form of detective agency could be created within the Justice Department by
executive action alone. Their reasoning was that the department

[40] *Ibid.* Don Wilkie, a Secret Service agent and the son of the Secret Service
chief, claimed that when Roosevelt's investigation of land and timber frauds
come to involve prominent politicians and businessmen, "the wire-pulling began" in an effort to prevent prosecutions. He interprets the restriction upon the
Secret Service as a direct result of Roosevelt's campaign against land thieves.
See Wilkie, *American Secret Service Agent*, 60–67.

[41] Cortelyou to Bonaparte, May 27, 1908, in Charles J. Bonaparte Papers,
Manuscript Division, Library of Congress.

[42] S. W. Finch to A. M. McNish, April 29, 1908, in Records of Bureau of
Investigation, Record Group 65, National Archives.

received an annual appropriation for "the detection and prosecution of crimes," and that funds from this appropriation previously expended for the services of personnel borrowed from the Secret Service could be used to bear the cost of a small detective force responsible directly to the attorney general.[43]

Shortly before July 1, 1908, the date the Sundry Civil Appropriation Act went into effect, President Roosevelt authorized the transfer of nine men in the Secret Service Division to the Justice Department.[44] Whether Roosevelt and Bonaparte viewed this as a permanent arrangement is not altogether clear. Chief Wilkie plainly viewed the transfer of agents to the Justice Department as a temporary expedient. Since the appropriation for counterfeiting had also been curtailed, the transfer of nine men to the Justice Department offered, in Wilkie's opinion, "a fortunate solution of what might otherwise be hardship to agents whose services could not be retained in this division beyond the close of the present fiscal year." So certain was he that the restriction would be removed during the next session of Congress that he virtually promised those agents transferred to the Justice Department reappointment in his division.[45] When a letter from Wilkie to one of the men to be transferred later came into Tawney's possession, it was cited as proof of the Secret Service chief's contempt for Congress in his campaign to build a "large central secret-service bureau under no limitations, under no restrictions, and responsible to nobody but himself." [46] That Wilkie strenuously objected to the limitations placed upon his division is a matter of record. But whether personal ambition or a desire for "the efficient pursuit of criminals" was the primary motive cannot be determined with any degree of certainty. It appears, however, that he, like Roosevelt and Bonaparte, was genuinely interested in the creation of a central bureau of highly trained detectives

[43] See Finch to Henry C. Smith, July 25, 1908, in Records of the Bureau of Investigation; Bonaparte to T. Roosevelt, December 31, 1908, in File 44–3–11–3, Department of Justice.

[44] See Don Whitehead, *The FBI Story: A Report to the People* (New York: Random, 1956), 21.

[45] John E. Wilkie to [?], June 27, 1908, quoted in *Congressional Record*, 60th Cong., 2nd Sess., 3135.

[46] *Congressional Record*, 60th Cong., 2nd Sess., 3135.

under the administrative direction of the attorney general, which would serve as an interdepartmental detective force. His anticipation of such a reorganization may help to explain why he was so eager to retain in government service those competent agents who otherwise would have been eliminated because of reduced appropriations.[47]

Whatever Wilkie's intentions may have been, Attorney General Bonaparte gave his personal attention to the modifications in his department's organization necessary for expanding its investigative and detective work. The nine men transferred from the Secret Service Division, together with thirteen other persons already employed in the department in connection with land fraud and peonage cases, were designated special agents, directly responsible to Chief Examiner Stanley W. Finch, who received from them daily reports, which he summarized for review by the attorney general.[48] In organizing this new force Bonaparte worked out the details in conjunction with Finch and several federal attorneys, especially Stimson of New York and Edwin W. Sims of Illinois.[49]

Although Bonaparte was careful to incorporate the nine men from the Secret Service into the Justice Department prior to the beginning of the fiscal year on July 1, 1908, the details of the administrative rearrangement were not completed until several weeks later. Reluctant to classify the reshuffled investigative personnel as a bureau, he usually referred to them as "the new Special Agent Force." Whatever its title, it represented, according to Bonaparte's successor, the first active step toward "the organization in this [Justice] Department of a comprehensive investigative service."[50] The

[47] See especially Wilkie's testimony in "Hearings before Subcommittee of House Committee on Appropriations," *House Reports*, 60th Cong., 2nd Sess., No. 2205, I, 32–40.

[48] Bonaparte to T. Roosevelt, December 31, 1908, in File 44–3–11–3, Department of Justice; *Annual Report of the Attorney General of the United States for the Year 1909* (Washington: Government Printing Office, 1909), 8–10.

[49] Edwin W. Sims to Bonaparte, June 25, 1908, Stimson to Bonaparte, June 30, 1908, Finch to Bonaparte, July 8, 1908, Bonaparte to Sims, July 7, 1908, in File 44–3–11–3, Department of Justice; Finch to Smith, July 25, 1908, in Records of the Bureau of Investigation.

[50] *Annual Report of the Attorney General, 1909*, p. 8.

investigative force created by Bonaparte was the origin of what later became known as the Federal Bureau of Investigation. In fact, by the end of 1908 the new branch of the Justice Department was generally known as the "bureau of investigation," a title which it did not officially receive until Taft became President. The date used by the present FBI to designate its official beginning is July 26, 1908, the date on which Bonaparte issued the following order:

> All matters relating to investigations under the Department, except those to be made by bank examiners, and in connection with the naturalization service, will be referred to the Chief Examiner for a memorandum as to whether any member of the force of Special Agents under his direction is available for the work to be performed. No authorization of expenditure for special examination shall be made by any officer of the Department, without first ascertaining whether one of the regular force is available for the service desired, and in case the service cannot be performed by the regular force of Special Agents in the Department, the matter will be called to the attention of the Attorney General . . . with a statement from the Chief Examiner as to the reasons why a regular employee cannot be assigned to the work, before authorization shall be made for the expenditure of any money for this purpose.[51]

Six months after issuing this order, Bonaparte stated with obvious pride that the new investigative force had already demonstrated its efficiency. "It is hoped," he concluded, "that its merits will be augmented and its attendant expense reduced by further experience." [52]

During the latter half of 1908, the "bureau of investigation" apparently surmounted most of the obstacles created by the congressional restriction upon the Secret Service. In view of the circumstances, one may well ask why Roosevelt renewed the controversy by a pointed reference to it in his last annual message in December, 1908. Despite what has been called the "impolitic" nature of the message generally, his "affinity for controversy" scarcely seems to offer a satisfactory explanation. Something more than merely a desire to strike back at a Congress which had stubbornly rejected his

[51] Order by Charles J. Bonaparte, Attorney General, July 26, 1908, in File 44-3-11-3, Department of Justice.

[52] *Annual Report of the Attorney General of the United States for the Year 1908* (Washington: Government Printing Office, 1908), 7.

proposals was involved. There is little doubt that Roosevelt intentionally provoked a discussion of the Secret Service issue in order to disclose to the public the motives of those members of Congress responsible for limiting his use of the "only trained detective force" in the government. He was convinced that his role in sending certain members of Congress to the penitentiary for violations of the land laws was the primary reason for the passage of the restrictive amendment. According to Roosevelt, corruption had "made its last stand just where it was least expected, namely in Congress." Therefore, he argued, his appeal had to be made to the public conscience rather than to "the conscience of Congress which had lain dormant so long." In discussing the matter with one of his aides, the President remarked, "How can I hunt out corruption, or even know that it exists unless I have the use of men who know where it is and how to get at the facts? I have pledged myself to wage war on corruption and graft wherever they can be found, and the higher up the criminal may be, the more necessary it is to strike him down. I want the people to know what I know and then it makes no matter how lenient a President may want to be, he will have to account to the people if corruption goes unchastized." [53] At the time many questioned whether Roosevelt's motives were as noble as such remarks suggested. The evidence seems to indicate that these suspicions were not altogether unwarranted, for in the process of protecting the machinery for waging his war on corruption the President went out of his way to incriminate those in Congress who had been persistent critics of his administration. It is also conceivable that Roosevelt, always concerned about his historical reputation, may have addressed his remarks on the Secret Service as much to posterity as to the public of his own day.

Yet there are other considerations which may have figured in his decision to reopen the discussion of the Secret Service. Fully aware of the temper of Congress, he not only came to see little hope for removing the restrictions upon the Secret Service but also feared that the new investigative agency in the Justice Department might

[53] Lawrence F. Abbott (ed.), *The Letters of Archie Butt* (Garden City, N.Y.: Doubleday, 1924), 239–40.

be subjected to similar limitations. Congressmen hostile to his vigorous exertion of presidential power had little reason to be more conciliatory in December, 1908, than they had been earlier in the year. Certainly the investigative activities of the executive departments which had been the source of congressional concern showed few signs of diminishing. Conceivably Congress might transfer its hostility to the new "bureau of investigation" and either limit its activity or legislate it out of existence. Such a possibility may help explain why Roosevelt devoted two paragraphs in his annual message to the question of the Secret Service. His treatment of the subject served to divert attention from the newly organized "bureau of investigation" and to raise questions about the motives which prompted Congress to curb the investigative functions of the government's only bona fide detective bureau. It was clearly a tactic designed to galvanize public opinion in opposition to further curtailments of executive investigative forces. In short, Roosevelt's remarks appear to have been calculated to elicit a public response which would act as a deterrent to any congressional effort to emasculate Bonaparte's force of special agents. If indeed this was his strategy, the popular reaction indicated that he could scarcely have calculated more accurately.

The message which Roosevelt released on December 8, 1908, not only contained many of the "radical" recommendations previously ignored by Congress but also included a defense of his administration against the charges of "executive usurpation" made by his legislative critics. The President charged that the congressional limitation upon the Secret Service had seriously diminished the effectiveness of the administration's war against some of "the wealthiest and most formidable criminals with whom the Government has had to deal." He specifically cited the violations of public land and antitrust laws as areas in which the investigations by Secret Service agents had been most useful. Stating publicly what he had told Speaker Cannon earlier, Roosevelt maintained that the restriction placed upon the Secret Service "could be of benefit only to the criminal classes." [54]

[54] Hermann Hagedorn (ed.), *The Works of Theodore Roosevelt* (24 vols.; New York: Scribner, 1924–26), XVII, 620.

Congress may well have been angered had the President said no more. But what actually unleashed congressional fury was the second paragraph of his comments on the Secret Service:

> The chief argument in favor of the provision [limiting the use of the Secret Service] was that congressmen did not themselves wish to be investigated by Secret Service men. Very little of such investigation has been done in the past; but it is true that the work of the secret service agents was partly responsible for the indictment and conviction of a Senator and a Congressman for land frauds in Oregon. I do not believe that it is in the public interest to protect criminals in any branch of the public service, and exactly as we have again and again prosecuted and convicted such criminals who were in the executive branch of the Government, so in my belief we should be given ample means to prosecute them if found in the legislative branch. But if this is not considered desirable a special exception could be made in the law prohibiting the use of the secret service force in investigating Members of Congress. It would be far better to do this than to do what actually was done, and strive to prevent or at least to hamper effective action against criminals by the executive branch of the Government.[55]

However impolitic his statement may have been, it tended "to put the co-ordinate branch in a hole." For Congress either to make the "exception" to which Roosevelt referred or to place additional limitations upon the government's investigative forces was to invite the charge that its members had something to hide. Certainly any effort to tamper with the Justice Department's "detective agency" would merely corroborate the President's position. Actually, Roosevelt's statement displayed a good deal of ingenuity. For anyone who checked the record of the congressional debates it was clear that his claim about congressmen fearing investigation was not the groundless, "wild charge" which some tried to make it. Nor did he accuse all congressmen of harboring such fears; his reference to "the chief argument" in favor of the Tawney amendment applied obviously to a handful of representatives. But, as one friendly editor pointed out, the President's use of the phrase "*a* chief argument" rather than "*the* chief argument" would have been more accurate and judicious.[56]

[55] *Ibid.*, 621.
[56] *Outlook*, XCI (1909), 58.

Whatever the validity or propriety of the President's statement, the reaction in Congress was immediate and vehement. Virtually ignoring the remainder of his lengthy message, members of both political parties seized upon the two paragraphs regarding the Secret Service as a studied insult to Congress. Representative Julius Kahn of California expressed the prevailing sentiment of his colleagues when he said that Roosevelt's reference to the Secret Service indicated that congressmen were "either rascals or fools." Democratic senators first considered a motion of censure but later assumed the position that they would leave "the disciplining of the executive to the majority party." Republicans, in the meantime, held a series of informal conferences in an effort to find an appropriate method of expressing their resentment.[57]

While both houses worked out their strategy, the Capitol corridors were filled with talk of recent "abuses" committed by Secret Service "spies." Tawney let it be known that Wilkie had sent an agent into his district during the campaign of 1908 for the purpose of bringing about his defeat. Although the accusation later proved to be utterly false, it served at the time to galvanize congressional hostility to Roosevelt and to lend credence to the idea that the Secret Service was being used for "political purposes." Several senators complained about being "shadowed," and rumor had it that a federal judge who rendered a decision unfavorable to the Roosevelt administration was investigated by "secret service sleuths" shortly afterward. A Democratic congressman who preferred to remain anonymous warned his colleagues through the press that Roosevelt possessed complete reports on their visits to a particular gambling house as well as other questionable places in Washington.[58]

No less hostile than the expressions emanating from Capitol Hill was the reaction of a sizable segment of the press. The primary issue, as many saw it, was whether a Secret Service with broad investigative powers was consistent with the welfare of a democratic republic. "The Secret Service," the *Wall Street Journal* declared, "is essen-

[57] Chicago *Tribune*, December 9, 1908; New York *Tribune*, December 10, 11, 12, 1908; New York *Times*, January 5, 1909.

[58] Washington *Post*, December 10, 1908; Atlanta *Constitution*, December 11, 12, 13, 1908; New York *Herald*, December 10, 11, 17, 1908.

tially antagonistic to the ideals of the Republic and whatever benefits may flow from its use by a wise executive, these benefits never can compensate for the perils and sinister potentialities involved in the expansion of secret and irresponsible power." [59] Newspaper cartoonists, who depicted Roosevelt in a Guy Fawkes setting, vied with editorialists, who characterized him as Napoleon and Wilkie as Fouché. In fact, one of the most persistent editorial themes of the anti-Roosevelt newspapers was the analogy drawn between the "government spies" of Roosevelt and Fouché's secret police. If critics read any significance into the fact that one of Napoleon's relatives, Attorney General Bonaparte, was Roosevelt's principal adviser in the Secret Service matter, they did not say so publicly.[60]

Although the President's remarks on the Secret Service provoked vociferous criticism in the press, public opinion from the beginning appeared to be overwhelmingly in his favor. Even some anti-Roosevelt editors admitted that the President had "the folks with him." Those who declared that the "people of the United States would never tolerate Fouchéism" also recognized that the people were even less likely to tolerate congressional interference with "the efficient pursuit of criminals." [61] Many editors were convinced that any attempt by Congress to "rebuke" the President would merely confirm the popular view of its members as something less than angels. The Philadelphia *North American* insisted that congressional retaliation

[59] *Wall Street Journal*, December 22, 1908.

[60] See "The President and Congress," *Harper's Weekly*, LII (December 12, 1908), 4; Des Moines *Capital*, December 12, 1908; Birmingham *Age-Herald*, December 19, 1908; Atlanta *Journal*, December 20, 1908; St. Louis *Republican*, December 10, 1908; New York *Sun*, December 10, 12, 1908; *Commoner*, VIII (December 18, 1908), 2; *Literary Digest*, XXXVIII (1909), 4.

[61] See Birmingham *Age-Herald*, January 10, 1908; Brooklyn *Standard*, December 12, 1908; James Lowth to James A. Tawney, December 18, 1908, A. O. Bright to Tawney, January 9, 1909, in James A. Tawney Papers, Minnesota Historical Society, St. Paul, Minn.; Norfolk (Va.) *Landmark*, December 16, 1908; New Haven *Morning Journal*, December 14, 1908; Philadelphia *Evening Telegram*, December 11, 1908; San Francisco *Call*, December 11, 1908; Omaha *Bee*, December 10, 1908; Columbus *Evening Dispatch*, December 11, 1908; Louisville *Herald*, December 17, 1908; "At Swords' Points in Washington," *Literary Digest*, XXXVIII (1909), 79–81.

would prove the validity of the old adage that "who excuses himself, accuses himself." [62]

While the public discussed the implications of Roosevelt's message, Congress took the initial steps toward assuaging its "wounded dignity" and defending its "maligned integrity." On December 11, 1908, Congressman James B. Perkins of New York, a sponsor of the restrictive amendment, proposed the appointment of a committee of five members by the Speaker to consider that portion of the President's annual message concerning the Secret Service and to report to the House "what action if any should be taken in reference" to it. Denying any "oversensitiveness to unfavorable criticism," Perkins claimed that the comments by Roosevelt could "not be lightly disregarded" by Congress without admitting "a lack of proper self-respect." His resolution was accepted without dissent, and Speaker Cannon immediately appointed Perkins chairman of the committee.[63]

On December 17, 1908, Perkins, on behalf of the committee, introduced a resolution calling upon Roosevelt to transmit to the House any evidence for his statement that the "chief argument" for restricting the use of the Secret Service was "that Congressmen did not themselves wish to be investigated." The resolution also requested the President to release "any evidence connecting any Member of the House of Representatives of the Sixtieth Congress with corrupt action in his official capacity." A Democratic member of the committee, John Sharp Williams, declared that if Roosevelt did not produce evidence to prove that "the entire body of the National Legislature has been actuated by the corrupt motive of shielding criminal congressmen," then the "country, which is the master of

[62] Philadelphia *North American*, December 12, 1908. See also Richmond *News Leader*, December 13, 1908; Philadelphia *Evening Telegraph*, December 15, 1908; Omaha *Bee*, December 20, 1908; Tacoma *Tribune*, December 22, 1908; Brooklyn *Standard*, December 12, 1908; James R. Garfield Diaries (James R. Garfield Papers, Manuscript Division, Library of Congress), December 15, 16, 1908; Lawrence Abbott to T. Roosevelt, January 15, 1909, in Roosevelt Papers.

[63] *Congressional Record*, 60th Cong., 2nd Sess., 140–41; New York *Tribune*, December 12, 13, 1908; Washington *Evening Star*, December 11, 12, 1908; Charles G. Washburn, *Life of John W. Weeks* (Boston: Houghton, 1928), 69–74.

both of us, will come to its own judgment of his conduct." The resolution, endorsed unanimously by the Perkins committee, passed the House virtually without opposition.[64]

On December 16, 1908, five days after the House established the Perkins committee, the Senate took under consideration proposals to create a similar body. A resolution by Senator Aldrich referred the President's statement on the Secret Service to the Committee on Appropriations with instructions for it to determine whether the restrictive amendment had "impaired the efficiency or sufficiency of the force employed in the secret service." It was also directed to ascertain "what persons other than those included in the Secret Service were paid from the Public Treasury during the fiscal year [1908] for services in connection with the enforcement of the laws or for work in the detection or investigation of possible crimes." As soon as practical, the committee was to recommend appropriate action by the Senate in response to the President. Senator Eugene Hale of Maine, who as chairman of the Appropriations Committee was in charge of the Aldrich resolution, promised "to proceed in a careful manner and dignified way." [65]

A group of southern Democratic senators voiced the suspicion that if Hale's inquiry was as "careful" as Aldrich's resolution, the President's insult to "the integrity of the Senate" would not be adequately dealt with. Senator Joseph W. Bailey of Texas accused Aldrich of having "been altogether too careful of somebody's feelings." Tillman claimed that the "manhood and self-respect" of the senators required vigorous action in view of Roosevelt's implication that they were "a lot of rascals and scoundrels who belong in the penitentiary." He concluded, "There may be men who feel that way, but God knows I don't." Tillman's remarks assumed greater importance shortly afterward because of revelations regarding his connections with a land speculation scheme under investigation by the Secret Service. If Democrats offered the greatest support to a stronger

[64] *Congressional Record*, 60th Cong., 2nd Sess., 373–75; Atlanta *Constitution*, December 18, 1908; Washington *Evening Star*, December 17, 18, 1908.

[65] *Congressional Record*, 60th Cong., 2nd Sess., 303, 311–15; Atlanta *Constitution*, December 17, 18, 1908; New York *Tribune*, December 17, 18, 1908.

rejoinder to the President, it was also a Democrat, Francis G. Newlands of Nevada, who made the only speech in his defense. Newlands reminded his colleagues that the President "was clearly within his constitutional power to make recommendations to Congress" and that an emotional response to his statement on the Secret Service was certain to have a more harmful effect upon the image of the body than any presidential comment. Newlands' plea was of no avail. The Senate easily adopted Aldrich's resolution directing the Appropriations Committee to recommend an appropriate response to the White House.[66]

Once Congress made clear its intention to take action on the President's message, the public interest in the Secret Service controversy assumed a new dimension. Many of those who attempted to find the broader meaning of the dispute agreed with the Seattle *News*, which interpreted the stand taken by Congress "as the opening gun in a campaign to win back for Congress the power and importance which Roosevelt has taken from it." "Undoubtedly, it has been planned," the *News* observed, "to serve the double purpose of defying the 'fangless lion' in the days of Roosevelt's waning power to fight back and also to serve notice to President-elect Taft that Congress does not intend to tolerate this same policy of intimidation." [67] Roosevelt's friends and foes alike generally agreed that the use of Secret Service agents in the land fraud investigations was the primary cause for congressional concern over "government spies." Critics charged that since agents were "too eager to show the connection of politicians with land fraud," they were "likely to embarrass innocent men." The example most often cited to prove this contention was the case of Senator William E. Borah of Idaho, whose "un-

[66] *Congressional Record*, 60th Cong., 2nd Sess., 313–14; Atlanta *Constitution*, December 18, 1908; New York *Tribune*, December 17, 1908. On December 19, 1908, even Senator Henry Cabot Lodge "turned against his friend in the White House," when he prevented an interruption in the Senate proceedings in order to take notice of a special message from Roosevelt. See Pringle, *Roosevelt: A Biography*, 340.

[67] Seattle *News*, December 12, 1908. For similar views see Lewiston (Maine) *Evening Journal*, December 11, 1908; Columbus *Evening Dispatch*, December 11, 1908.

justifiable prosecution" in connection with land fraud had resulted in his acquittal.[68] Such incidences convinced the Rochester *Post-Express* that Congress should administer a strong rebuke to Roosevelt and serve notice on his successor that the Secret Service was not to be used as "a private detective agency for the president." [69]

Other newspapers, which refused to discuss the matter in terms of a quarrel between Roosevelt and "the controlling clique in each house of Congress," insisted that the basic issue concerned the place of a secret government detective agency within a democratic society. Their concern focused not so much on the allegedly improper use of the Secret Service in the past but on the dangers inherent in the existence of a "free lance" investigatory bureau. Unless it were "placed upon a more satisfactory basis," the Secret Service might easily become a threat to the very democratic institutions it was designed to protect. But those few editors who attempted to discuss the ramifications of a greatly expanded Secret Service without dealing in accusations against either the President or Congress apparently made little impression upon the public. There was, in fact, no popular inclination to reflect upon the larger issues involved in the squabble.[70] Of far greater interest at the moment was the manner in which Roosevelt would react to the position assumed by Congress.

When the House demanded that President Roosevelt release any information in his possession regarding the misconduct of its members, the anti-Roosevelt press was overjoyed that Congress had at last called his bluff. But the President himself described the action as foolish. "I was careful," he confided to a friend, "never to con-

---

[68] Chicago *Tribune*, December 9, 1908; Omaha *Bee*, December 14, 20, 1908; Kansas City *Times*, December 11, 1908. For Roosevelt's interest in the Borah case see T. Roosevelt to William Allen White, May 8, July 30, 1907, T. Roosevelt to Bonaparte, August 24, 1907, in Morison (ed.), *Roosevelt Letters*, V, 662–63, 736–37, 767, 771. Despite the widespread acceptance of the idea that the use of the Secret Service agents in land fraud investigations was the source of the agitation, the vast majority of the agents lent to the Justice Department were employed in antitrust cases.

[69] Rochester *Post-Express*, December 14, 15, 1908.

[70] Pittsburgh *Telegraph*, December 15, 1908; New York *Evening Post*, December 14, 1908; St. Louis *Republican*, December 18, 1908; Milwaukee *Sentinel*, December 28, 1908; Wilmington (Del.) *Every Evening*, January 4, 1909; Houston *Post*, January 4, 1909; *Wall Street Journal*, December 22, 1908.

demn all Congressmen, but my business is to war against all crookedness wherever I find it, and I am not going to let up as long as I am President." [71] He was not only careful in framing his response to the House request but also delayed its release so as to reap maximum advantage. According to one veteran journalist, "Roosevelt let the idea circulate through his well organized press service that reports of secret service men on Congressmen would prove interesting reading if sent in in a special message." [72] Roosevelt's delay in responding to the House did seem to encourage rumors to the effect that he was busy compiling evidence to support his contention that congressmen had reason not to wish to be investigated. Reliable political observers noted that such reports, coupled with the fact that Roosevelt still delayed his response, had caused considerable anxiety among congressmen, who had come to doubt whether the decision to call his bluff had been wise. A common view was that for all its "snarling," Congress would "not bite" lest the President be provoked into releasing information "damaging to the careers of congressmen." [73]

Throughout the Christmas recess the controversy continued to dominate editorial and news columns. On December 21, 1908, the New York *Tribune* reported that Roosevelt had under consideration a plan to abolish the Secret Service and to consolidate all detective work in a division of criminal investigation within the Justice Department. The new division would also include revenue agents, pension examiners, and customs and postal inspectors, as well as those already employed in the new "special agent force." Because the report appeared in the *Tribune*, it was generally agreed that it originated with the White House.[74] The pro-Roosevelt press praised the plan as embodying the principles of economy and efficiency. But other newspapers, including some which had not been especially

[71] T. Roosevelt to William V. Sewall, December 18, 1908, in Morison (ed.), *Roosevelt Letters*, VI, 1492.

[72] Arthur Wallace Dunn, *From Harrison to Harding: A Personal Narrative Covering a Third of a Century, 1881–1921* (2 vols.; New York: Putnam, 1922), II, 89.

[73] Brooklyn *Eagle*, December 18, 1908; Buffalo *Express*, January 3, 1909; Cleveland *Ledger*, January 5, 1909; Omaha *Bee*, December 20, 1908.

[74] New York *Tribune*, December 21, 22, 1908.

partisan to Congress, characterized the proposed reorganization as merely a scheme for getting Roosevelt out of his "present difficulty." It was, according to the New York *Evening Post*, "a red herring across the real trail." [75]

Convinced that any hope for removing the limitations on the Secret Service was futile, Roosevelt did explore with both Attorney General Bonaparte and Chief Wilkie, the possibility of consolidating all detective work in the Justice Department. Interestingly enough, the organization and functions ascribed to the proposed "division of criminal investigation" closely paralleled those of the existing bureau of investigation. Apparently, Roosevelt envisioned a broadening of the scope of the bureau by having it absorb all agents of the detective kind, including those in the Secret Service, who had been attached to various executive departments.[76]

On January 14, 1909, Bonaparte set forth his views on the proposed reorganization in a lengthy letter to the President in which he explained the rise and expansion of investigative activities by the federal government. The attorney general endorsed the idea of a partial consolidation of government detective forces under his jurisdiction, but raised serious objections to any attempt to dispense with investigative agents in all departments except Justice. He rejected any proposal for a grand consolidation of all detective work into a single agency. "I think," he wrote, "it is important—indeed, indispensable—to the proper discipline of each Executive Department that investigations relating to the conduct of its business, the care of its records and the efficiency of its personnel, should be directed by the Head of the Department in question." In fact, the work of the detective force in the Justice Department "should not begin until the need for a criminal prosecution or some civil proceeding against somebody shall become at least reasonably probable." Although Bonaparte did not explicitly state that the Secret Service should remain an agency within the Treasury Department, this was apparently his intention. As far as he was concerned, the new bureau of

[75] Brooklyn *Eagle*, December 22, 1908; Birmingham *Age-Herald*, December 23, 1908; New York *Tribune*, December 24, 1908; New York *Evening Post*, December 21, 24, 1908.
[76] New York *Tribune*, December 21, 24, 1908.

investigation in his department "could if necessary furnish to other departments suitable men to discharge exceptional duties." In short, he argued that the perfection of the new force of special agents in his department obviated the need for further reorganization in the government's detective personnel. "I believe," he assured the President, "that if it [bureau of investigation] is maintained by my successor and receives, from time to time, the improvements suggested by experience, it will develop into a highly efficient and trustworthy detective agency." Bonaparte's argument was sufficiently convincing to cause Roosevelt to abandon plans for further reorganization of the government detective forces.[77]

In the meantime, the President had completed his special message in response to the House resolution demanding that he release any evidence of corrupt action by its members. By the time it was presented to the House on January 4, 1909, popular opinion appeared to be solidly behind the President in the Secret Service matter. The message was at once conciliatory and belligerent. But it did not reveal the slightest retreat from his earlier statement. "I have made no charges of corruption against Congress," Roosevelt began, "nor against any Member of the present House." But he made it eminently clear that whenever proof of corruption came into his possession, he would not hesitate to take the same kind of action as he had taken previously against two senators and three representatives. Roosevelt, assuming for the moment a position as defender of the separation of powers, informed the House that it was not within his "province" to report on the "alleged delinquencies" or "supposed corrupt action" of a House member. For him to do so would be an infringement upon the constitutional power of the House, which alone had authority over its membership. Following some soothing remarks about his opposition to "indiscriminate attacks upon Congress," Roosevelt proceeded to single out for special criticism Congressmen Tawney, Smith, Sherley, Fitzgerald, and Cannon because of their roles in placing the restriction upon the Secret Service. Tawney was accused of intentionally misrepresenting the scope and function of the Secret Service, while Speaker Cannon

[77] Bonaparte to T. Roosevelt, January 14, 1909, in Roosevelt Papers.

was chastised for his failure to make the House aware of the President's letter protesting the enactment of any restrictions upon the Secret Service. In an additional strike at Cannon, Roosevelt traced the origin of the agitation over the Secret Service to the publication of an article in the Chicago *Inter-Ocean* in 1904 by L. W. Busbey, a journalist who later became secretary to the Speaker. Then, in the course of an elaborate review of cases in which the Secret Service had participated, the President described in detail the frauds committed by Charles T. Stewart, the friend and associate of Congressman Smith. The lengthy references to the Stewart case were so phrased as to convey the impression that it was the basis for Smith's desire to place restrictions upon the agency. The President emphatically denied that Secret Service men had ever been used "in the investigation of purely private or political matters" during his administration. In "the name of good government and decent administration," he urged the House to rescind its action of the previous session. Then, in a final paragraph, he paid a tribute to Chief Wilkie and requested that his annual salary be increased from $4,500 to $6,000. The message was an extraordinary state paper not only for what it said but also for what it did not say. Particularly notable was the omission of any reference to the bureau of investigation, which at the time was performing many of the functions formerly assigned to the Secret Service.[78]

When the message was laid before the House on January 4, 1909, it was referred to the special committee chaired by Perkins and originally created to consider that portion of the President's annual message dealing with the Secret Service. While awaiting the committee's recommendation, those congressmen who had been mentioned by name in the special message were free in their expressions of hostility. Speaker Cannon interpreted the message as primarily the work of Secret Service Chief Wilkie, who had "constructed for the President a fantastic story," and as "more offensive than the one to which the House had [already] taken exception." Cannon was convinced that Roosevelt had attempted to place the responsibility "for the whole mess" upon him by citing an article by his secretary. "The

[78] "Special Message of the President," 3–30.

use of that old newspaper article by President Roosevelt," he concluded, "was the weakest political move I ever knew him to make." Busbey, the author of the article, later explained that it had been written a year before he became Cannon's secretary and that it had actually been inspired by Roosevelt himself. But what neither made public at the time was the old enmity which had existed between Busbey and Wilkie ever since their days as rival newspapermen in Chicago.[79]

Even more strongly than Cannon, Tawney expressed resentment at what he considered the President's attack upon his personal integrity. He denied that he had misrepresented Secretary Cortelyou's views on the Secret Service and accused Roosevelt of quoting him out of context. In reacting to Roosevelt's statement, Tawney made no effort to hide his contempt for Wilkie. His criticism of the Secret Service chief seemed to confirm rumors that the two men were old adversaries. Tawney claimed that Wilkie either wrote or inspired the controversial paragraphs in the President's annual message because he was the only official who lost any power or patronage as a result of the restrictive amendment. The powerful congressman, in effect, served notice that what he called the Roosevelt-Wilkie campaign against him would not go unchallenged.[80]

On January 8, 1909, Congressman Perkins introduced, with the unanimous approval of his "spanking committee," a resolution to table that portion of the President's annual message on the same subject. The introduction of the measure precipitated a long and acrimonious debate in which those congressmen resentful of Roosevelt's "executive usurpation" unleashed the full fury of their wrath upon him. The most extensive discourses were made by those members of the Appropriations Committee who had been largely responsible for the restrictions upon the Secret Service. Of these none elicited more enthusiastic applause than a speech by Tawney in which he defended his personal "veracity" as well as congressional

[79] Cannon, *Uncle Joe Cannon*, 232, 240–41; Atlanta *Constitution*, January 5, 1909; Washington *Evening Star*, January 4, 5, 1909; New Orleans *Times-Democrat*, January 13, 1909.

[80] Tawney to J. P. Hurley, January 9, 1909, Tawney to Charles N. Mitchell, January 9, 1909, in Tawney Papers.

"integrity." [81] Others claimed that the passage of the resolution was necessary to prevent the curtailment of civil liberties by a large, irresponsible force of government detectives whose zeal frequently carried them "beyond the needs of the service." The most effective critic of the greatly expanded activities of the Secret Service was Congressman Swagar Sherley of Kentucky, a member of the Appropriations Committee, who was particularly bothered by the prospect of a governmental detective force which would be immune to criticism and accountable to no other authority. "If Anglo-Saxon civilization stands for anything," he declared, "it is for a government where the humblest citizen is safeguarded against the secret activities of the executive of the Government. It stands as a protest against a government of men and for a government of law." Sherley warned his colleagues of the threat to the Fourth Amendment posed by the investigative techniques of government detectives and concluded with the declaration, "Sir, when it shall come to the formulation of a new law that shall govern the use of the secret service, I trust that this Congress, representing the individual citizens of this country, may as heretofore guard with jealous care the sacred rights of those citizens, and hedge about such service with all the safeguards essential to the preservation of the people's liberties." [82]

Only a handful of congressmen, designated either as "Roosevelt men" or as "insurgents who are glad to take a fling at the House organization," rallied to the defense of the President. Again, Congressman Bennet of New York delivered a lengthy address justifying Roosevelt's position on the Secret Service issue, and Augustus P. Gardner, the son-in-law of Senator Henry Cabot Lodge, tried in vain to secure the passage of a substitute motion which would have snatched victory from the old-guard Republicans by taking the "sting" out of the House rebuke to the President. But despite a frenzy of parliamentary maneuvering by Gardner and his colleagues, the Perkins resolution passed by a vote of 212 to 36.

[81] *Congressional Record*, 60th Cong., 2nd Sess., 645–83; New York *Tribune*, January 9, 1909; Council Bluffs (Iowa) *Nonpareil*, January 5, 1909.
[82] *Congressional Record*, 60th Cong., 2nd Sess., 645, 658, 660, 671, 680.

"Here was the culmination of past grievances," the *Independent* declared.[83]

The tabling of the presidential messages by the House was a method of rebuking the Chief Executive which had rarely been invoked. In fact, Speaker Cannon characterized the passage of the Perkins resolution as the most significant triumph of the legislature over the executive since Henry Clay's resolution censuring Andrew Jackson for his bank policy. Once the House had administered its rebuke to Roosevelt, it proceeded immediately to pass a resolution introduced by Tawney calling for a searching investigation of all aspects of the Secret Service and its activities. Congressman Marlin E. Olmsted of Pennsylvania was appointed chairman of a special committee to undertake the investigation, which was to be "distinct and separate" from the probe of the Secret Service already underway in the Senate.[84]

But such actions by the House did little to enhance the popularity of its position with the public. No amount of rebukes or protests could offset the effect of Roosevelt's charge regarding congressional interference with his pursuit of criminals. The President still had the popular side of the controversy; neither resolutions nor rhetoric by Congress prompted any substantial shift in public opinion. Actually, the more vigorously Congress reacted to his message, the more unpopular its position seemed to become. The heavy volume of letters and messages which congressmen received from their constituents and from organizations such as the Good Government Association suggested that the people were indeed with Roosevelt.[85] If the correspondence received by Tawney on the Secret Service question was any indication of the sentiment in his district, it revealed that a vast majority of his constituents was in hearty disagreement with his position. Several of those who wrote him implied that he would have to answer for his behavior "in the next election."

[83] *Ibid.*, 645–83; "Rebuking the President," *Independent*, LXVI (January 14, 1909), 104.

[84] *Congressional Record*, 60th Cong., 2nd Sess., 645–83; New York *Times*, January 9, 1909.

[85] New York *Times*, January 9, 10, 1909.

And one confidently predicted that the people of his district "will get you . . . someday on this incident." [86] According to the Chicago *Evening American*, the popularity of Roosevelt's position could be explained by the fact that he showed less interest "in the little thief in the customs house" than in the big criminals who shielded their crimes behind a façade of respectability and legal sanctity. It maintained that congressional charges regarding the misuse of the Secret Service sounded like so much bluster in view of Roosevelt's record of ferreting out violators of the land, antitrust, and lottery laws. Whether the President had been indiscreet in his messages or whether Congress had misinterpreted them was of no real concern to the ordinary citizen. But what was important, the *Evening American* declared, was that Roosevelt had dared to "go down under the dome of the Capitol, and catch us some of those cheap 'certificate of deposit' scamps that sell us out." [87]

Fully aware of the popular support for his cause, the President missed no opportunity to keep Congress on the defensive. While the House was preoccupied with administering its rebuke, Roosevelt was preparing to make another move which would lend credence to his suggestion that Congress itself was not composed altogether of angels. In response to a Senate inquiry regarding the number and activities of agents of the secret service type, he compiled a formid-

[86] E. A. Agard to Tawney, January 9, 1909, J. E. Engstad to Tawney, January 6, 1909, in Tawney Papers. See also O. H. Hawley to Tawney, January 6, 1909, W. E. Jones to Tawney, January 6, 1909, Phoebe Cousins to Tawney, January 7, 1909, Fred Cogswell to Tawney, January 8, 1909, S. T. Jones to Tawney, January 15, 1909, Theodore M. Knappen to Tawney, January 14, 1909, *ibid.*; St. Paul *Pioneer Press*, January 7, 1909; Omaha *Bee*, January 20, 1909; Chicago *Tribune*, January 4, 5, 6, 1909; Cleveland *Ledger*, January 5, 1909; Washington *Evening Star*, January 4, 5, 6, 7, 1909; New Haven *Register*, January 5, 1909; Detroit *Free Press*, January 5, 1909; Philadelphia *North American*, January 5, 1909; Philadelphia *Public Ledger*, January 5, 1909; *Literary Digest*, XXXVIII (1909), 79–81; *Current Literature*, XLVI (1909), 115–18; "Rebuking the President," *World To-Day*, XVI (February, 1909), 126–27. A common reaction was expressed by an Illinois attorney: "I have voted against Theodore Roosevelt at every election . . . and this in spite of the fact that I am an ardent republican: yet in the matter of the rebuke . . . I am with him, as is, in my opinion eighty per cent of the people of this country." Agard to Tawney, January 9, 1909, in Tawney Papers.

[87] Chicago *Evening American*, January 14, 1909.

able dossier of reports from various officials in the executive department corroborating his own testimony about the need for detectives "by which alone the Government can effectually safeguard itself against wrongdoing." In a letter accompanying this material Roosevelt took occasion to strike at his old enemy Benjamin R. Tillman by including information about a case which had recently come to his attention. The case raised serious ethical questions about the attempt of the South Carolina senator to acquire certain tracts of land in Oregon for himself and various members of his family. The President was careful to point out that this case demonstrated how Secret Service agents inadvertently stumbled upon damaging evidence against a member of Congress while investigating the activities of private individuals. When Roosevelt released the text of his letter on January 9, 1909, the controversy over the Secret Service for the moment was obscured by the renewal of the old enmity between Roosevelt and Tillman.[88]

According to the documents on the Tillman case presented by the President to the Senate, the senator first expressed an interest in purchasing some Oregon timberlands in 1907 while on a speaking tour in the Northwest. The land in question was "wagon-road and grant-land" claimed by railroads. With Tillman's aid in Washington, the way seemed to be cleared for a land and timber syndicate to acquire extensive tracts of land at $2.50 an acre. Tillman immediately got an option on several "desirable quarter sections." Then, in February, 1908, Bryan Dorr, a real-estate agent working with the syndicate, distributed a circular in which he advertised Tillman's connection with the land deal in an effort to attract purchasers. The publicity of his relationship with the scheme prompted Tillman to call for an investigation of Dorr by the Post Office Department. In discussing the Dorr circular in the Senate on February 19, 1908, he stated that he "had not bought any land anywhere in the West nor undertaken to buy any." Among the documents transmitted to the Senate by Roosevelt were several letters and telegrams from Tillman which revealed the true nature of his negotiations for the purchase

[88] T. Roosevelt to Eugene Hale, January 5, 1909, in Morison (ed.), *Roosevelt Letters*, VI, 1459–64. See also *Congressional Record*, 60th Cong., 2nd Sess., 719–39.

of the reclaimed lands whenever they became available. These documents had been acquired by postal inspectors and Secret Service agents in the course of making the investigation of Dorr, which ironically had been instigated by Tillman himself. In a telegram of October 20, 1907, Tillman informed the syndicate, "I want nine quarter sections reserved. Will forward applications and money at once." Roosevelt emphasized the obvious contradiction between Tillman's statement to the Senate and his previous actions regarding the purchase of Oregon lands. Furthermore, the President maintained that if Tillman was the protector of the public welfare he claimed to be, then it was his duty to compel the railroad companies to restore the lands to the public domain so that they might be sold for their actual value. It was scarcely in the public interest for Tillman to apply his well-known pitchfork to railroad companies for the purpose of acquiring for himself valuable lands at a ridiculously low price. The fact that the lands he proposed to purchase were exempt from the law requiring sale to actual settlers may have acquitted him of conspiracy to defraud the government, but it hardly justified his use of his official position for personal profit.[89]

On January 11, 1909, Senator Tillman rose in the Senate to defend his "integrity and character" from this presidential assault. His lengthy discourse, interrupted by noisy ovations from the floor as well as from the galleries, included bitter denunciations of Roosevelt for "striking below the belt" in what he called the unprecedented public chastisement of a senator by a President. "Theodore Roosevelt enjoys to the limit," he declared, "the feeling of getting even with Ben Tillman, and lays on the big stick with the keenest relish, doubtless believing that the pitchfork has gone out of business." Although Tillman challenged the President's interpretation of his connection with the Oregon lands, he did not deny the essential accuracy of the data presented to the Senate. Nor did he deny

[89] The documents pertaining to Tillman's interest in Oregon lands were reprinted in the *Congressional Record*, 60th Cong., 2nd Sess., 719–39. See also "Senator Tillman's Case," *Public*, XII (January 15, 1909), 53–58; "Mr. Tillman's Disingenuousness," *Outlook*, XCI (1909), 129–30; Francis B. Simkins, *Pitchfork Ben Tillman: South Carolinian* (Baton Rouge: La. State, 1944), 445–54.

his interest in purchasing some of the land. But he insisted that Attorney General Bonaparte had fully approved his resolution forcing the railroads to comply with the terms of the land grant and claimed that "Secret Service sleuths" had ransacked his office in an effort to obtain incriminating evidence. "Of course, the President is sure that I have done something very discreditable and outrageous," Tillman maintained. "He hates me and would destroy me if he could." Admitting that he may have been "disingenuous" in his earlier explanation of his connection with the land deal, Tillman nonetheless advised Roosevelt to put his energies to better use in efforts to regain lands stolen by E. H. Harriman and "others of his ilk" rather than harassing an impoverished senator who merely desired to acquire a few paltry acres. He welcomed "the most searching investigation" by the Senate and promised to abide by any verdict reached by his colleagues.[90]

Although the Senate avoided any such verdict, the press was quick to render one. And Tillman was the loser. Outside the South the senator had few advocates except for the labored editorial defenses of the New York *Times* and the Chicago *Inter-Ocean*.[91] The anti-Roosevelt press was generally less concerned with a defense of Tillman than it was in citing the case as proof that the President did indeed use the Secret Service to spy upon his opponents. Most editors, however, agreed with the *Outlook*'s contention that although Tillman had committed no crime, his conduct was discreditable because it involved "a plan to make personal pecuniary gain out of a matter which he had to consider and legislate upon as a Senator." [92] Other newspapers claimed that Roosevelt's exposure of Tillman was all the more telling because it impugned his honesty—"the one virtue for which Tillman has been given credit universally." [93] For

[90] *Congressional Record*, 60th Cong., 2nd Sess., 887–93.

[91] New York *Times*, January 12, 13, 14, 1909; Chicago *Inter-Ocean*, January 13, 1909.

[92] *Outlook*, XCI (1909), 129. See also "How Senator Tillman Emerges," *Literary Digest*, XXXVIII (1909), 124–26.

[93] Des Moines *Register*, undated clipping, in Secret Service Scrapbook; Peoria *Star*, January 11, 1909; Buffalo *Express*, January 12, 1909; Wilmington (Del.) *Morning News*, January 13, 1909; Philadelphia *North American*, January 13, 1909.

obvious reasons Negroes in general rejoiced at the turn of events. In exposing the senator, Roosevelt was credited with freeing "the Negro and the nation of a millstone about their necks." According to one Negro editor, the case did not involve "another good man gone wrong" but rather, "a bad man just found out." [94]

No one was more pleased with the public reaction to the exposure of Tillman than the President himself. It not only dealt a blow to one of his most virulent critics but also served notice on Congress that he did indeed possess evidence reflecting upon the ethics of its members. "I think," he confided to his son, "I have knocked the paint off of Tillman, who is one of the foulest and rottenest demagogs in the whole country; and I do not see how the House can get away from what I have said about it." [95] The successful strike against Tillman, coupled with the rising tide of public support for his position regarding the Secret Service, convinced Roosevelt that Congress would be reluctant to place further restrictions upon the investigative agencies of the executive department. Although it might continue the limitation upon the Secret Service as a face-saving device, he could be reasonably certain that the force of special agents in the Justice Department was safe from legislative emasculation.[96]

By mid-January, 1909, according to the Milwaukee *Sentinel*, Congress had "reached the smokeless powder stage in its row with the President." Visits to the White House by members of Congress, which had virtually ceased, gradually returned to normal after the Tillman episode. Evidence that some congressmen were having "second thoughts" about their warfare against the President over the Secret Service was provided by the action of the House in Jan-

[94] New York *Age*, January 23, 1909.

[95] T. Roosevelt to K. Roosevelt, January 10, 1909, in Morison (ed.), *Roosevelt Letters*, VI, 1472.

[96] Congressman Frank Clark of Florida, a critic of the Secret Service primarily because of its involvement in peonage investigations, introduced a resolution in the House demanding that the attorney general provide information on the new special agents in the Justice Department. Anticipating Clark's resolution, Bonaparte furnished the Judiciary Committee with a routine statement regarding the new investigative force. That the House did not use the Clark resolution as an occasion to criticize the force of special agents indicated it would not impose further restrictions on such agencies. See *Congressional Record*, 60th Cong., 2nd Sess., 615, 1167–68.

uary, 1909, in expunging from the record the bitter personal attack on the President made by Congressman William Willet of New York. It was generally agreed that the new attitude evident in Congress toward the President was prompted more by the hostile popular reaction to "its childish actions over the Secret Service" than to the imminent departure of Roosevelt from office.[97]

Even though Congress may have reached the "smokeless powder stage," there were still a few of its members, as well as some anti-Roosevelt editors, bent upon having the last word in the controversy. In an obvious attempt to demonstrate that the President was not the paragon of virtue he claimed to be, the anti-Roosevelt press made much of his use of Secret Service agents and private detectives in the Brownsville investigation. The charge was that the President had resorted to such illegal tactics in an effort to justify his hasty dismissal of three companies of Negro troops accused of terrorizing the town of Brownsville, Texas.[98] The opportunity of congressmen interested in clearing "the good name of the co-ordinate branch" came during the hearings on the Sundry Civil Appropriation Bill for 1910 and during the discussions of the reports finally delivered by the House and Senate committees instructed to inquire into the Secret Service. Tawney in particular was determined to combat what he considered the popular misconception of Congress's attitude toward the Secret Service. He released a lengthy document which purported to prove that Congress, rather than restricting the government's "secret service work," had in fact made possible its expansion through vastly increased appropriations. He claimed that $23,500,000 had been spent in crime detection by the federal government in 1908–1909. Roosevelt partisans were quick to characterize such a claim as a calculated attempt to mislead the public about the issue in question. The New York *Tribune* analyzed the figures cited by Tawney and concluded that they had little relevance to the

---

[97] Milwaukee *Sentinel,* January 19, 1909; New York *Times,* January 19, 1909; New York *Tribune,* January 10, 11, 12, 13, 14, 1909; Omaha *Bee,* January 29, 1909.

[98] Baltimore *Sun,* January 11, 1909; New Orleans *Times-Democrat,* January 13, 1909; Springfield *Republican,* January 16, 1909; Wilmington (Del.) *Every Evening,* January 4, 1909.

cost of the Secret Service and other detective activities of the government. Actually Tawney had included under the cost of "secret service work" such items as the maintenance of the police force in Washington, D.C., and virtually the total cost of the Revenue and Forest services, as well as that of the inspection required under the Meat Inspection Act and the customs laws. Such a mistake, according to the *Tribune*, might be excused in anyone else other than in the chairman of the House Appropriations Committee, who obviously knew better. Tawney's argument was further weakened by the publicity given several cases in which federal investigations had to be abandoned because of the restrictions placed on the Secret Service. One of these concerned the disappearance of $178,000 from the subtreasury in Chicago. If Tawney had intended to refute Roosevelt's contention that the limitation on the Secret Service had hampered the government's war on crime, he had utterly failed.[99]

During the hearings on the Sundry Civil Appropriation Bill for 1910, Tawney joined with Smith, Sherley, and Fitzgerald in a futile attempt to place the Roosevelt administration on the defensive. Bonaparte, Garfield, and Wilkie were their chief targets, and each was subjected to what was described as a "grilling." Bonaparte was questioned closely regarding the establishment and activities of the special agents in the Justice Department. Although Tawney and his colleagues raised no specific legal objections to the agents, they made much of Garfield's testimony that the restriction upon the Secret Service had not impaired the work of the Interior Department. But even the use of Garfield's statement as evidence that Roosevelt had deliberately misled the public about the effects of the restrictions was of little avail. The pro-Roosevelt press hastened to explain that the statement had been lifted out of context. Actually what Garfield told the committee was that although his department had not suffered because of its failure to employ Secret Service agents, it might well have been embarrassed if the Justice Department had not been able to supply its needs for detectives. Of those

[99] New York *Tribune*, January 14, 16, 17, 1909. See also Rochester *Post-Express*, January 20, 1909; Wilkie, *American Secret Service Agent*, 70–71; E. W. Clark to Tawney, February 10, 1909, in Tawney Papers.

appearing before the committee none was subjected to a more thorough "grilling" than Wilkie. The exchange between him and Tawney lent credence to the interpretation that the whole controversy over the Secret Service stemmed from a long-standing feud between the two men. Wilkie insisted that despite opposition by the committee to a proliferation of separate investigating agencies, its action in restricting the Secret Service had had precisely the effect of forcing each department to organize its own group of detectives. Like many others, including Roosevelt himself, the Secret Service chief claimed that the committee had imposed limitations on the use of his personnel by other departments without providing any sensible alternatives. He again advocated the centralization of all detective forces in the Justice Department on the grounds that such a change would promote economy and administrative efficiency. "That is where investigating forces really belong in my opinion," he declared. "They should be in the Department of Justice. The cases have to go there eventually. All our cases go to the department for prosecution." [100]

When Wilkie protested that the published version of his testimony had been edited and certain key phrases omitted, Tawney characterized his charge as an "act of impertinence and insolence" which warranted disciplinary action. Tawney, in fact, advised Secretary Cortelyou as Wilkie's superior to take such action immediately. Clearly Tawney had come off second best in the confrontation with Wilkie, who, among other things, laid to rest once and for all the charge that a Secret Service agent had been in Tawney's district during the campaign of 1908 for the purpose of bringing about his

---

[100] "Hearings before Subcommittee of House Committee on Appropriations," *House Reports*, 60th Cong., 2nd Sess., No. 2205, I, 5–45, 123–65. Congressman Sherley, as usual, questioned both Bonaparte and Wilkie about the consistency of "secret service" agencies with democratic institutions. He was especially alarmed by the prospect of an ever-expanding detective force and was convinced that the tendency was for the heads of government detective forces to become a power unto themselves answerable to no one. "The idea that some of us have in mind," he declared, "is how to safeguard an instrumentality, which, in the past . . . , has frequently been used for oppression and for the continuation in power of men having the instrumentality at their command."

defeat. Wilkie revealed that the "government sleuth" to whom Tawney had made so many references was actually a private detective employed by a department store in the congressman's hometown.[101]

By the time the Sundry Civil Appropriation Bill came up for consideration in Congress it was clear that the status of the Secret Service and the Justice Department's bureau of investigation would not be substantially altered. If congressional pride demanded the retention of the Secret Service limitation, the popularity of the President's campaign against violators of public laws was a deterrent to any inclination by Congress to tamper with the bureau of investigation. Congressmen rather freely admitted that their correspondence from constituents on the Secret Service issue was "running ten to one" in the President's favor. On February 1, 1909, the House excused the Olmsted Committee, originally instituted to make a sweeping inquiry into the Secret Service, "from all but the most perfunctory investigation." Members of Congress, including Tawney, conceded that although the Secret Service should be confined to its activities regarding counterfeiting and protection of the President, the attorney general "had full power to organize a detective force under the appropriation for the prosecution and detection of crime." The question at this juncture was whether there should be a central detective bureau responsible to the attorney general or two separate detective agencies located in different departments.[102]

When the subcommittee chaired by Senator James A. Hemenway of Indiana finally delivered a report on its Secret Service inquiry on February 11, 1909, it paved the way for an exchange of views on the organizational aspects of the problem. Characterized as a "conservative document," the Hemenway Report specifically denied that the restrictions upon the Secret Service had in any way hampered government investigations and emphasized the liberality of congressional appropriations for such activity. The Senate committee weighed the feasibility of placing all government detectives under

[101] Wilkie to Tawney, February 17, 1909, Tawney to Cortelyou, February 20, 1909, in Tawney Papers; Congressional Record, 60th Cong., 2nd Sess., 3125.
[102] New York Times, February 2, 4, 1909; New York Tribune, February 4, 5, 6, 1909; Omaha Bee, January 29, 1909; Indianapolis Star, February 5, 1909; W. H. Thompson to Tawney, January 18, 1909, in Tawney Papers.

the Secret Service Division in the Treasury Department but strongly counseled against it. Clearly the committee's position was colored by a personal animosity toward Wilkie, who was described as an ambitious man desirous of having "all the inspection service of the United States under his control." But the senators were hesitant to recommend the other alternative, the transfer of the Secret Service to the Justice Department, because they were fully aware of the difficulties involved in any reorganization which enlarged one executive department at the expense of another. In effect, then, the Hemenway Report favored a continuation of the dual system whereby the Secret Service Division concentrated upon counterfeiting and the detective force in the Justice Department assumed responsibility for other types of investigations.[103]

On February 19, 1909, the President expressed his views on the Hemenway Report in a lengthy letter to Senator Hale, chairman of the Committee on Appropriations. "In not one single instance during these seven years," he declared, "has it been shown that their action jeopardized any man who was not connected with illegal transactions." But the most remarkable feature of the letter was Roosevelt's praise and defense of Wilkie as an exceptionally efficient public servant who had been "one of the main stand-bys of the Government." Wilkie's efficiency, Roosevelt argued, made him "dreaded and hated by lawbreakers," who alone delighted in the restriction placed upon his activities. Strangely enough, the President interpreted the Hemenway Report as favorable to his idea "that the secret service be placed under the Department of Justice." Roosevelt concluded, "Chief Wilkie should be transferred to the Department of Justice and placed at the head of the force therein organized." In view of the congressional hostility toward Wilkie, it is difficult to imagine a recommendation less likely to be implemented. The Senate, of course, ignored it and allowed the Hemenway Report to stand as its final action in the Secret Service controversy.[104]

The House, always more sensitive and belligerent about the issue, indicated that it too was ready to "climb gracefully down off its high

---

[103] "Inquiry . . . of Secret Service," 1–10.

[104] T. Roosevelt to Hale, February 19, 1909, in Morison (ed.), *Roosevelt Letters*, VI, 1527–33.

horse." The debate over the Sundry Civil Appropriation Bill on February 25, 1909, allowed Tawney, Smith, and Fitzgerald one last opportunity to defend their honor and integrity. Smith attempted to besmirch the reputation of the Secret Service by casting aspersions upon the character and efficiency of its agents. He characterized them as "liars" who were "worthless in land fraud cases" and in preventing presidential assassinations. He concluded that the Secret Service was composed of men who by the very nature of their profession were dishonest. In his opinion it took a thief to catch one and no amount of "vainglorious boasting by Wilkie" could obscure this fact. Again, Bennet of New York made a futile effort to remove the restriction upon the Secret Service and was joined by George W. Norris and other "insurgents," who used the issue as an occasion to tackle the House's "ruling clique." Not only was the restriction retained in the final version of the Sundry Civil Appropriation Bill but Tawney also managed to incorporate another amendment which Roosevelt's friends described as "pure spite." It forbade the President to appoint any commission of inquiry unless Congress gave him specific authority.[105]

On March 3, 1909, the Olmsted Committee delivered to the House a report of its investigation of "secret service work" which covered much the same ground as the various hearings and debates on the subject. It differed from the Hemenway Report primarily in its concern for the legal status of the Secret Service Division and the bureau of investigation. Both, wholly dependent upon annual appropriation acts, existed "without permanent authority of law." The Olmsted Committee reported, "Whether the separate forces of secret service men now existing in the Treasury Department and in the Department of Justice should be combined in one, under control of the Attorney General, we do not attempt to decide, but suggest that, whether separately maintained or under one control, they should be permanently provided for and their duties clearly

[105] *Congressional Record*, 60th Cong., 2nd Sess., 3121–36; New York *Tribune*, February 26, 27, 1909; Theodore Roosevelt, *An Autobiography* (New York: Macmillan, 1913) 430–31; Gifford Pinchot, *Breaking New Ground* (New York: Harcourt, 1947), 343; *United States Statutes at Large*, 60th Cong., 2nd Sess., Pt. 1, p. 1014.

defined and limited by law." On this note the House concluded its considerations of the secret service agencies of the government.[106] On the day following the presentation of the Olmsted Report, Theodore Roosevelt left office.

Congress did not choose to reopen the issue after Roosevelt's departure. The new President, William Howard Taft, was probably happy to allow the question to lie dormant despite his desire to place the circle of law around Rooseveltian innovations. Taft had been indirectly involved in the Secret Service controversy when as secretary of war he had been accused of employing Secret Service agents and private detectives to gather incriminating evidence against the Negro troops accused of the Brownsville affray. Whatever his reasons, Taft offered no encouragement to those in Congress who desired to provide both the Secret Service and the bureau of investigation with the "permanent authority of law." When Bennet offered to introduce such legislation, Taft's attorney general, George W. Wickersham, merely promised to give the matter his consideration.[107] That Wickersham had other plans became clear on March 6, 1909, when he issued an order officially establishing the Bureau of Investigation under the direction of Stanley Finch. His order formalized the arrangement already worked out by Bonaparte. It also gave the Justice Department's investigative service "a secure place and the dignity of a name." But it did not delineate the areas of investigation for which the bureau and the Secret Service would be responsible.[108]

[106] The Olmsted Report was reprinted in *Congressional Record*, 60th Cong., 1st Sess., 3795–3801. Bonaparte was anxious for his force of special agents to acquire more specific legal standing. He urged the Appropriations Committee to include the phrase "for secret or detective work" in the portion of the Sundry Civil Appropriation Bill pertaining to the Justice Department. The committee ignored his suggestion and the law passed without any specific reference to the department's "secret or detective work." See "Hearings before Subcommittee of House Committee on Appropriations," *House Reports*, 60th Cong., 2nd Sess., No. 2205, I, 165; *U. S. Statutes at Large*, 60th Cong., 2nd Sess., Pt. 1, p. 1014.

[107] William S. Bennet to George W. Wickersham, March 8, 1909, Wickersham to Bennet, March 9, 1909, in File 44–3–11–3, Department of Justice.

[108] Order by George W. Wickersham, Attorney General, March 16, 1909, in File 44–3–11–3, Department of Justice. The new bureau included "all persons

After 1909, the bureau periodically underwent adjustments to clarify its relations to other departments and to specify its sphere of authority. The first major stimulus to the bureau's expansion was the Mann White Slave Act of 1910, which provided its "first big assignment." [109] That the agency was renamed the *Federal* Bureau of Investigation in 1936 suggested that its metamorphosis was near completion. According to one authority, the bureau "sloughed off its chrysalis" in the same year when it was relieved of the function of examining judicial officers. Its agents "were now armed, trained, mobile, active in the pursuit of criminals, rapidly developing a legend of invincibility, and kept in the spotlight." But as the FBI assumed more and more functions previously performed by the Secret Service, friction developed between the two agencies. In 1951 Congress finally defined in law the authority and jurisdiction of the Secret Service, and four years later a "Memorandum of Agreement" between the Justice and Treasury departments supplemented the statutory delineation between the two services in an effort to prevent further difficulties over the jurisdictional scope of their respective investigative powers.[110] Regardless of these later developments, the FBI was indisputably a creature of the Roosevelt administration.[111]

The controversy over the Secret Service was in a sense a dramatic episode in the adjustment of the federal governmental machinery to the new responsibilities placed upon it during the opening years of the twentieth century. The struggle came to a climax during the

---

whose compensation or expenses are paid from the appropriation 'Miscellaneous Expenses, United States Courts,' or the appropriation, 'Detection and Prosecution of Crimes,' and who are employed for the purposes of collecting evidence or of making investigations or examinations of any kind for this Department or the officers thereof."

[109] Cummings and McFarland, *Federal Justice*, 380–81; Whitehead, *FBI Story*, 24–25; Max Lowenthal, *The Federal Bureau of Investigation* (New York: Sloane, 1950), 10–21.

[110] Arthur C. Millspaugh, *Crime Control by the National Government* (Washington: Brookings, 1937), 79. For an analysis of jurisdictional and administrative problems between FBI and Secret Service, see *ibid.*, 87–128; Bowen and Neal, *The United States Secret Service*, 192–93.

[111] Louis Brownlow, *The Autobiography of Louis P. Brownlow: A Passion for Anonymity* (Chicago: U. of Chicago, 1952), 45.

last months of Roosevelt's term of office and assumed the appearance of a battle by Congress to prevent further aggrandizement of the executive power at the expense of the legislature. Congress may well have enjoyed the less popular side in the controversy but it at least served notice that "no spy system" would be allowed to grow up within the government. The persistence of this attitude helps explain why agents of the Bureau of Investigation remained "purely investigative officers" who exercised their function "in aid of executive officers of the United States." Not until 1934 were these agents allowed to carry arms, serve warrants, and make arrests and seizures. Later revelations of abuses committed by certain Secret Service agents during the Roosevelt administration lent credence to the charges made by congressmen in 1908–1909.[112] Such revelations may not have warranted their claims that Roosevelt himself practiced "Fouchéism," but later disclosures regarding the investigative techniques of the FBI convinced some Americans of the prophetic quality of the arguments by Sherley, Tawney, and others. The issue raised by those who advocated limitations upon the Secret Service was of profound significance because it concerned the place and role of secret government detectives in a democratic society. The failure of the civil-libertarian objections to elicit more popular support may be explained in part by the circumstances under which they were raised: the motives of the old-guard Republicans and southern Democrats who most strenuously opposed the free-wheeling activities of government detectives appeared to be considerably less lofty than their rhetoric. Ironically, many of the arguments employed by the so-called reactionary elements of the Roosevelt era were later invoked by liberals, especially in the 1920's and 1950's,[113] when the FBI's war against subversion involved the "investigation of beliefs." The later critics, no less than Congressman Sherley, saw in the activities of the government's detective force a threat to "the preservation of the people's liberties."

[112] Cummings and McFarland, *Federal Justice*, 381; Whitehead, *FBI Story*, 18–19.

[113] See Lowenthal, *Federal Bureau of Investigation*, 4–13, 444–65. See also the special issue of the *Nation*, CLXXXVII (October 18, 1959), which is devoted to the FBI.

During the struggle over the Secret Service Roosevelt assumed the role of a crusader for righteousness who had been denied the use of his most effective weapon against wrongdoers—a St. George forced to confront the dragon without his sword. Impatient with those who objected to the expanded activities of the Secret Service on high civil-libertarian grounds, Roosevelt appealed to the public conscience with the argument that federal detectives were necessary to combat the lawlessness and corruption which menaced the very institutions essential to democracy. But by focusing upon specific members of Congress who had been his perennial critics he left himself open to the charge of pursuing noble ends by dubious means, of risking the destruction of the very thing he claimed to be protecting. His action in this instance indicated that his distinction between moral and immoral behavior was not devoid of political and personal consideration. Whatever the ethical verdict, his tactic was effective. Even Tillman, for all his animosity toward Roosevelt, chose not to make good his threat to expose the "long list of abuses" committed by the Secret Service. His failure to pursue the issue allowed the President the personal satisfaction of having the last word in a public quarrel which had been in progress since 1902. The effect of Roosevelt's indictment of Tawney, though belated, was perhaps even more significant. During the congressional campaign of 1910, when Tawney was fighting for political survival, Roosevelt hastened his demise by publicly criticizing him for his role in the Secret Service incident. "Looking back a bit," the Washington *Evening Star* commented following Tawney's defeat in 1910, "Mr. Tawney can and does attribute most of his recent political troubles . . . to his big row with President Roosevelt over the Secret Service." [114]

Roosevelt preferred to explain the dispute over the Secret Service in terms of morality and efficiency, but he also used it to defend the powers and prerogatives of his executive office. In fact, his role in the controversy graphically demonstrated his conception of the President as a steward of the people who was ever the watchful guardian of the commonweal. For him, adequate performance in this capac-

[114] Washington *Evening Star*, September 21, 1910. See also Philadelphia *North American*, September 22, 1910.

ity required the assistance of a corps of competent detectives such as those in the Secret Service. As a means of achieving greater efficiency in the detection of crime, Roosevelt desired to consolidate the government's detective forces into a central bureau under the jurisdiction of the attorney general. When Congress clearly indicated that it was in no mood to sanction such a thoroughgoing consolidation, Roosevelt as usual was willing to compromise. The result, after all the smoke had cleared, was a dual arrangement of two "secret services," one limited to investigation in the Treasury Department and the other ranging broadly in both the civil and criminal fields.

Index